This Crested Hill

This Crested Hill

*An Illustrated History of
the University of Idaho*

Keith C. Petersen

University of Idaho Press • *Moscow, Idaho*

The University of Idaho Press
Moscow, Idaho 83843

Printed in the United States of America
9 8 7 6 5 4 3 2 1

Library of Congress Cataloging in Publication Data

Petersen, Keith C.
    This crested hill.

    Bibliography: p.
    Includes index.
    1. University of Idaho—History. 2. University of
Idaho—Description—Views. I. Title.
LD2323.P48   1987   378.796'86   87-13760
ISBN 0-89301-120-7

"Here upon this crested hill is the spot to which the entire State should look for intellectual leadership."

Alfred A. Upham
Sixth President, University of Idaho
Inaugural Address, 1921

Dedication

Lillian Woodworth Otness, Class of 1930, first
introduced me to the pleasures of researching and
writing on Latah County's rich history. She is a former
student and member of the faculty, as well as a long-
time friend of the university. An ardent supporter
of history and historic preservation, she is also a
personal friend. I am honored to dedicate this book
to her.

Table of Contents

Acknowledgments

1 • Prologue

1

15 • "It Would Be . . . An Olive Branch":
Moscow Gets a University

2

23 • The University is Built, 1889-1906

3

47 • Sectionalism, Politics, and Finances,
1906-1989

4

77 • Life on Campus

5

111 • Athletics

6

155 • The University and the Military

7

189 • "We Want . . . a Just and Equal Treatment":
Minorities at Idaho

8

213 • Reaching Out to Community, State,
and Nation

233 • A Note on Sources

239 • Photograph Credits

242 • Index

Acknowledgments

Officials of the University of Idaho probably had some apprehension when they hired me to write this history. I am a graduate of Washington State University, and anyone who has resided in the Palouse need not be told about the hesitation some might have in asking a "Cougar" to write a "Vandal" history. But let me allay any fears. Those of us at Idaho's sister university have long known that there is another fine school just ten miles east. It was truly a pleasure to learn more about that institution, and I thank those who had enough confidence in my abilities to allow me to undertake the task.

Roy Fluhrer, coordinator of the University of Idaho Centennial, found time among all his other duties to meet with me regularly during the course of writing, to make appointments for me with people on campus, and to oversee the editorial, design, and publication process. I am indebted to him for his untiring efforts.

I spent many days in the university library's Special Collections and Archives, and I am grateful to the fine staff for their untiring helpfulness and friendship: Terry Abraham, Lois Ackaret, and Judy and Ralph Nielsen. Warren Owens, dean of library services, found room in a crowded library to provide me with much appreciated office space. I am also indebted to Terry Gray of the library staff, who patiently photocopied hundreds of pages of research material.

Mary E. Reed, director of the Latah County Historical Society—who is also my wife—and Christine Talbott, the society's librarian, assisted me in finding university-related research materials and photographs at the society. Others who opened valuable materials for my inspection included Elizabeth Jacox at the Idaho State Historical Society Library; Matt Telin, university registrar; Joanne McCroskey at the Alumni Center; and Leo Ames, supervisor of the university's publications design.

All books are truly team efforts, and over the years I have been fortunate to find two extremely competent colleagues who catch many of my mistakes prior to publication, not only saving me immense embarrassment but also making for vastly improved final products. Once again, I am grateful for the editorial skills of Judy Austin and for the typing and editing skills of Kathleen Probasco.

Several people reviewed parts or all of this manuscript in draft form, and their comments made for a better book. In addition to Warren Owens and Mary Reed, these reviewers included Richard Gibb, president of the university; Kent Hackmann, chair of the Department of History; Major Andrew Haygood and Lieutenant Colonel Edward Lindahl, professors of military science; Terry Armstrong, executive assistant to the president; and Bill Belknap, director of athletics. I would also like to thank book designers Debra Moloshok and Emily Silver and all those people who shared personal experiences of their times at the university, particularly Frank B. Sutherland, G. A. Riedesel, Bill McGowan, Bob Curtis, and Annette M. Getty.

It may seem silly to some, but I would be remiss if I did not also acknowledge the help of Clio. Getting up every morning to write—facing four walls and a stack of research notes on a crowded desk—can be a lonely task. Clio the cat is not only good company but a fine warmer of laps. She is, after all, named for the muse of history.

I have no doubt left many out who should appropriately be acknowledged, and for that I apologize. I hope all of you know that your assistance has been truly appreciated.

Keith C. Petersen
Pullman, Washington
November 1986

Prologue

Surely it was difficult for James Alexander MacLean, who loved the University of Idaho, to describe the appearance of its grounds in 1906 as "something to be deplored and forgotten." MacLean, who served thirteen years as president of the school, believed "a College campus should carry memories of a thousand delightful and ennobling associations," and he endeavored to improve the school's looks. Because of his efforts and those of twelve other presidents, hundreds of faculty and staff, and thousands of students, the University of Idaho approached its centennial anniversary as a beautiful campus holding easily a thousand pleasant memories.

Almost exactly eighty years after MacLean wrote his critique, I toured the grounds. It was the opening day of classes in August, 1986, a hot afternoon with a dry east wind. I am neither staff nor alumnus. I came to the task of writing this book as an "objective historian." Yet even for me, after months of sifting through records, photographs, and reminiscences, the campus evokes a thousand memories.

People touring these grounds take different routes, and there was no real reason for the way I chose to walk that day. But let me tell you about my course, and the things I saw.

I started from my office on the lower level of the University Library—the same office Rafe Gibbs used when he wrote *Beacon for Mountain and Plain: Story of the University of Idaho* in the early 1960s. I enjoyed my time in that

In 1906, President James MacLean wrote that the campus grounds were "something to be deplored and forgotten."

office. It seemed a sort of continuing legacy between that earlier history
and this one. But Rafe might not recognize the space if he returned today,
for I shared the room with high-tech, expensive machinery placed there to
assist the visually impaired, just one of many efforts undertaken in the past
twenty years to make the university more accessible.

Outside, students hurried on their way to classes: a multicolored mixture of
shorts and T-shirts; well-worn cords and new designer jeans; expensive
shirts with high-fashion labels; tennis shoes; sandals; dresses and high
heels; sunglasses slung low from gold chains around necks. Almost
anything seems acceptable stylistically; it is a democratic campus. I moved
into the flow, past booths offering information for new students.

University Classroom Center, Memorial Gymnasium, and the
University Library (1970s).

Across from the Library I paused to look at Memorial Gymnasium,
constructed to honor Idahoans who died during World War I. Football-
carrying gargoyles adorn the building's side. On the roofline is a decorative
frieze with a cowboy-and-Indian motif. If these signals seem somewhat
mixed, one can argue that the decoration is at least much more spirited
than our modern architectural ideals allow. Inside the gym are large
photographs of Vandal sports heroes and cases filled with trophies and
game balls. The old gym floor—long a place of intercollegiate basketball
games and boxing matches—gleamed with a lacquer finish.

Moving outside, beyond the gym, I found a crowd at the Administration
Building Annex. Like others there, I picked up a catalog. It takes 200 pages
of squinty-sized type to list the course offerings, from Accounting and
Aerospace Studies to Vocational Teacher Education and Wildland
Recreation Management. Grateful that I no longer have to struggle with
registration and exams, I stepped back outside, where summer
maintenance crews had poked flowering plants into nearly every patch of
usable ground. The place blazed with color.

Graduation at Memorial Gymnasium (right, 1930s), and football gargoyle on gymnasium exterior (above).

I strolled through the Price Green picnic area adjoining the Shattuck Arboretum, past the fireplace and tables—people sketching and reading and visiting in this quiet nook—to the school's dominating structure, the Kibbie-ASUI Dome, ten years old in 1986, winner of national engineering awards, holder of memories for those who attend football or basketball games or track meets or graduation ceremonies, or simply enjoy jogging around its sheltered track on cold winter days. The Vandal football team was practicing on this day, a padless session, shorts, shirts, and golden helmets. They ran pass patterns under banners proclaiming the Vandal men as Big Sky Conference basketball champions in 1981 and 1982 and the university's women cagers as conference victors in 1985.

South of the Dome I walked to the top of the Arboretum. It was quiet there—none of the jostling crowd of students finding their way to new classes. To the north and east is Moscow. A tiny, disheveled western town when the university was founded, it has grown with the school into a community of about 15,000. From here I could see grain elevators, now bursting from another bumper Palouse harvest; Main Street's graceful brick buildings; hundreds of trees lining residential neighborhoods; and beyond, the forested slopes of Moscow Mountain. To the west is Kamiak Butte, and on the prairie in between, though invisible from this spot, lie Pullman and Washington State University—itself the repository of thousands of memories of Vandal–Cougar athletic contests.

Across Nez Perce Drive is the golf course Francis James designed, crowned by the clubhouse dedicated to his memory. Across the street again, diagonally from me, at the edge of the Arboretum, is the President's house, shadowed by the elevated water reservoir most old-time Moscowans still insist upon calling ''the new 'I' tank'' although it has stood here for over thirty years. Surely this spot holds well over a thousand memories.

Golf course (1930s).

Two prominent landmarks: the Spanish-American War Statue and the old I tank (c. 1940s).

New I tank (1950s).

Through a gap in the Arboretum's trees I spotted the ''old I tank,'' moved to the university farm north of campus when workers completed the current reservoir. How many Washington State students climbed its steps when it stood on this hill to paint crimson ''W''s on its sides? How many Idahoans dutifully trudged up the next morning to readorn its metal shell with golden ''I''s? The old I tank now stands unpainted and rusty. Most current students do not know its past. No one climbs the new I tank anymore. Its large, bold ''I''s seem permanently safe from marauding Cougars. Nearby is a huge communications dish, a modern landmark on the I tank hill.

East of the I tank is the new ''Greek Row,'' lined with fraternity and sorority houses constructed here since the 1950s. Directly across the street is Tau Kappa Epsilon. Perched in the yard on freshly painted wheels is Old Bertha, the cannon that has been on campus nearly 100 years. I walked down Nez Perce Drive to Ridenbaugh Hall, constructed as a women's dormitory in

Ridenbaugh Hall and the campus' most handsome walkway (1920s).

1902, the oldest building on campus, ivy vining up its brick walls. Besides containing the University Art Gallery, it is now a place for musicians to practice. From one window drifted the sound of classical trumpet; from another a synthesizer and drums pounded the beat of Van Halen rock. The sounds epitomize the diversity of the school.

Just north, across the street from Ridenbaugh, tennis players hit balls on asphalt courts at the site of the pond earlier students knew as "Lake Huntley," a murky puddle President MacLean drained to help eliminate the campus's "deplorable" appearance.

The walkway from Ridenbaugh to the Administration Building is the university's most handsome. Gnarled trees edge the path, and beyond sweeps the Ad Building lawn. Along this winding parkway are several reminders of the university's history. One is the Home Economics Building, constructed in the 1950s on the site of the former Engineering Building. Inside I found an exhibit on Mary Hall Niccolls, who left nearly a half-million dollars to the school for home ec scholarships. "A Remarkable Legacy," the exhibit label accurately headlined—just like the many other gifts donated over the years by appreciative alums. Outside the Home Economics Building are two stone benches made from stair treads of the old Engineering Building, the only reminders—aside from photographs in the archives—of that handsome structure.

Beyond the benches is a sixteen-step, uneven stairway leading to two peaceful seats overlooking the Administration Building. They used to form the main entrance to the "old" Ad Building, the university's first structure, destroyed by fire in 1906—the year of President MacLean's pessimistic

Gnarled trees line the Ridenbaugh walkway (1970s).

The old-steps memorial (1940s).

statement. They are all that is left of the building. In the 1930s Congressman Burton French, Class of 1901, offered a prize to the student designing the best memorial to that structure. The plan of reconstructing the "old steps" won. After a nationwide search—because some of the stones adorned gardens and yards as far away as Florida—the steps were collected and repositioned into a new campus landmark.

Across the street is the "new" Administration Building, opened in 1909, a massive central tower surmounting its main entrance. The building is a

Administration Building lawn (c. 1920s).

place for plaques. Bronzed tablets recognize the David family for donating the carillon of bells; memorialize students and staff who have died in five wars; recognize donors of scholarship and loan funds. On the exterior of the north entry, just past the renovated auditorium, a mosaic seal of the university greets the building's visitors.

At the front of the building rests the I Bench. In earlier days non-seniors found sitting here could expect healthy paddlings. Current students do not recognize that tradition, however: the bench can be used by anyone, though in truth it receives only a fraction of the visitation of earlier times when students practiced school yells here weekly.

The fountain in front of the Ad Building—site of many duckings of wayward underclassmen—has been replaced with a landscaped flagpole. Across the drive is the Presidential Grove: trees planted by Teddy Roosevelt, William Taft, Eleanor Roosevelt, and other luminaries. Beyond the grove stands the school's oldest monument, the Spanish-American War statue. Wrote a student poet in 1903:

> Silently he stands, year in year out
> With eyes unclosed and vigilant
> Gazing upon the busy world below.

He still stands and gazes, but his world is considerably less busy than in earlier times: as the campus grew it expanded to the north and west, leaving the Ad Building lawn an oasis for those seeking a quiet walk under a canopy of mature trees.

"Silently he stands, year in year out
With eyes unclosed and vigilant
Gazing upon the busy world below."

Views of the Administration Building in the 1920s.

Administration Building fountain in the 1940s; the area filled in and landscaped in the 1960s.

Administration Building auditorium (1920s).

View from north entry of the Administration Building (c. 1920s).

Hello Walk (1930s).

The most famous path through that lawn is the ''Hello Walk.'' No one said ''Hello'' to me as I passed—another tradition lost. Still, it is a special route. Memories linger here, for sure.

Hello Walk entrance (1940s).

The Hello Walk opens out to the older fraternity and sorority houses, the Perch Grocery, the Music Building, and the Campus Christian Center. The Christian Center occupies the site of Jay Glover Eldridge's home. Eldridge, first and only dean of the faculty, arrived in 1901. He was disappointed to find that although he lived on Elm Street the town had no elm trees. So he obtained one from New Haven, Connecticut, "City of Elms," and planted it here. It still grows in front of the center, surrounded by a concrete bench.

The University Bookstore was packed—empty-handed students going in, those exiting carrying bagged books. It was nearly as busy as Permeal French's Blue Bucket Inn—which formerly occupied this site—used to be at the opening of school. Next door, the Student Union Building's restaurants and candy counter buzzed. I went out the union's back door and crossed through the small "People's Park" established during a time of rising environmental awareness in the 1970s. I walked along Paradise Creek, where freshmen and sophomores formerly held tug-of-war contests. On this day it was quiet and calm here.

My tour ended along the creek. I left more unvisited than visited—residence halls, athletic complex, greenhouses, university farm, classroom and office buildings, intramural fields, student apartments. The university catalog's campus map lists 162 buildings and sites stretched over dozens of acres. It was too much to see on one hot day. Clearly, however, James Alexander MacLean would find the place anything but deplorable. It is now a beautiful campus, suitably representing a mature institution. What follows is the story of how the school grew during its first hundred years from undeveloped farmland into a major university.

1

"It Would Be . . .
An Olive Branch"

Moscow Gets
a University

William J. McConnell, one of the university's founders and most ardent supporters.

William J. McConnell loved to gamble—"Poker Bill," some of his friends called him. His fondness for the game was an extension of his gambler's approach to life. Born in Michigan in 1839, he moved west as a young man and accumulated a considerable fortune in California's gold fields. Eventually, lured by new gold strikes in the Boise Basin, he moved to the Horseshoe Bend area of southwestern Idaho Territory and amassed another tidy sum by selling fruits and vegetables to miners. Still restless, McConnell in 1871 transported his family to Yamhill, Oregon. After again succeeding in business, he entered Oregon politics and served a term as president of the state senate. He refused an offer to be the Republican candidate for governor, preferring to move once more.

By 1886 McConnell was firmly established in Moscow, Idaho Territory, owner of one of the region's largest stores. This gamble paid off, too, and McConnell became the small town's most influential merchant. Along with several of his contemporaries, McConnell looked for ways to make Moscow prosper. Landing a university for the small town would provide just the economic boon he sought.

Willis Sweet, one of McConnell's Moscow contemporaries, also hoped that an investment in the town's future would help him and the community—and it did. Sweet's advocacy of a university at Moscow enhanced his rising political career. Born in Vermont, Sweet arrived in the panhandle town in 1881 and founded one of its first newspapers. By the time he was admitted to the bar in the late 1880s, he was a major figure in northern Idaho politics, leader of a Moscow machine capable of delivering support to office-seekers who proved willing to assist his town.

Willis Sweet, pictured at the left in the back row, posed for this photograph with some Moscow friends in the late 1880s. At about the same time, he began working toward establishing a university in Moscow.

Fred T. Dubois was just such a politician. Though he never lived in Moscow, he became a friend of the community, primarily because he needed Sweet's support to win election as Idaho's territorial delegate to Congress. A native of Illinois and graduate of Yale, Dubois moved to southeastern Idaho in 1880. He served as United States Marshal from 1882 until 1886, when he was elected territorial representative. Dubois combined a fierce dislike of Idaho's Mormons with a staunch belief that the territory's panhandle should remain a part of Idaho and not be annexed to Washington. In the process he became the territory's first major national political figure.

Together these three men—all relative newcomers to Idaho and all with ascending political fortunes—played major roles in securing the state university for the small town of Moscow. For one hundred years, many Idahoans and tourists alike have pondered the question of how this isolated farming community in Idaho's panhandle became the home of a major university. That choice was intricately tied to the political atmosphere of Idaho Territory in the mid-1880s.

Idahoans of the late twentieth century joke that their state has three capitals—Spokane for the north, Salt Lake City for the southeast, and Boise for the southwest. But the issue was hardly a laughing matter to territorial politicians of the nineteenth century who struggled for years to keep the region intact. While religious preferences drew the Latter-day Saints of southeastern Idaho toward Salt Lake, geographical barriers forced the residents of Idaho's panhandle to look to Spokane rather than Boise for supplies and services. There was no north-south route within Idaho, and treacherous, slow roads through Washington and Oregon made communication between north and south difficult. Idaho's first capital was located in Lewiston with the establishment of the territory in 1863, but within a year and a half it was moved to Boise. With a small population base, the north had little influence in territorial affairs. Yet it held many of Idaho's richest natural resources—mines, forests, and agricultural lands. Northern Idahoans increasingly feared that their region was becoming an exploited colony as the south seemingly reaped the economic advantages of these resources while providing few benefits in return.

Not surprisingly, many northern residents sought to remove the panhandle from Idaho and annex it to Washington Territory—a move with some geographical merit. In 1878, 96 percent of northern Idaho voters ratified a constitution that would have united them with Washington. That sentiment remained strong in 1887, when Idaho came perilously close to splitting.

Nevada's congressional representatives had lobbied for years to append southern Idaho to Nevada. To gain support for their proposal, in 1887 they backed the idea of removing the panhandle to form part of Washington, a plan endorsed both by Washingtonians and by many northern Idahoans—particularly those living in Moscow and Lewiston, hotbeds of annexationism. A bill adding the panhandle to Washington Territory passed both houses of Congress, and in early March 1887 signature by President

Fred T. Dubois, Idaho's most powerful politician in the 1880s and early 1890s, helped soothe sectional difficulties and land the state university for the panhandle.

In the mid-1880s, Moscow was a typical small western town featuring a main street lined with wood frame buildings (right). By the mid-1890s, the town's business section boasted handsome brick structures (below). The university spurred this economic growth, and the community and school continued to grow together.

Grover Cleveland was all that remained for northern Idaho to become eastern Washington. The north would be freed at last from the "cold-hearted, avaricious scheming leeches" of southern Idaho, as one northern resident ecstatically proclaimed.

Idaho's territorial governor, Edward A. Stevenson, firmly opposed the bill and upon its passage telegraphed President Cleveland that the majority of Idahoans did not favor splitting the territory. Stevenson convinced Cleveland to study the measure further, and the president's pocket veto preserved the territory's unity. Another annexation proposal appeared in the next session of Congress but was never seriously considered. By then, Fred Dubois had joined Stevenson in the effort to preserve Idaho.

Dubois had narrowly won election as territorial delegate to Congress in 1886, owing much of his success to Willis Sweet, whose Moscow machine turned out Dubois supporters both at the nominating convention and during the election. Sweet was one of the few politically active residents of Moscow who did not favor annexation. Dubois likewise wanted a united Idaho. With Dubois working against annexation in Washington, D.C., while Governor Stevenson fought it in Idaho, the idea lost momentum. The majority of Idahoans probably never favored splitting the territory, although a vocal group in the north, aided by ambitious politicians in Nevada and Washington, kept the idea alive for years.

Willis Sweet's endorsement of Dubois shocked many of his northern colleagues who supported annexation. Sweet's motivation may have been to ally himself with a dynamic and rising political figure like Dubois. In any event, Sweet's support was essential to Dubois. The two men were amply rewarded for their cooperative pact: Dubois was elected to Congress; Sweet received significant political favors from his friend. Years later, Sweet would reminisce that "the 'southeast' was grateful for the support given Mr. Dubois. . . . For one thing, the 'southeast' was . . . in favor of anything within reason that north Idaho asked for. . . . North Idaho had come into her own; and all we had to do was ask for what we wanted."

One of these favors was to create a new county—Latah—by dividing Nez Perce County and giving Moscow a county seat. It remains the only county in the United States formed by an act of Congress. As a second concession to northerners, Dubois had Sweet appointed as United States Attorney for Idaho Territory. After Dubois was re-elected as territorial delegate in 1888, again with Sweet's help, Sweet and his Moscow associates began formulating a final favor: a university for their town.

The first serious move to establish an Idaho university came in 1887 when a bill proposing a college at Eagle Rock (Idaho Falls) appeared before the legislature. The measure passed both houses, but Governor Stevenson reluctantly vetoed it. While he supported the idea of a university, he believed this particular bill suffered from serious omissions. Only because of a carelessly worded piece of legislation did southeast Idaho lose the university to the north.

John Warren Brigham

John Warren Brigham was the "kid legislator" of Idaho's last territorial assembly. Born in California in 1857, he migrated in 1879 to the Palouse hills near Genesee, where he took a homestead. He farmed that land for the rest of his life and was buried nearby—a fitting resting spot for a man who loved to work the soil.

When John Brigham arrived in Boise for that last territorial legislative session in 1888 he assumed a position of leadership, even though he was only thirty-one. With Willis Sweet he wrote the act creating the University of Idaho, then introduced the bill to the legislature, and stood by the governor's shoulder as he signed it into law on January 30, 1889. Later that year, as one of Latah County's representatives at the state constitutional convention, Brigham helped pass the clause permanently locating the university in Moscow. Once Idaho was accepted into the union, he served three terms in the state legislature.

Mostly, though, John Brigham enjoyed farming—and watching the university he helped to create grow. His wife, Nellie Wilson, was among the first students to enroll when classes began in October 1892. Over the *years, John and Nellie sent six of their children to the university to receive degrees. The youngest, Morton, graduated in 1939, when the university celebrated its fiftieth anniversary. It was the same year the college awarded an honorary Bachelor of Arts degree to John, recognizing his unfailing support of the institution. He was eighty-two when given the award, and Life Magazine ran a photograph of John and Morton Brigham, standing together, receiving their degrees.*

John Brigham, shown below in 1939, was a prominent figure on campus during the fiftieth anniversary observances. As the last of the original founders still living he gave speeches, spoke on the radio, and buried his reminiscenses in a time capsule. He liked to tell his audiences that he had persuaded southern Idaho's legislators to vote for the university bill by convincing them that they could walk the streets of Moscow without falling off into Canada.

Just a year after the semi-centennial, John Brigham died at home. "It was an inspiration to see this old gentleman, white-haired and gnarled like an old oak tree,

Agitation for a university continued, but by the time the next territorial legislature convened, the Idaho political situation had changed drastically. Now it was clear that the north would remain as part of Idaho and should be included in the list of prospective university sites. Representatives from the southeast, cheered by the north's support of their favorite son for territorial delegate to Congress, proved willing to compromise on the location. Moscow civic leaders such as William McConnell believed there would never be a better time to request the institution for their town. And Willis Sweet was prepared to cash in on one last political favor. When Idaho's last territorial legislature convened in 1888, Sweet was one of the first representatives to arrive. He came bent on an overriding mission: to shepherd through a bill creating a university at Moscow.

Now that the threat to separate north and south had been thwarted, Idaho's political leaders began working feverishly to gain statehood. Yet two pockets of discontent needed appeasement before a successful constitutional convention could be held: the powerful anti-Mormon forces of southeast Idaho, led by Dubois, who hoped to permanently disenfranchise the Latter-day Saints; and the few but influential annexationists remaining in the north.

Although Sweet began drafting legislation to establish a university, he soon became entangled in anti-Mormon battles. Back in Moscow, William McConnell grew impatient with Sweet's lack of progress on the university bill. He convinced legislator John Warren Brigham of Genesee to expedite the proposal.

Early one morning, while Sweet was still in bed, Brigham strode into his Boise room and pressed upon him the importance of introducing a university bill before the session adjourned. Sweet agreed to dictate the concluding sections of his bill, which Brigham dutifully transcribed. Shortly afterwards Brigham introduced Council Bill 20, creating a university at Moscow. With the territorial legislature preoccupied in its bitter fight over anti-Mormon legislation, and with southern representatives seeking ways to appease the north, the bill passed easily, receiving only one dissenting vote in both houses. Noted one legislator when endorsing the bill:

> It would be recognized as an olive branch in the interest of peace and good-will extended by one section of the Territory to another, between which there has been long and bitter contention. In the place of discord and threats of disunion, [it] would unite the sections in the march of progress and improvement for the entire Territory, and a speedy admission into the sovereignty of States.

Governor Stevenson signed the act into law on January 30, 1889. Brigham was the only legislator present.

Having satisfied the north with the promise of the university, Governor Stevenson called a constitutional convention for July 4, 1889, in Boise. Latah County sent the third largest convention delegation, with six representatives, including Sweet, Brigham, and McConnell. McConnell's political savvy—gained while in the Oregon legislature—was soon apparent, and he became an influential leader of the session. He and the other Latah

County delegates maneuvered an unusual coup: they wrote the location of the university at Moscow into the state constitution, making it one of only a handful of universities nationwide afforded such protection. Once Idahoans had approved the constitution in November 1889 the university could be relocated only by constitutional amendment; legislative whims were not enough. The provision proved invaluable in later years as various legislators threatened to dismember the institution by moving certain colleges or departments to other parts of the state.

By 1890 the university had been firmly established in Idaho's legal codes. Fred Dubois steered the statehood bill through Congress, and Idaho became a state in 1890. Dubois would later become a United States senator from the new state, and William McConnell and Willis Sweet emerged from the proceedings as significant political figures and recognized friends of the new university. McConnell became one of the state's first United States senators and later served as governor; Sweet was elected as the new state's first member of the House of Representatives. Sweet was named to the university's first Board of Regents; McConnell was its first recipient of an honorary degree. Later, both would have men's dormitories on campus named after them, reminders of their many efforts to garner the University of Idaho for Moscow.

his eyes twinkling with the light of remembered battle, retell the struggles and hopes that he and the rest of the backers of the University of Idaho endured to make this institution possible for the young men and women of Idaho," Dean Herbert Wunderlich noted upon his death. "His entire life was interwoven in the pattern of the growth of the University and should serve as a shining example to students and faculty members."

In John Brigham's last year, the campus—which had been nothing but an undeveloped field when the kid legislator journeyed to Boise in 1888—served over 3,000 students.

Willis Sweet Hall, a men's dormitory, was constructed in 1936 to honor one of the school's founders.

2

The University Is Built
1889-1906

Willis Sweet and Henry Blake, the first president and secretary of the Board of Regents, returned home to Moscow in the spring of 1889 from a board meeting in Boise. They had just received authorization to purchase land for the new university, but they had only $15,000 to acquire the property, improve it, and develop plans for a building. They hoped for a bargain. "Parties interested should bear in mind that the Territory does not expect to pay exorbitant prices," they admonished in an advertisement in the Moscow *Mirror*.

Seven people responded to the ad. After considering the offers, the search committee finally purchased a twenty-acre tract of hilly land for $4,000 from James Deakin, one of Moscow's largest landowners. In the romanticized view of the town's newspaper editor, "probably [no] more sightly location could . . . be found in Idaho. The location . . . command[s] a perfect view of Paradise valley and the spur of mountains beyond, while by glancing along the side of Tomer butte, one can see the tops of the Bitter Root mountains."

While later generations might agree with that rosy assessment, it took some imagination to envision the property's potential in 1889.

Although a Moscow newspaper bragged that "probably [no] more sightly location could be found in Idaho" for a university, the hill was actually nothing more than a field overlooking a rather ramshackle town when construction began.

It lay completely undeveloped. Only Jim Deakin's wagon road connected the land to the community of Moscow. At one end stood a swamp surrounded by a few willow bushes—the only "trees" on the site. The hill was about a mile from downtown Moscow, which still consisted primarily of small wooden frame buildings and had the disorganized look of a young western town. A standard joke about the community's muddy, unpaved streets circulated frequently in those early years: "One rainy day I saw a black hat floating down the middle of the street. I put planks out and went out to get the hat and underneath I saw a man. I said, 'Can I help you?' And he said, 'No thanks, I'm riding a horse.'"

With money remaining after the purchase, the regents began making improvements. In the fall of 1889 workers excavated a building site, but nothing was constructed until the summer of 1891, when the state finally released additional funds. By the fall of 1892 the thirteen-room west wing of what became known as the Administration Building stood completed. Financial difficulties continued, however, and the structure was finished piecemeal, with the central section and east wing added later. In fact, the entire Administration Building was not done until 1899, ten years after ground-clearing had begun with such optimism.

By the early 1900s, the campus—dominated by Ridenbaugh Hall, the Mines Building (later known as Engineering), and the Administration Building—took on a collegiate air.

In 1891 the regents appointed an acting president. They needed a person willing to serve without pay, preferably someone already living in Moscow who could oversee construction. They chose Regent James H. Forney to lead a university that had no students and no faculty. Forney was a newcomer to Moscow but was well known in Idaho political circles, having served for many years as a territorial prosecuting attorney.

In the summer of 1892 the regents hired their first salaried president, Franklin B. Gault. Gault had been superintendent of public schools in Tacoma, Washington, where he had largely organized that community's

Judge James H. Forney, first acting president of the university.

Franklin Benjamin Gault, the university's first president, poses on the Administration Building steps in the 1890s.

school system and raised money for several new buildings. Since the "university" was to consist of both collegiate and preparatory departments, Gault's experience as both fundraiser and secondary-school educator seemed especially valuable.

Gault arrived on campus in September 1892, and Forney showed him around. They walked up the hill along a dusty path laid across a plowed field. Winding among piles of lath and lumber, they entered the partially completed Administration Building with its unplastered walls. Forney reminisced later that he could almost "see Gault wilt" as the new president viewed the unfinished building and grounds. But Gault stuck it out. A few weeks later, on October 3, 1892, the University of Idaho opened its doors.

On that day Gault and John Edwin Ostrander, the only other faculty member, greeted approximately forty students, the first enrollees. "There was no sidewalk then; no graveled path that wound in sinuous curves across a grass-grown campus," student Florence Corbett Johnson recollected some years later. "Only a wagon road. . . . The dust in this road was ankle deep, and through it waded eager boys and girls in search of education."

With the Administration Building still unfurnished, students sat on windowsills and boxes. "There being no furniture of any sort the programme for the day was brief," Gault later wrote. He and Ostrander jotted down the names of the prospective students and asked about their prior education. On the following day the president administered a short entrance examination, and two days later he announced the results. He deemed no one eligible to undertake collegiate-level work and placed all students in three levels of the preparatory school. The university would

Prep school class of 1899. Until the 1900s, enrollment in the "university's" prep department consistently outnumbered the collegiate department. As high schools proliferated around the state, the university dropped its prep department in 1913.

Lawrence Henry Gipson

The quality of a university is perhaps best judged by the achievements of its alumni. Although the University of Idaho had a collegiate enrollment of less than 100 in 1899 when Lawrence Henry Gipson began his studies, it must have offered those students a good education if his later career is any indication.

Gipson was born in Colorado in 1880, the fourth of eight children of an extraordinary family: four of the siblings would later be listed in Who's Who in America. His parents were civic minded, but his father, Albert, was a restless businessman who grew dissatisfied as a lawyer and went broke as a banker. A multi-talented man, the elder Gipson had published two books on irrigated farming and, upon the failure of his banking business, moved his family to southern Idaho's irrigated farmland region in 1891. Two years later he permanently settled in Caldwell. There he farmed, sold real estate, published two newspapers, and dabbled in politics. His wife, Lina, played a prominent role in establishing the Caldwell Public Library.

Lawrence Henry Gipson was a shy child, and hardly a successful student in his early years. He would later write that his educational career at Caldwell "by no means reflected credit" on the family. When he was elected secretary of his school's Literary Society in the seventh grade his teachers refused to let him serve because they feared he would ruin the society's publication. But, although his formal schoolwork was undistinguished, like many brilliant individuals Gipson voraciously and independently studied in the field that interested him most—history.

By October 1892 the Administration Building—one of Idaho's largest structures, which loomed above the small town of Moscow—stood completed to the point that classes could begin.

operate for a dozen years before students in the collegiate department consistently outnumbered those in the prep school.

The first day of class came on Monday, October 10, 1892. By then Gault had hired Annette Bowman to teach drawing and Nellie Brown as a general instructor in the prep department. It was perhaps the only time that the university had as many women as men on the faculty.

As word of the university's opening filtered through the state, more and more students arrived to register. By the end of the year there were 135 on campus, with a half dozen having advanced to collegiate-level work. President Gault worked hard to encourage more students to come. "It matters not how plainly you are clad, how poor your scholarship, the University offers you its benefits," he wrote in the school's first calendar. "If you are determined to learn, if you will make the efforts and the sacrifices, a liberal education is possible." The inducements worked. By the second academic year the university had attracted 232 students. While many Idahoans had thought that a university for the young state was premature and would remain largely unused, just the opposite occurred. By its second year, the school already faced the chronic budgetary and space problems that would plague it throughout most of its first century.

In fact, the university survived its early years only because of federal largesse. While the state provided some money to purchase land and partially erect the Administration Building, it was not until 1895 that it provided any general operating revenue. Until then, all bills were paid from federal funds.

On July 2, 1862, at the height of northern fear and frustration over the course of the Civil War and with Confederate troops regularly winning significant victories, President Abraham Lincoln had signed into law an act that has been called "the most important single . . . enactment ever made in the interest of education." The law was known as the Morrill Act, named for United States Representative Justin Smith Morrill of Vermont, who worked years for its passage. Commonly called the Land Grant Act, the Morrill Act granted every state 30,000 acres of land for each of its senators and representatives. Proceeds from sales of these lands were to be devoted to the support of at least one college in each state. Morrill envisioned these land-grant colleges as being different from existing institutions that were largely "based upon the classic plan of teaching those only destined to pursue the so-called learned professions, leaving farmers and mechanics . . . to the haphazard of being self-taught or not scientifically taught at all." While states would have the freedom to include classical studies in their land-grant college curriculums, the primary focus would be agricultural and engineering sciences. In view of the existing political situation, the land-grant colleges were also to provide instruction in "military tactics." Except for a few private academies and West Point, the nation had virtually no facilities for military training prior to the Civil War. After that conflict, the country's land-grant colleges would turn out thousands of soldiers for America's armed services.

Twenty-five years after the Morrill Act, Congress had passed another piece of significant educational legislation, the Hatch Act, named for Representative William Hatch of Missouri. It provided that an agricultural experiment station be established at each land-grant institution "to aid in . . . diffusing among the people of the United States useful and practical information on subjects connected with agriculture." An annual grant of $15,000 would be provided to each state that accepted the act's provisions.

Idaho's lawmakers were well aware of these land-grant provisions when they passed legislation creating the university. Since this was Idaho's only college, it was natural that legislators should designate it as the state's land-grant institution. In the early 1890s the university's regents, desperate for funds to finish the Administration Building and hire a staff, took the steps necessary to qualify for federal land-grant funding. They organized the Idaho Experiment Station, immediately receiving $15,000 under the Hatch Act. Thus, agricultural outreach, which has played a prominent role at the university for 100 years, actually began before the university itself. This initial $15,000 enabled the university to open its doors. On December 25, 1892, Secretary of the Interior John Noble presented U.S. Representative Willis Sweet with a Christmas present in Washington, D.C.: another $15,000 check, the university's first funding under the Morrill Act.

The money helped the school survive, but that is about all it did. The University of Idaho had the misfortune of beginning just as the nation slipped into one of its most serious economic recessions. What has come to be called the Depression of 1893 was an economic malaise that actually

It was fortunate for Gipson that his family moved to Caldwell, for Presbyterians had founded the College of Idaho in that town in 1891 under the presidential leadership of the Reverend William Judson Boone. Frustrated at school—having failed some subjects completely—Lawrence Henry Gipson, fifth from left in this

1890s photograph of his family, dropped out and learned the printing trade. But Boone, an energetic recruiter for the young College of Idaho, met with Gipson and convinced him to try once again. Gipson enrolled in the institution in 1897. It was the turning point in his life. He would later dedicate one of his books to Boone.

Gipson did not excel in all subjects at the College of Idaho, but his grades markedly improved. As the "College" at this time offered only preparatory work, Gipson enrolled at the University of Idaho in 1899. His first few semesters in Moscow were passable but hardly noteworthy. The only history class offered was American Constitutional History. But when James MacLean became president of the university in 1900, he greatly expanded the history and political science offerings, teaching many classes in those fields himself. MacLean was the first to truly spark Gipson's intellectual curiosity. The student found the president "a very careful scholar," who first awakened in him "an interest in the study of political institutions." In his junior year Gipson won the university's oratorial contest; during his senior year he got straight A's. Following his graduation in 1903 Gipson became an assistant professor in history and economics at the university.

In 1904 Lawrence Henry Gipson became a Rhodes Scholar in the first year of that program and joined 41 other Americans who studied in Oxford for the next three years. The spark of academic interest that had first flickered at the College of Idaho and University of Idaho burned most brightly at Oxford. It was a perfect location for Gipson to study his favorite topic—English history. He emerged from Oxford, earned a doctorate at Yale, and became one of the outstanding historians of his generation.

Gipson returned to the University of Idaho as a professor of history from 1907 to 1910. Later he taught at Wabash College and Lehigh University. During this time he began work on his magnum opus, The British Empire Before the American Revolution. Before Lawrence Henry Gipson died in September 1971 at age 91—the acknowledged dean of American historians—he saw the fifteenth and concluding volume of his epic history published, a scholarly labor characterized as the "greatest single work by an American historian of our time." It was "a work of synthesis on a scale that few historians could have the temerity to attempt or the longevity to complete," noted one awed observer.

University President James MacLean called the Administration Building a structure "unique in its architecture . . . but with a certain attractiveness and appropriateness."

lasted for several years. States like Idaho, which relied heavily upon agriculture, were especially affected. The market virtually dropped out for many farm products. In the Palouse region of Idaho these difficult times were compounded by a disastrous wet harvest, when wheat sprouted in shocks and went unthreshed. It was the first crop failure ever in the lush Palouse countryside, and the financial reverberations affected everyone. Even Moscow's most prominent merchant, Idaho's Governor William J. McConnell, went bankrupt and lost his huge store and fine house.

Up the hill, the university also faced bleak times as the financially beleaguered state legislature could not provide money to maintain the institution. And in 1895 President Gault received disheartening news from the federal government: the Department of the Interior demanded that $1,410 of Morrill funds be returned because the university had improperly used it to pay the salaries of professors of ancient and modern languages. Gault had no contingency fund, yet he realized that if he neglected to return the money he would jeopardize the university's future federal support. He rushed to Boise and presented his dilemma to the legislature. Almost miraculously the assembly granted the university $16,230 in general operating support. Aside from appropriations for land purchase and building funds, this was the first state aid the institution received.

For the next several years, the state's contributions were erratic at best. Gault continually pleaded for more money, but the legislature could not or would not provide a viable annual maintenance fund. In 1898, James Forney, now president of the Board of Regents and well aware of Gault's difficulties, attempted to embarrass the state into providing its share of the university's budget. "The United States Government . . . does not intend that this or any other state should become a parasite upon Federal bounty," he wrote in his annual report to the governor. "The Morrill and Hatch endowments are not intended as a temptation to sloth and indifference. . . . Neither Idaho nor any other state is doing its duty when it seeks to contribute the least possible amount to meet this government generosity."

Still, the state continued to provide only the minimal amount it could without jeopardizing federal funding. For example, the budget for the 1900-01 school year totaled $45,000, with only 18 percent coming from the state. Morrill and Hatch funds paid the salaries of a history professor, librarian, and professor of physical culture and purchased half of the janitor's supplies. While the legality of utilizing these funds in this way was rather dubious, the university had no choice. By 1902 Idaho stood at the bottom of the list of all western states in the amount of state funding provided for higher education.

Despite the recurring difficulty of obtaining operating support, the legislature continued to fund building construction, and the campus grew steadily during its early years. The crowning achievement was the Administration Building. The structure, as James MacLean described it, was "a building unique in its architecture . . . but with a certain attractiveness and appropriateness and an air of assured completeness which dominated the imagination of all believers as the Mecca and end of their university pilgrimage." The imposing red-brick structure stood four stories high, over half a football field long, its interior finished in California redwood. When finally completed in 1899, it contained forty-five rooms encompassing

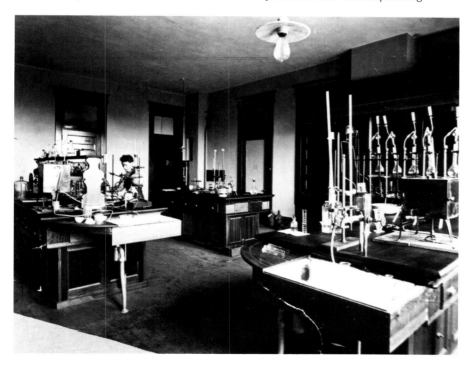

Lawrence Gipson won virtually every major honor awarded to historians in his field— the Justin Winsor Prize, the Loubat Prize, and the Pulitzer Prize. He was perhaps just as satisfied, however, with the award presented to him by his alma mater in 1953. In that year Gipson returned to Moscow to receive an honorary doctorate, shown below. It was a fitting tribute for one of the school's most distinguished alumni. At the same time it was for Gipson a return to the state and the school that had first sparked the curiosity of a great scholar. "The failure of the North Denver Bank in 1890 seemed to our family a cruel stroke of fortune," Gipson reminisced late in life. "But it brought us to Idaho, where in time I became Idaho's first Rhodes Scholar. Had the bank prospered and had we

remained in Colorado . . . I should never have become a Rhodes Scholar. The competition would have been too great. How little can one judge the effect upon his future of the events of the moment!"

The Administration Building—for some years the only structure on campus—housed all university functions, including classrooms and labs.

In the university's early years, the Administration Building also housed the library (below), and a museum in the entrance hall (right).

virtually all university functions. The basement's laboratories emitted rich odors that permeated the entire building. Most of the upper floors served as classrooms. There were also offices for administration and staff, a furnace room, an assembly hall, and a small area euphemistically called the "library." Despite the fact that one early observer termed this "the most substantial and the most attractive building in Idaho," it was overcrowded from the beginning.

For several years the Ad Building stood alone, but in the mid-1890s it was joined by a wooden structure known as the Annex. This small building housed a variety of functions. The entire Agriculture Department fit into one end. "There were bags of wheat that they had secured from the U.S. Government . . . a pair of scales, a cream separator, and a churn," recalled Homer David, a graduate of 1901. "Underneath was a stable for the team of horses which was kept in one corner. In another corner were kept the drill, harrow, and other implements." A small gymnasium occupied the other end. Sandwiched in between was the armory, which stored rifles for students taking military training.

The Annex, a frame building, was the second structure built on campus. In addition to housing the gym and agriculture department, it also served as the armory.

A worker measures feed at the University Farm. In 1896 Moscow residents purchased ninety-four acres adjoining the campus and presented the land to the university. This became the school's farm.

A corn binder on the University Farm.

In 1896 citizens from Moscow purchased ninety-four acres adjoining the campus and presented it to the school. This became the University Farm, and soon workers constructed barns and outbuildings. On the campus proper, the regents authorized construction of a horticulture building and attached greenhouse in 1898. Later this small frame building became known as Liszt Hall, and then Music Hall, serving the campus until 1952.

The regents authorized construction of a horticulture building in 1898. The third major building on campus, this later became known as Liszt Hall and still later as Music Hall. It was dismantled in 1952.

These small wooden buildings hardly relieved the serious campus overcrowding. Enrollments increased each year, from 135 students in 1892 to 358 by 1900. Perhaps no need proved more pressing than dormitory space for women. All students were forced to room in Moscow in the early years. While this arrangement presented no serious problem for men, many parents refused to send their daughters to the school unless they could be properly supervised and housed. Consequently, the state legislature appropriated $25,000 for the erection of a women's dorm. Construction began in 1901 and officials dedicated the building in 1902. It became the first structure on campus named for a person—Mary E. Ridenbaugh, then vice president of the Board of Regents—and was dedicated "to the young women of Idaho." In 1977 the building, the oldest still standing on campus at that time, was listed on the National Register of Historic Places in recognition of its important role in the university's development.

The legislature also appropriated $25,000 for a science hall, and in 1902 workers completed the handsome three-story School of Mines, later known as the Engineering Building. In addition to housing the Departments of Mining and Geology, it also provided space for woodworking shops and the Department of Mechanic Arts. It was torn down in 1951 to make way for a Home Economics building.

By the early 1900s the Annex was completely antiquated, having little room and a leaky roof. Because the university needed a proper gymnasium and

1899: the university's first horticulture class gathers in the new horticulture building's greenhouse.

Ridenbaugh Hall, a women's dormitory, opened in 1902. The second brick building on campus, it brought an elegance heretofore missing, as evidenced in the entrance hall (top), and dining room (bottom).

armory, President MacLean pleaded for additional money from the legislature. He was successful: that body granted $25,000 for building construction. In 1904 laborers completed a handsome red-brick gymnasium and armory, designed by Idaho's most famous architect, J. E. Tourtellotte of Boise. When the larger Memorial Gymnasium was constructed in 1928, this smaller building became the women's gym, and still later Art and Architecture South.

Despite this new construction, the setting remained rustic. Raw sewage drained from the Ad Building onto an open field, then flowed into Paradise Creek. A boardwalk ran from the northeast corner of the campus to the Ad Building, and a gravel road, slushy in spring, led from the eastern edge to that structure. The stagnant pond remained on the corner of campus, nicknamed ''Lake Huntley'' after Frederick Huntley, head of the horticulture department. A barbed-wire fence encircled the campus. The stiles used for crossing this fence proved awkward—especially for women in long dresses. After students and staff had managed to negotiate the barbed wire they were greeted by ''Idaho Violet,'' the College of Agriculture's only cow, a purebred Jersey who was, as some students remembered, ''a wild-eyed flighty bovine, ready and willing to [give] chase . . . on the least provocation.''

When James MacLean became president of the university in 1900, one of his goals was to beautify the campus. Believing the reputation of a university depended partially upon its appearance, he ordered Lake

Workers completed the handsome School of Mines in 1902. Later known as the Engineering Building, it stood until 1951 when it was razed to make way for the Home Economics Building.

Huntley drained—no doubt to the relief of Professor Huntley—and the barbed-wire enclosure removed. In 1903 he persuaded the legislature to provide sufficient funds for campus improvements, and workers began planting trees, flowers, and shrubs.

At the same time, the university's educational structure matured. Lawmakers and university officials agreed that the institution should not be limited only to agriculture and engineering, which were mandated by the Morrill Act. The Organic Act of 1889 creating the university ordained that

As the university grew, class offerings and extracurricular activities proliferated: a zoology class in 1896 (top), and student production of ''The Rivals'', 1900 (bottom).

the institution "provide the means of acquiring a thorough knowledge of the various branches of learning connected with scientific, industrial and professional pursuits." The act mandated departments of arts and letters and once classes began, various other departments proliferated including applied science, engineering, agriculture and mechanic arts, mining and metallurgy, music, and industrial arts.

The expansion was quite impressive, especially in view of the persistent financial difficulties and numerous controversies. In fact, the school was nearly torn apart almost before it began. Statewide sectional disputes had given the university its start when southern Idaho interests attempted to appease the north. But there were many in the south who never liked the idea of having the state university in the panhandle, and for decades university administrators and sympathetic politicians struggled to keep the institution intact.

The first serious attempt to dismember the university came in 1895 when representatives from southeast Idaho introduced legislation to relocate the Department of Agriculture in the south. Had they succeeded, the University of Idaho would have lost its Morrill and Hatch funding. President Gault worked diligently to preserve the institution. His defense of the university during the 1895 crisis was eloquent: "[To] separate the magnificent

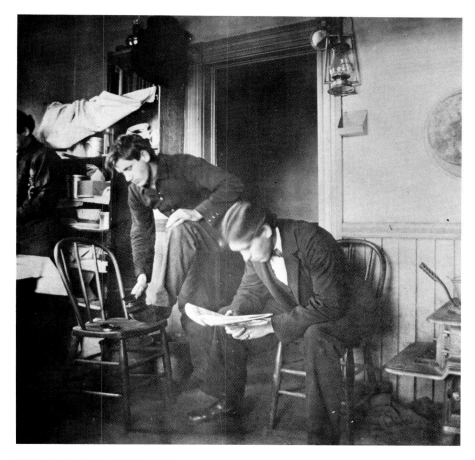

Student housing in 1897, in the days when everyone lived off campus.

University building and the munificent Federal benefactions and . . . maintain two schools is to starve both or crush the people with taxation."

While Gault's warnings were influential, perhaps more decisive was the legal issue raised by some friends of the university: the school could not be split without an amendment to the state constitution. Southern opponents then adopted another strategy. In that same legislative session they introduced a bill to create an entirely new college at Idaho Falls. Although the idea of establishing a separate university would ultimately succeed, the 1895 legislature defeated the bill, realizing it could hardly afford one such institution, let alone two.

One of the most serious problems facing the university was its isolation in a state only loosely linked by a weak transportation system. One of the first students to enroll at the university recalled the two-day trip from his home in Grangeville to Moscow, only 100 miles away. He rode by stage to Lewiston, then crossed the Clearwater River by ferry, then rode another stage up the steep hill to Genesee and on to Moscow.

Trains would eventually connect Grangeville with Moscow; but even when rails created a network through the state the university remained unreachable for many. "It is a pity to have been living in Idaho for nearly twenty years, paying quite heavy taxes, and not be able to benefit from our own schools," wrote one Idahoan. "The University is built so far from the center of the state that we cannot afford to send our children there." The Regents labored for years to obtain reduced railway rates for students, and in 1898 the state's two major railroads agreed to lower student rates substantially. In later years, the "Student Special" trains, which snaked their way throughout Idaho, became extremely popular.

The class of 1901 planted a tree on the Administration Building lawn on Arbor Day, 1900 (right), then reunited every five years to have their photograph taken in front of it (facing page).

Even with improved and cheaper transportation, many residents of the southeast remained discontented with the university's location. In 1901 the legislature passed a bill creating the Academy of Idaho at Pocatello, the forerunner of Idaho State University. The bill also set aside 40,000 acres of the University of Idaho's land grant for the exclusive use of the academy. Northern Idaho's representatives supported the bill, which passed easily. Their action might seem surprising, since they gave away part of the university's land grant, but in actuality they were returning a favor to legislators of the southeast who had voted for the Moscow institution a dozen years earlier. They may also have hoped that the creation of the Pocatello academy would defuse future attempts at segregating the university. If so, they must have been disappointed when the segregation battles continued.

In 1905 the legislature considered a proposal to relocate the School of Mines at Hailey. Once again, supporters of the university pointed out the illegality of the action. Swayed by these arguments, the legislature defeated the bill. Legislators then halfheartedly considered a proposal to create a second School of Mines but in 1905 decided—as they had in 1895—that the state could not afford two institutions. Still, the segregation battles of 1895 and 1905 merely presaged many more to come.

As the new university struggled for survival, it experienced some rocky relations between its presidents and Board of Regents. In fact, the regents forced the university's first two executives to resign.

Franklin Gault was in many ways an ideal first president. He was an excellent administrator of an institution that had more high school than collegiate students. He was also very instrumental in developing the strong public-school system in Idaho that eventually made the preparatory

The Silver and Gold Book

Protected in the University of Idaho Library is perhaps the school's most cherished memento, one of the few artifacts to survive the Administration Building fire of 1906, an object that links the university of the twentieth century to its embryonic predecessor of the nineteenth century. It is known as the Silver and Gold Book.

The 1893 Columbian Exposition held in Chicago, the famous "White City," captured the imagination of the nation. Here Americans put on a show for themselves and the world. It was a gaudy affair, participants attempting to outdo one another in the grandiosity of their exhibits. The new state of Idaho hoped to make a spectacular appearance at its first world's fair.

In 1892 an Idaho selection committee chose Spokane's Kirtland K. Cutter, one of the Northwest's preeminent architects, to design its fair building. The structure, shown below, was a three-story log cabin, with virtually all of the construction materials coming from Idaho. The building, a decided hit, attracted 10,000 visitors a day. Residents from throughout Idaho worked to fill the building with materials to show off their new state. There were Indian artifacts and chairs

made of antlers; paintings, photographs, and needlework; stuffed animals and pressed wildflowers; forty-five display pieces of timber, including the largest at the fair—an eighty-foot section of Idaho red cedar; apples, prunes, peaches, and a yard-long sweet potato. Some of the items did not survive the Exposition. Somebody stole a silver cup, a $1,000 silver brick, and opals from Owyhee County.

Women around the state organized several clubs to ensure that their communities would be represented. In Moscow, some formed the Ladies' Columbian Association, with Mrs. J. H. Forney as president. In seeking an appropriate representation for the college town they turned to Franklin Gault, president of the university; Annette Bowman, the school's first art teacher; and R. M. Crockett, a Moscow jeweler. Together the three developed the idea of a Silver and Gold Book. The "book," seen below, is actually a jewelry box resembling a book. Its cover is adorned with scenes from Idaho: mining, lumbering, hunting, and agriculture. The center medallion is an engraving of the university's Administration Building, "a perfect

department superfluous. At the same time, he was not unaware of the needs of the university and its college-level students. He fought aggressively and successfully to prevent the school from being segregated, encouraged the growth of campus clubs and organizations, and was largely responsible for the early social development of the student body.

Despite his obvious skills, Gault became a victim of Idaho's political system. Until 1898, the governor appointed a whole new Board of Regents every two years. The system proved manageable during Gault's first years, when his friend William McConnell held the governor's office. But in 1897 Frank Steunenberg succeeded McConnell and appointed a new board that was unsympathetic to Gault. In the summer of 1898 the regents forced the president's resignation. The legislature eventually passed a law giving regents staggered terms, thus ensuring board continuity. But it was too late to help the school's first administrator.

Joseph P. Blanton, the regents' choice as successor, lasted only two stormy years. A native of Virginia, Blanton was forty-eight years old when he became president. Tall, well groomed, and with an ample mustache, Blanton was a brilliant public speaker. He had been a public-school teacher, a professor, and a college dean before he arrived in Moscow. Though he was at the University of Idaho only a short time, Blanton's administration made some significant contributions. Chief among them were the first summer school in the Pacific Northwest, held in 1899, and advances in the work of the Experiment Station. In fact, Blanton, an indefatigable worker, named himself director of the station as well as professor of political science and history, in addition to his administrative duties.

Within a year of his taking office a significant number of faculty members began to openly criticize the president. At the same time, the Board of Regents assumed many administrative duties that Blanton thought were his responsibility. In 1899 the board fired two faculty members without consulting Blanton; when the regents continued to interfere with day-to-day operations, the president exploded, writing the Board in 1900 that "you cannot be indifferent to the fact that during the whole of this scholastic year you have studiously ignored the President in your dealings with members of the faculty, students and even the janitors." At the same time, Blanton accused two regents of graft in connection with the completion of the Administration Building.

By the spring of 1900 relations between the board and its hand-picked executive could hardly have been worse. When the regents returned a report to the president and requested that it be altered, Blanton refused. Consequently, in June 1900 the board asked for Blanton's resignation. The president again refused and filed a lawsuit against the board, claiming he was being wrongfully deprived of his office. A court ruled that the regents could hire—and fire—whomever they pleased, and Blanton quietly left town, devastated.

The next president proved a more fortunate choice. James A. MacLean was a tall, thirty-two-year-old Canadian bachelor when he became president in

The university's third president, James MacLean, advertised widely in an effort to lure students to Idaho.

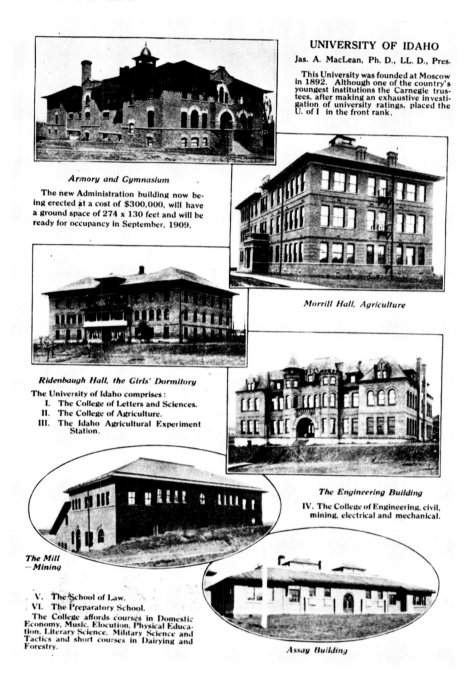

UNIVERSITY OF IDAHO
Jas. A. MacLean, Ph. D., LL. D., Pres.

This University was founded at Moscow in 1892. Although one of the country's youngest institutions the Carnegie trustees, after making an exhaustive investigation of university ratings, placed the U. of I in the front rank.

Armory and Gymnasium

The new Administration building now being erected at a cost of $300,000, will have a ground space of 274 x 130 feet and will be ready for occupancy in September, 1909.

Morrill Hall, Agriculture

Ridenbaugh Hall, the Girls' Dormitory

The University of Idaho comprises:
I.   The College of Letters and Sciences.
II. The College of Agriculture.
III. The Idaho Agricultural Experiment Station.

The Engineering Building

IV. The College of Engineering, civil, mining, electrical and mechanical.

The Mill —Mining

V. The School of Law.
VI. The Preparatory School.
The College affords courses in Domestic Economy, Music, Elocution, Physical Education, Literary Science, Military Science and Tactics and short courses in Dairying and Forestry.

Assay Building

1900. He was in some ways eccentric. Frequently he appeared on campus apparently well dressed—until one noticed he had forgotten to exchange his bedroom slippers for shoes. He regularly taught classes at his home, sometimes from his bed. He was also an abysmal public speaker. Yet despite his quirks and shortcomings, MacLean was an outstanding administrator. He came to Idaho from the University of Colorado, where he

and correct likeness'' in the opinion of a Moscow newspaper reporter writing in 1893. The Idaho state seal, a covered wagon, a pack train, and a railroad train embellish the spine. The book was handmade in New York, then shipped to Moscow, where Crockett adorned it with rubies from Ruby Creek and opals from the Moscow opal mines.

The Ladies' Columbian Association displayed the book at the home of Mrs. A. T. Spotswood so Moscow's residents could preview their masterpiece. The Moscow reporter was ''surprised to behold such an artistic piece of workmanship. We expected to see something real nice, but our expectations were not pitched to such a high state but that we were surprised on seeing.'' He encouraged the town's residents to support the Association's fundraising efforts to defray the $290 cost of the book.

By accepting private contributions, charging club membership dues, and hosting fundraisers, the Ladies' Association raised the amount needed to pay for the book, purchase a protective case, and ship it to Chicago. In fact, they had $1.25 left over. After the Columbian Exposition, the club displayed the book at a fair in San Francisco, then donated it to the University of Idaho.

The book remained in the university president's office until 1906, admired by all who visited. When the Administration Building caught fire on March 30, some heroic students burst into the office to save what they could. In the smoke and heat they were unable to find much and had to leave quickly with only two objects: the Silver and Gold Book, and a rather moth-eaten stuffed mountain sheep. While rescuers saved some valuable university records from other parts *of the building, these were the only two mementos salvaged. For a number of years the university displayed the sheep in the school's gymnasium. Officials eventually discarded it. The Silver and Gold Book remains—a treasured reminder of the university's early history and of the dedicated efforts of Moscow women to see that their town was appropriately represented at the grandest celebration of the 1890s.*

had witnessed many attempts to separate various parts of that institution. This experience served him well in Moscow, where virtually every legislature during his tenure introduced a segregation bill. MacLean repeatedly rushed to Boise to lobby the legislature just when things seemed the most hopeless, and he always returned victorious. That the university remained intact during his thirteen-year tenure as president is largely a credit to MacLean's keen administrative and political abilities.

MacLean needed all of his considerable administrative skills to rebuild the campus after a fire destroyed its most important landmark. Early in the morning of March 30, 1906, Moscow residents awakened to fire bells and the clatter of hose carts. The Administration Building was ablaze. At first it hardly seemed possible that the entire building would burn, but fire swirled up the open stairway, engulfed the redwood interior, and within a few hours left nothing but "the gaunt, staring walls of the great building," in the words of Jay Glover Eldridge, dean of the faculty. Heroic action by students and staff saved some important university materials: registrar's records, the chemical library, some laboratory equipment. Eldridge enlisted the help of a student, commandeered a ladder, and entered his office through a window. He tossed out desk drawers filled with deans' records to a crowd below, who carried them to safety.

In spite of these efforts, virtually everything was lost. At first people believed the walls remained strong enough to support a rebuilt structure, but that proved impossible and they were dynamited. It was a crushing

The Administration Building burns, March 30, 1906.

For a while, some people believed the Ad Building walls remained sound enough to rebuild, but the idea proved infeasible and workers dynamited the structure.

A crew cleans brick from the destroyed Administration Building.

blow to a young university. The school's dynamic president had just won another battle to prevent dismemberment; the collegiate department was finally larger than the prep department and growing steadily; the grounds were improving; the campus had just been graced with the construction of new, substantial buildings. Some people were disconsolate when virtually the entire town gathered on the morning after the blaze to view the damage. Not James MacLean, an eternal optimist. He used the fire as a tool to prod the legislature into increasing its support.

The Ad Building fire of 1906 was destined to become a turning point in the university's history. To many it appeared that the direction would be toward a future of retrenchment, when the small college would cease growing and might even lose its long struggle for survival. With MacLean at the helm, the university turned in just the opposite direction. Upon the ashes of the old Administration Building MacLean supervised the erection of an even larger Ad Building. That structure symbolized the University of Idaho's growth and maturity as a major institution of higher education—a maturing process begun by MacLean in the days following the fire and continued by the administrations that followed.

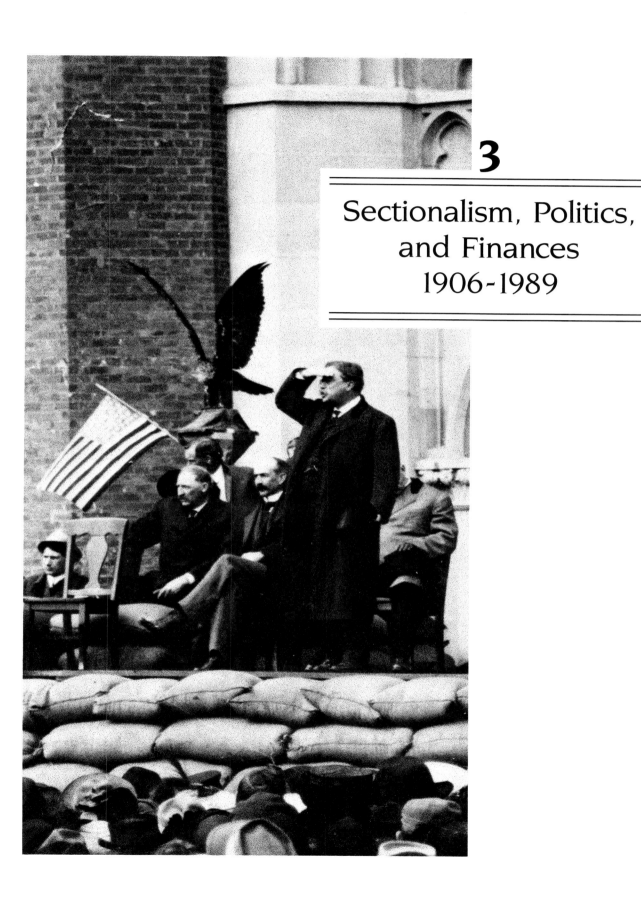

3

Sectionalism, Politics, and Finances
1906-1989

The Administration Building was still smoldering when James MacLean called a meeting of the faculty early on the morning of Saturday, March 31, 1906. The president insisted that classes be held as scheduled the following week, and he sent staff members throughout Moscow looking for space where students could meet. He feared that cancelling classes would provide ammunition for southern Idaho politicians who wanted to dismember the university. He was relieved to receive a telegram from Governor Frank Gooding that weekend: the Administration Building would be rebuilt, and no part of the university would be moved. In fact, for a time after the fire, the university enjoyed a level of legislative support it had not experienced since its founding.

Campus officials and townspeople met the day after the Administration Building fire in 1906 to plan for the continuation of classes.

Destruction of the Ad Building did create administrative headaches, however. The most pressing was finding space in which to carry on the university's functions. Staff offices and the library moved into the gymnasium. The residents of Moscow offered their new Carnegie Library, the Methodist church, and various lodge halls to the university. The facilities were not completely suitable for instruction, as Harold Axtell recalled of his experience teaching preparatory classes in the Carnegie Library: "This was not conducive to learning for these rooms were open, and more than once I discovered amorous couples among the book stacks." Though somewhat inconvenienced, campus life continued, and students completed their term without losing a day.

At the same time, MacLean began making plans for constructing new buildings. The president convinced the regents to construct a building for the College of Agriculture, to be named Morrill Hall, with insurance money from the fire. MacLean's idea of using insurance money to build Morrill was a gamble. If the state legislature agreed to appropriate additional funds to

Until workers completed the new Administration Building, classroom activity had to shift elsewhere. Some classes met downtown in Moscow's new Carnegie library (top), while the gymnasium doubled as the library (bottom).

also construct a new Administration Building, the university would come out of the fire with two buildings instead of one. However, if that body refused the appropriation, the school would be without a main building and would be in a weakened position to defend itself against the inevitable future segregation battles. Fortunately for MacLean and the school, the legislature agreed to the request, and two new buildings rose on campus. MacLean had greatly strengthened the school's position, because most of the separation battles had centered on removing the agricultural college. With a handsome, expensive new agriculture building on campus, it would be more difficult for segregationists to garner support for removing the college.

With insurance from the Administration Building fire,
President MacLean built Morrill Hall (right) to serve as an
agriculture building for such classes as Dairy Science,
shown in this 1908 photograph (below).

The regents hired Boise architect J. E. Tourtellotte to design a new Administration Building. Tourtellotte worked closely with MacLean, and the two came up with a plan for a three-story Gothic structure with a 130-foot tower to be located on the site of the burned building. The legislature approved $275,000, and construction started in 1907. The building opened in 1909 with only one major change from the original design: in order to save money, the front tower stood only eighty feet high.

The legislature appropriated $275,000 to construct a new Administration Building. Work began in 1907, and the doors opened in 1909. It took several more years, however, before wings on the north and south completed the structure.

The Presidential Grove

Good publicity never hurts. The university has always sought all the good publicity it could get, especially during its early years, as it struggled to convince the state legislature to provide the support needed for survival and growth. Few publicists have come upon a better gimmick than gracing their organizations with the presence of famous people. The usefulness of this technique has not escaped University of Idaho administrators, and many visits by luminaries have been marked by permanent reminders of their coming: the planting of trees in the Presidential Grove.

In the latter part of the twentieth century, campus growth shifted northward so that the historic core of the university's grounds—the area between Ridenbaugh Hall and the Administration Building—is not as well traveled as it was in earlier days. Just in front of the southern edge of the Ad Building rests a grove of mature trees. Though each has a plaque describing who planted it and on what date, most people casually walk by the grove today, unaware of its significance. Though somewhat misnamed—only one sitting American president has ever planted a tree here—this is the university's Presidential Grove, a living reminder of important publicity events in the school's past.

The first tree-planting ceremony was perhaps the best. On April 9, 1911, former president Theodore Roosevelt came to Idaho, and, in his inimitable way, made a bully time of it. He arrived by train, and thousands of people greeted him. He was driven in an open car to the Hotel Moscow, grinning and waving the entire way, followed by a motorcade four blocks long.

A large crowd gathered the next morning to watch Teddy leave for breakfast at Ridenbaugh Hall. By eight in the morning people began to mass in front of the Administration Building around a platform of wheat sacks draped in bunting, backed by an American flag and stuffed eagles. Thousands of them came—between 8,000 and 20,000 depending upon whose estimate you believed, Teddy's naturally being the highest. There they stood in the rain, waiting for the great man. "At 9:03 Mr. Roosevelt mounted the pile of wheat sacks," reported the Argonaut. "The rain ceased, the sun almost shone and 'Teddy' grinned. . . . Then the crowd yelled, every man after his own fashion and at the top of his own voice." TR gave an address expressing his ideals for a university education, then dismounted the platform and departed on a train to Spokane. The nation's twenty-fifth president had "honored the University of Idaho and the city of Moscow with his presence for sixteen hours."

On his stroll from Ridenbaugh Hall to the platform of wheat, Teddy paused long enough to "honor a little tree [a blue spruce] by planting it on the campus," in the words of the Argonaut reporter, while university students gave an Idaho yell. Thus began the Presidential Grove.

In many ways the university's immediate recovery from the fire was impressive. Yet the old battles to prevent segregation and obtain adequate funding soon resumed. Indeed, the University of Idaho has never enjoyed long-term lush times, and seldom have revenues kept pace with the institution's steady growth. The university's enrollment—which stood at 202 in 1906—reached 1,000 shortly after World War I, 4,000 in the 1950s, and 9,000 in the 1980s. With this rising student population came increased needs for faculty, staff, and buildings. Urgent requests for more money to meet these demands became a familiar refrain. The task was never easy, as Idaho's legislators, working in a state with a small population and limited revenues, wrestled with the continuing problem of allocating scarce resources to various state agencies.

The nearly completed Administration Building in 1909 (above) and Poultry marketing class (below).

The university's financial difficulties often led to innovative policies, particularly in paying for new buildings. For example, several structures—such as Memorial Gymnasium—were built using money donated by individuals. Funds provided by the national Young Men's Christian Association built the Y-Hut, or U-Hut. Unable to squeeze money from the legislature to construct dormitory space, the Board of Regents in 1920 came up with a unique idea: they asked Moscow businessmen to pass a bond issue to construct a building. The businessmen retained ownership until the university paid off the indebtedness with student rental income. The university constructed Lindley Hall in this way in 1920, and Forney Hall in 1923. The system became an Idaho trademark, and over the years many of the school's most prominent structures were financed by similar bonds. The plan was copied by other state universities around the nation.

Forney Hall during construction (top), and its ceremonious dedication on June 11, 1923 (bottom).

The tree stood alone for only six months. On October 4, 1911, William Howard Taft became the only president of the United States ever to visit Moscow while still in office. Taft, who lacked Roosevelt's charisma, drew a crowd only about half as large. The president was in Moscow only an hour, just long enough to speak on foreign relations to people assembled on the Ad Building lawn and plant a Port Orford cedar in the Presidential Grove.

Vice President Thomas R. Marshall visited campus in November 1917, while the university was on wartime alert. He addressed a small crowd on international affairs and the nation's need for university-educated people. Then, appropriately for a native Indianan, he planted an Indiana red oak in the grove.

For fifteen years the three trees stood by themselves. The planting of the fourth was not nearly so festive an event as the earlier ceremonies had been, even though university officials hoped it would be. On October 12, 1932, the university celebrated the fortieth anniversary of the beginning of classes with a large convocation in Memorial Gym. President Mervin Neale thought he had negotiated a coup when he convinced Vice President Charles Curtis to take time out during a western campaign swing to visit the campus. Curtis came, but despite Neale's pleading he refused to say a word to those gathered in the gymnasium. He did, however, consent to plant an Engelmann spruce in the Presidential Grove.

Considerably more fanfare attended the 1938 tree-planting ceremony of Teddy Roosevelt's niece—First Lady Eleanor Roosevelt. But then, ceremony always seemed to surround the Roosevelt family. The Borah Foundation had invited Roosevelt to speak on world peace. President Harrison Dale agreed to greet her at the Spokane airport and transport her to Moscow but, after experiencing two flat tires on the way, had to ask with great embarrassment for a limousine to assist. Dale fixed his flat tires in time to intercept the official party in Spangle and drove the First Lady the rest of the way. At each small town along the route crowds cheered and waved flags as she passed. Only Pullman was silent— perhaps miffed that the president's wife chose to visit Washington State College's arch-rival. After meeting with the press and before giving her speech, Roosevelt planted a Douglas fir on the Ad Building lawn, shown below.

Although it is still called the Presidential Grove, other people have also planted trees here. There is a fir commemorating the bicentennial of George Washington's birth, a pine marking the fiftieth anniversary of the university's Borah Foundation, and trees planted by Idaho's senator Frank Church and university alumnus and diplomat Philip Habib. The ceremonies surrounding these plantings have been less grandiose than the visits of the Roosevelts, but all have served to publicize the university—and beautify the Ad Building lawn.

The Life Science Building under construction in August 1924 (above), and dedicated in September 1924 (below).

The university faced another critical situation in the 1930s. At a time when the legislature reduced state appropriations, enrollment climbed rapidly. Despite the difficult financial situation, the school experienced one of its most impressive building booms during this period. Again, creative financing proved the key. Major additions during the decade included Neale Stadium, Sweet and Chrisman dorms, and a Student Union Building—all financed by bonds. The infirmary and a library addition were funded by the federal Public Works Administration.

The heating plant is shown under construction in 1927 (left). The university library was overcrowded by the 1930s (below). Not until 1957, however, did a new facility provide comfortable space (following page).

With state appropriations lagging behind needs, university officials sought other ways to finance needed buildings. Funds from the federal Public Works Administration paid for the infirmary. Students and staff broke ground in 1936 (left), and the building was ready for use the next year (below).

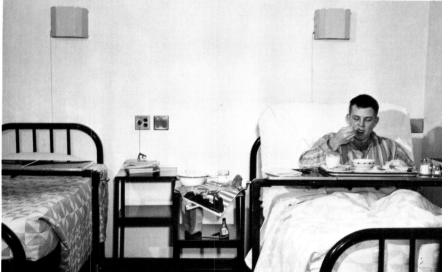

The late 1940s and 1950s brought yet another major building expansion, the beginning of the most dramatic period of construction in the school's history—mostly paid from appropriations provided by "a suddenly progressive legislature."

The Music Building (right) was one of many constructed during the building boom of the 1950s. However, no structure added during that decade brought a more dramatic change to campus than the "new" I tank, replacing the long-time landmark, the "old" I tank (below).

As enrollment continued to rise in response to the nation's "baby boom," university officials struggled to keep pace. They authorized millions of dollars' worth of construction in the 1960s, 1970s, and 1980s. The state financed some buildings, student fees paid for others, private donors helped build some, and throughout the period bonds remained an effective money-raising method. The rapid construction in this period drastically changed the campus, yet in such a way that the school's central core encircling the Administration Building lawn retained its historic integrity.

Millions of dollars worth of construction in the 1960s, 1970s, and 1980s changed the complexion of the university. Structures completed during this time included the renovated Student Union Building (top), the University Classroom Center (left), and the Education Building with its distinctive Kiva (following page).

The structure gaining the most publicity at this time was the Kibbie–ASUI Dome, a covered football, basketball, and track complex named the nation's outstanding structural engineering achievement of 1976.

The Kibbie-ASUI Activity Center, named the nation's outstanding structural engineering achievement of 1976, is shown here while under construction in 1975.

While school officials generally found imaginative ways to keep up with building needs, money for staffing and programs proved more difficult to obtain. The university's low salary scale made it harder to secure and retain "first-class men and women to instruct the young people of the state," noted President Alfred Upham in 1923. "It is no exaggeration to say that the survival of the University . . . as the present generation has known it depends not on expanded but simply on restored appropriations," lamented President Harrison Dale in 1939. Yet another president wrote seventeen years later that the "salary situation at the University of Idaho is serious—in fact, is becoming alarming." In 1972 President Ernest Hartung, noting that funding increases continued to lag behind growth rates, stated: "I don't think people realize how desperately bad off we are." And the university's financial situation led directly to the resignation of three presidents: Melvin Brannon in 1917, Ernest H. Lindley in 1920, and Harrison Dale in 1946.

While university administrators struggled with the funding problem, they also had to withstand continued attempts to dismember parts of the school. The legislative spirit of unanimity in the immediate aftermath of the Administration Building fire quickly faded as old sectional differences resurfaced. During every legislative session following the conflagration until his resignation in 1913, President MacLean fought bills attempting to remove the College of Agriculture to the southern part of the state. And

Charles Houston Shattuck

Charles Shattuck debarked from a train at the Moscow depot on September 1, 1909, to begin a new job as the first head of the university's recently created department of forestry. Compared to his surroundings at South Carolina's Clemson University, the small Idaho community appeared a bit forlorn—"a dust-covered little town . . . without one foot of pavement." As he made his way up the hill to the university his disappointment must have increased. This was not a campus of lush greenery like older institutions in the East. Here was a college that had spent its first twenty years merely trying to survive. School administrators had so far been unable to pay much attention to beautification. In 1909 Shattuck found the grounds "practically void of trees and shrubbery," and "the surroundings . . . lonesome . . . the solitude oppressive." Charles Houston Shattuck would change all that in the next eight years. He, more than any other individual, was responsible for transforming the University of Idaho from a group of buildings into a beautiful campus. Along the way he also developed one of the nation's earliest university forestry programs.

the battles continued for several years after MacLean left. As the years wore on, campus officials were able to take these legislative moves less seriously. After the legislature defeated a bill to move the university to "some other place than Moscow" in 1917, the *Argonaut*—the student newspaper—hypothesized that these "biennial threats" had merely become bargaining chips introduced to force friends of the university to vote for the pet measures of representatives from other parts of the state.

By the 1920s the long segregation disputes had largely subsided. But sectional fights continued, with the end result that while the University of Idaho retained all of its colleges and departments, it had to increasingly compete with other institutions for meager state revenues. In Pocatello, an ambitious Miles Frank Reed, a University of Idaho graduate of the class of 1901, served as principal of the Academy of Idaho and aspired to make it into a four-year, degree-granting institution. In 1915 he succeeded in changing its name to the Idaho Technical College, and the rapidly growing school became a rival for legislative funding. The University of Idaho's backers believed most state money for higher education should go to one institution—in Moscow. People in the southern part of the state viewed the matter differently. The south had 70 percent of Idaho's population, yet the only public southern institution of higher education received merely 30 percent of legislative appropriations for higher education. Southerners maintained that Idaho's growing population and the difficulty of travel between south and north justified another major university in Pocatello.

In 1925 state senators introduced a bill that would have changed the name of the Institute to the Idaho College of Agriculture and Mechanics and transferred all federal Morrill and Hatch Act funds from Moscow to Pocatello. "Idaho has not the population nor the wealth adequately to support two degree-granting institutions," the Spokane *Spokesman-Review* editorialized. "The state could better afford to make an appropriation yearly to pay the railroad fare of all southern Idaho students going to Moscow than to plunge into the stupendous mistake of making another four-year college in Idaho."

Despite the warning, the bill came within one vote of passing. Northern Idaho's representatives realized some type of compromise was necessary to keep the Pocatello institution from becoming an even larger drain upon the university's appropriations. Similarly, southern Idaho representatives saw that it was not yet an opportune time to pass legislation creating a four-year institution in Pocatello. University of Idaho President Alfred Upham and Idaho Technical Institute President Jesse Retherford agreed that a melding of the two institutions would better serve both. Thus, in 1927, the institute became the Southern Branch of the University of Idaho—a school that now had two campuses, separated by 600 miles.

For twenty years administrators at the University of Idaho supervised activities on the two far-flung campuses. The relationship between the two remained amicable, and the system served the state's needs. But residents of southern Idaho continued to demand a four-year institution, and bonds

Sectionalism, Politics, and Finances

between the two were not strong enough to withstand the old sectional differences between north and south.

In order to make the school more accessible to all residents of the state, and dampen the movement to dismember the university, campus officials persuaded railroads to provide special trains to transport students to Moscow. The trains began in the southeast part of Idaho and snaked their way northwest. The arrival of the "Student Special" in Moscow was always a festive occasion marking the start of another year.

Charles Shattuck was a handsome forty-one-year-old Missouri native with dark hair and a well-trimmed beard when he arrived in Moscow. He had just recently received his master's and doctoral degrees in the comparatively new field of forestry from the University of Chicago. Shattuck was not immediately accepted on the campus. "The forestry course was considered as more or less of a fad—an untried experiment," he later wrote. "Its faculty and students were regarded as rather outside the family of colleges." Indeed, even his use of the term "faculty" was a little presumptuous, for Shattuck at first was the faculty—"one lone Prof to do everything," he lamented.

But Shattuck, a dedicated, loyal, and hard worker, plunged into his new task. During his first year he offered three forestry courses. He taught his classes in a combined classroom and laboratory, and met with his eleven students in a "7 x 9 office on the first landing of the stairway in Morrill Hall, [with] one office desk, one office chair, [and] one other chair."

Shattuck often worked well past midnight, laying the groundwork for what he hoped would become an important department. He utilized the local area to make up for resources the university lacked. He talked Potlatch Lumber Company officials into allowing him to use its large mills and numerous logging camps as teaching facilities. The company also donated timber and equipment for experiments. Shattuck became intimately familiar with the local landscape and what it had to offer. "We went to the forests, the logging camps, and the mills to get the facts," he wrote. Frequently Shattuck could be seen leading a group of students on twenty-mile hikes across the Palouse hills, sometimes slogging through snow, leaving before dawn, returning at dark, wet, cold, and tired. Shattuck asked his students to endure no more than he did, and his efforts to provide a forestry program of high quality paid off. He gained the respect of his academic colleagues and university administrators, and the department grew rapidly. So did Shattuck's stature on campus.

The administration added more faculty members to the department. In 1913 the department was transferred from the College of Agriculture to the College of Letters and Science, and a few months later officials appointed Shattuck as the first dean of that college. From then until 1917 he held the joint titles of head of the forestry department and dean of the college.

One of Shattuck's plans for improving the department's teaching ability was to create an arboretum on campus. During his first year at the university Shattuck began to covetously eye "an unsightly disfiguration back of the campus which no one seemed to want, and which could not be kept free from noxious weeds of every kind." At President James MacLean's request, Shattuck presented a proposal to the regents to turn the thistle patch into an arboretum. He argued that the arboretum would not only train students, but also help beautify the campus. The regents approved the plan.

In the spring of 1910 Shattuck, nurseryman Clement L. Price, and all the students of the forestry department planted seeds and nursed them through one of the driest, hottest springs in Latah County's history. Price made numerous wagon trips to Moscow Mountain, returning with small

The battle to split the campuses began in earnest in the late 1930s. The Idaho Southern student newspaper in 1938 requested that "Idaho Southern be entirely removed from the domination and inexcusable strangling it now suffers as a result of Moscow dictation." The University of Idaho Alumni Association denounced the call for another four-year college, while the

The university honored its prize cow, Idaho Violet Rosch Ormsby, in 1923. She stood at the head of the banquet table and provided the meal's beverage.

The Little International agricultural show was one of the major annual campus events and normally included a parade—such as this one in 1936—through campus and downtown.

Southern Branch Alumni lobbied for just such an institution. Legislators regularly introduced bills to separate Idaho Southern and make it a four-year college.

Debate over severing the campuses subsided during World War II but resurfaced again immediately afterward when a series of events caused residents throughout the state to seriously reexamine the issue. Large numbers of Idaho veterans returning from the war were anxious to obtain four-year educations under the GI Bill. The University of Idaho simply could

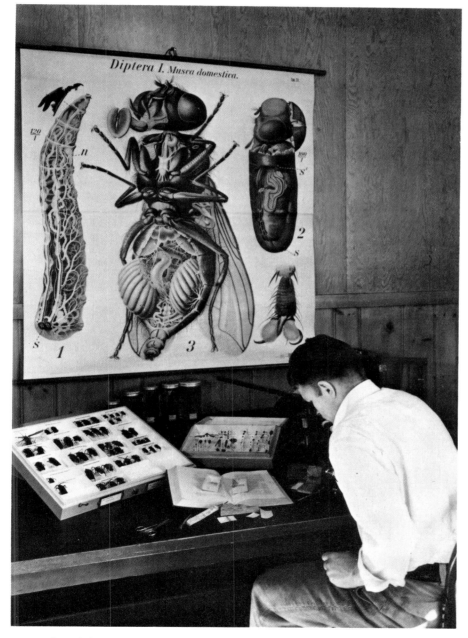

Entomology lab (1937).

conifers for the arboretum. Through their diligent efforts over 12,000 trees representing 150 species survived, including the four-year-old black cherry shown here with Shattuck in 1914. The former weed patch on the edge of the campus thrived through the years—largely due to the untiring work of Clement Price—and became the cornerstone of a landscape-beautification project that eventually encompassed the entire university grounds. It was also the first university arboretum in the West.

Shattuck meanwhile became embroiled in a continuing feud between Idaho's governor Moses Alexander and university president Melvin Brannon. Shattuck—always loyal—spoke out strongly in defense of his president. Despite his outstanding and widely recognized accomplishments, the Board of Regents forced him to resign at the end of 1917 in a housecleaning effort after Brannon left. Not only was the move controversial, it cost the university one of its most gifted educators.

For two years Shattuck taught at the University of California at Berkeley. Then he returned to Idaho, serving as manager of the Mountain States Building and Loan Association at

65

Idaho Falls. He died at that city in 1931.

Two years after his death a new generation of university officials finally gave Shattuck posthumous honor for his untiring work on campus. They named the former weed patch—now a beautiful wooded lot used by walkers, picnickers, recreationists, and researchers—the Charles Houston Shattuck Arboretum. A clearing in the arboretum, formerly used as a rifle range, was planted to grass and decorated with picnic tables and a fireplace. It became known as Price Green in honor of Clement Price, Shattuck's friend and assistant, seen here in 1924 with black locust seedlings.

not meet the increased demand. Facing this pressure, C. A. Robins, a northern Idahoan who was elected governor in 1946, supported the idea of a second four-year college. The willingness of an important state leader to compromise on an issue that had heretofore divided politicians along geographical lines opened the door to legislative change. In 1947 both houses of the legislature unanimously passed a bill creating a four-year Idaho State College at Pocatello, making it completely independent of the University of Idaho.

If University of Idaho supporters believed decentralization of the state's higher-education program would end with the formation of Idaho State College, they were mistaken. The Lewiston State Normal School had been founded in 1893, eventually changing its name to the Northern Idaho College of Education. In 1949 the state legislature closed the college amid much bitter sectional strife, with northern representatives opposing the move. The campus opened again in 1955, under a new name and new administration. Lewis-Clark Normal School was then operated as a division of the University of Idaho and consisted of a two-year program to train elementary-school teachers. Once again the university maintained two campuses. Then, following the pattern of the Southern Branch, in the 1960s Lewis-Clark Normal split away from its parent school, becoming a four-year, tax-supported institution known as Lewis-Clark State College.

In the southwest, residents of the state's largest city had long clamored for a university. Had it not been necessary to appease the north in the 1880s, the state university would in all likelihood have been located in Boise, which was in many ways the most logical site. Residents of the capital city had formed an academy in 1882, and the Episcopal Church had turned this into a private junior college by the early 1930s. In 1939 the state legislature passed a law permitting the organization of junior-college districts. Under this ordinance, Boise Junior College became a tax-supported institution. But the residents of Boise—like those in Pocatello and Lewiston—demanded a four-year college, something they received by legislative action in 1965 when Boise Junior College became Boise State College; in 1974 it was granted university status.

"Can Idaho really support another state university at Boise or anywhere else in the state at this time?" questioned the *Argonaut* during the debate surrounding the establishment of Boise's new four-year school. The issue was a familiar one. Though the University of Idaho survived many segregation efforts, it was powerless to stop the infusion of new four-year institutions elsewhere in the state. As both the university and the state approached their centennials in the late 1980s, many residents continued to ponder whether a state with such limited financial resources could adequately maintain four four-year institutions, three with graduate programs. Throughout the 1960s, 1970s, and 1980s some legislators called for the closing of one or more of the campuses. As Idaho neared the end of its first 100 years of statehood, many residents could not help but wish that legislators had paid more attention when University of Idaho president James MacLean, early in the twentieth century, warned about the dangers

Art class (1947).

of attempting to support too many schools: "Would Idaho throw in its lot with those states which had declared for a unified University and a unified State, or with those states . . . which had followed the policy of segregation, leading to unending war?"

The state's political situation, stirred by sectionalism, also played a role in the selection and tenure of several of the university's presidents. James MacLean resigned in 1913 to become chancellor at the University of Manitoba in his native Canada. During his thirteen years in Moscow, MacLean guided the University of Idaho through some of its most difficult times. The three-year tenure of MacLean's replacement, Melvin Brannon, was marked by feuds with numerous influential state politicians. Chief among his adversaries was Governor Moses Alexander, who won election in 1914 on a promise to reduce taxes. Alexander spent his four years in office attempting to cut some state taxes by reducing the budget of the university, claiming the school was extravagant. Alexander continually attacked Brannon, his salary, and his policies, and in 1915 the legislature attempted to cut the president's salary. In January 1917 a frustrated Brannon resigned, but his departure touched off an even greater controversy. The Board of Regents, now primarily composed of individuals appointed by Alexander, also asked for the resignations of Charles

Melvin A. Brannon, fourth president of the university.

Shattuck, dean of the College of Letters and Science, and George Ayers, dean of the College of Law, without conferring with Edward Sisson, state commissioner of education. Both Shattuck and Ayers had supported Brannon, and Alexander wanted them removed. Protesting this action of the regents, Sisson also resigned.

For the first twenty-eight years of its history, the school had been drawn into an intricate web of political squabbling. It is doubtful that the university could have survived had the political intrigue continued unabated. Fortunately, most of the presidents following Brannon—while not immune to changing political winds—did not have to endure the difficult times faced by those preceding them.

Ernest H. Lindley, who replaced Brannon in 1917, served the university through one of its most difficult periods. Not only did he arrive on campus at a time when it was bitterly divided over the recent firings, but the campus was gearing up for its new role as a military training camp during World War I. Despite these difficulties, Lindley's tenure was highly successful—but short. He left in 1920 to become chancellor at the University of Kansas.

The university then found a successor who remained for eight years. Alfred H. Upham, president from 1920 to 1928, came to Idaho with an outstanding reputation as an educator at Miami University of Ohio. He left to become president of that school, which was also his alma mater.

President Ernest H. Lindley, center, with English professor George Morey Miller, right, and an unidentified man (c. 1919).

Two university presidents, Alfred Upham, its sixth on left, and James MacLean, its third on right, pose in 1924 with Prince Gelasio Caetani and Governor C. C. Moore.

Frederick J. Kelly, whose tenure was not nearly so smooth, replaced Upham. Kelly organized a junior college within the University of Idaho, a program unpopular with many faculty members in the professional schools. He also irritated influential alumni by refusing to provide intercollegiate athletics with the amount of money they believed it deserved. The Board of Regents forced Kelly to resign two years after he accepted the job.

Mervin G. Neale replaced Kelly and served during the most difficult years of the Great Depression. Neale aggressively sought federal financial aid and brought the university its first great building boom since its early history.

The university's eighth president, Mervin Neale, points out campus landmarks from MacLean Field to its third president, James MacLean in 1937 (below left). Frederick J. Kelly, seventh president of the university (below).

The school's enrollment nearly doubled in size during his tenure. Neale resigned in 1937 to resume his former teaching duties at the University of Minnesota. Before he left campus, the regents named the school's new football stadium after him.

Harrison C. Dale became the school's next president; like Upham, he came from Miami University of Ohio. He served from 1937 until 1946, guiding the university through its second incarnation as a military training camp. Dale resigned at the close of the war, believing the state had not fulfilled its obligations to those former instructors who had left the university for the armed services, then returned to find they would not be rehired despite the president's commitment to doing so.

President Harrison Dale, second from left, welcomes First Lady Eleanor Roosevelt, far right, to Moscow at a reception in the President's House (1938).

On September 1, 1946, Jesse E. Buchanan became the first alumnus to hold the rank of president. Buchanan graduated in civil engineering in 1927, the first University of Idaho student to receive four years' worth of straight A's. Upon graduation he began teaching at the school, and advanced to dean of the College of Engineering in 1938. In 1946, at age forty-one, he became one of the youngest university presidents in the United States. In 1954 he resigned to become president of the Asphalt Institute. During his tenure he launched the university on another impressive building boom, adding several permanent brick structures to the campus. His successor would oversee the completion of most of those buildings.

When the Class of 1927 assembled on campus for its twentieth reunion, it welcomed member Jesse Buchanan. He had become university president the previous year—the first alumnus to head the school.

University bookstore (1950s).

71

Idaho State College President Donald Walker, left, and U of I President Donald Theophilus sign an athletic pact (1960).

Hello Walk (1960s).

That successor was Donald R. Theophilus, like his predecessor a man advanced to the presidency from within the university's ranks. Theophilus came to Idaho in 1927 as an associate professor of dairy husbandry. He later became dean of the College of Agriculture and, upon Buchanan's departure, acting president. Theophilus was popular with his faculty colleagues, some of whom nominated him for the permanent position of president. While he was honored by the nomination, when asked whether he would accept the position he replied, "I have never applied for a position and do not expect to start now. Should the Regents offer me the position I would give the offer serious consideration." The Regents did offer, Theophilus did accept, and he served as president until 1965.

Ernest W. Hartung replaced Theophilus, serving until 1977, when he was succeeded by Richard D. Gibb. They served during a period of student activism and increasing federal equal rights requirements, such as Affirmative Action. Theirs was a time of continued growth in enrollment,

The university's twelfth president, Ernest Hartung, addresses a group of students who came to his house to wish him a merry Christmas in 1969.

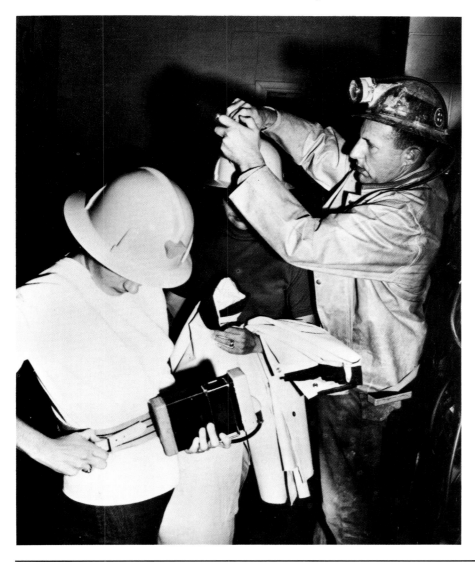

Summer Institute in Geography students prepare to descend into a Coeur d'Alene mine (1965).

Chemistry lab (1968).

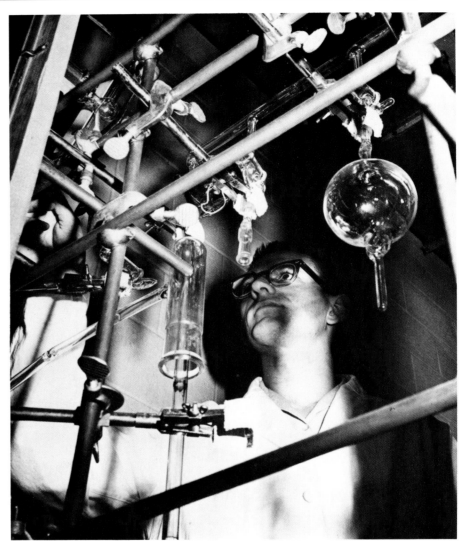

Summer Theater rehearsal (1969).

with an increasing emphasis on outreach, research, and graduate-level instruction. They were years of impressive building construction, and growing inter-institutional cooperation. Yet this was also a frustrating period for administrators, a time when long-term budgetary difficulties climaxed. "The nagging problem of underfinancing" that Hartung warned of in 1972 eventually forced the university to eliminate or curtail several programs in the 1980s, when it laid off numerous faculty, staff, and administrators.

As the University of Idaho approached its centennial under the leadership of its thirteenth president, it could look back upon its origins as a single building perched on a muddy hill above a small western town, a school with a faculty of two, teaching forty students. It had grown into a complex of dozens of buildings on 320 acres, valued at hundreds of millions of dollars, with a staff of nearly 2,000 and a student body of 9,000. During that time nearly 60,000 graduates had joined the ranks of the first four to go through commencement in 1896. The school had a past of which it

Avid gardener Richard Gibb, the university's thirteenth president, guided the school during its centennial observance.

could be proud, and although budgetary constraints continued to cause problems—as they had for ten decades—it justifiably approached the future with considerable optimism.

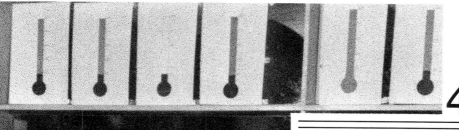

4

Life on Campus

A person's experiences on the Moscow campus largely depended upon the years spent there. Activities changed over time. Among the most popular outings of the early 1900s, for example, were excursions to the Woodman's Hall in Joel, with hayrides in warm weather and sleigh rides in winter. "Saturday evening about 50 members of the first year college men and their ladies set out for Joel in hayracks," reported the *Argonaut* in 1908. "After arrival, the evening was taken up with dancing and getting acquainted. At a late hour the young ladies brought out heavily loaded baskets." Few college students of the post-World War II era attended basket socials, rode on hayracks—or had even heard of Joel. Generalizations about college life are a little risky.

Regardless of when people attended the University of Idaho, however, most could sympathize with Hazel Marcellus, who recalled her first day in 1919:

> That was a miserable day! I don't suppose the day itself was miserable, but I was. Everything was strange, everybody was strange and even the

In the days before good roads, the arrival of the Student Special—such as this one in 1924—marked the beginning of each school year.

atmosphere itself was strange. Strange words and queer phrases came floating to my ears. Ad Building, Morrill Hall, registration, committee on admissions, dates, Freshman-Sophomore fight—what on earth were they and what did they mean?

The 1912 student handbook outlined some procedures to help new students through the first traumatic days:

Write home
Fix up your room
Buy University colors
Buy a season's ticket and support athletics
Run over all the yells and songs
Buy your books
Choose associates carefully
Boost class spirit
Be at football rallies
Join some active society, musical, debate, scientific or all
Attend social affairs.

Debarking from the Student Special (1938).

By the 1970s U-Haul trailers dotted the campus at the beginning of each year, replacing the hectic scene at the train depot.

Notably missing from the list was attending classes; but that was the reason everyone gathered in the first place, and registration was one of the students' first communal activities. A writer in the 1973 *Gem*—the university annual—described the process:

> It's unamerican |sic| not to hate registration. If you like registration you must be some kind of a pervert. To begin with your name is always in the wrong part of the alphabet so you spend three hours finding an advisor. Half the classes you want have been cancelled or the times changed so you have to rework your entire schedule. When your time to register finally rolls around, you stand outside the gym waiting for half an hour, usually in the rain. When you get inside, the lab you wanted is closed and

Although a writer in the *Gem of the Mountains* once stated that "It's unamerican not to hate registration," the event has marked the introduction to college life for several generations of students (right and following page).

you have to change sections in everything else. The only class you really wanted is full, and the guy in line ahead of you just got the last card for the last English class. So you fork over the money for a list of classes you didn't want and fill out a lot of pointless questionnaires. Finally after you've been drug through hell backwards, they want to take your picture.

Through the 1920s, university students attended regular student-body assemblies. Some of these featured talks by faculty members and outside speakers on topics such as "courtesy and good behavior" and "use of the library." In the school's earliest days, students organized some of the assemblies themselves and provided their own speeches. In fact, oration or "rhetoric" was mandatory for all students in the 1890s, and for freshmen for some years after that. The 1903 *Gem* looked back upon the "old days" of those student speeches:

The greatest horror known to students then was the terrible "rhetorical" system, when two orations a year had to be given by every student of college grade from the rostrum on Assembly days. 'Twas a pitiful, as well as a ludicrous sight, to watch each poor victim tremble up the aisle, bow to the faculty which sat in a rigid line behind him, and then tremble and shake through an oration before the eyes of his fellow students.

Oratorical and debating contests remained among the most popular of student activities in the first twenty years of the university's history, and sometimes as many people attended meets as viewed sporting events. The Watkins Medal for Oratory, presented annually, was the first award ever offered at the school. The college's first two student clubs—the Amphyctyon Literary Society, organized in 1892, and the Websterian Debating Society, founded in 1893—were formed to improve forensic ability. The school entered an intercollegiate oratorical association in 1896, two years before it joined its first athletic conference. In 1902 President James MacLean hired Edward Maslin Hulme to fill the newly created position of professor of history and oratory. In addition to coaching successful intercollegiate debating teams for many years, Hulme taught such popular classes as Public Speaking, Writing of Orations, Construction of Briefs, and Oral Debate.

C. W. Gibson, Miles Reed, and Burton French, the university's 1901 debating team.

As the popularity of debate was declining after 1910—with freshmen no longer required to give orations in assemblies—campus upperclassmen began devising other ways to segregate themselves from their less esteemed younger colleagues. Since it was difficult to distinguish a freshman from a sophomore, junior, or senior, the upperclassmen decided a dress code was in order. In 1907 the *Argonaut* editorialized in favor of distinctive clothing for each class—particularly for men students:

It's time we were drawing the line of demarcation somewhere. Under the present system . . . it requires several mathematical deductions to find out the difference between an upper and lower classman, although after contiguous association a person can tell the difference. But we are all in a hurry. We wish to know and we want to know quickly.

By 1911 the Idaho student body had adopted a dress code for men. It dictated that freshmen wear green caps; only juniors and seniors could sport derby hats, use a cane, or dress in corduroy trousers. Freshmen could not wear dress suits at any college function. While various components of the dress code gradually fell into disuse, the regulation requiring that freshmen be topped in green beanies remained for over two decades. The university's "I Club," made up of varsity lettermen, enforced the rule. They would appear without warning on campus wielding paddles, and punish those found disregarding the regulation. By the 1930s, some people began questioning the policy. "The school is still supporting a set of worthless outgrown customs," admonished the *Argonaut*, and in 1931 the upperclassmen dropped the requirement. Beanie-wearing made a brief revival in the mid-1930s but then gradually faded away.

In the days when the school was small and students knew most of their classmates, the strongest units on campus were the various classes. Identity as a freshman, sophomore, junior, or senior was important, and most associations were with other members of the same class. Naturally, such a system encouraged rivalries, with the most competitive divisions being those separating freshmen from sophomores. Tremendous frosh-soph wars were a campus tradition for years.

At first, the contests were little more than disorganized brawls between the two classes that occasionally got out of hand. In 1905 a group of freshmen captured some sophomores and painted them with shoe polish. In retaliation, some sophomores painted a freshman with silver nitrate, a hazing incident exposed by the press throughout the Pacific Northwest. "Sophs haze Freshman and may have scarred him for life," reported the Moscow *Journal*, while the Boise *Statesman* claimed the student was "branded

A long-standing campus tradition mandated that freshmen wear green beanies to distinguish them from "superior" upperclassmen (above). Ducking a frosh in the Administration Building fountain (left, 1920s).

and disfigured for life." In fact, the student was not permanently scarred, but the negative publicity encouraged campus administrators to crack down on class brawls. They threatened students with suspension and encouraged more organized contests between the two classes. Under the direction of history professor Edward Hulme, class members began participating in wrestling matches, tug-of-war, football games, and something called the "Hulme contest" in which fifteen brawny men from each class attempted to carry or drag members of the other team across opposing goals. In this more organized form, these class battles—followed by a "Bury the Hatchet" dance—remained a campus tradition for years.

The Hulme Contest in 1922. When rivalries between freshmen and sophomores became too unruly, history professor Edward M. Hulme organized the "Hulme Contest" to encourage more wholesome competition.

Much of the class rivalry revolved around the annual posting of edicts, when sophomores placed signs around campus "enlightening" freshmen as to their proper role. Freshmen just as diligently attempted to tear down the posters. The sophomore edict directed toward the class of 1942 is typical of the genre:

> You, the droopy-drawered swaddlers, will henceforth obey, the following rules of freshman conduct set forth by us, the superior sophomores, your masters:
> - You shall, from this day forward, wear green caps atop your empty heads
> - When you meet your superiors, the sophomores, you will step into the street and grovel while they pass.

Following World War II, as the school's enrollment grew rapidly and contained a large percentage of older and married students, the class loyalties—and rivalries—gradually faded.

Like all aspects of campus life, the university's traditions changed over time, but a number lasted for several years:

- Every student tipped his hat upon meeting the university president.
- Idaho men never attended athletic events with dates.
- The "I Bench" in front of the Administration Building was reserved for seniors.
- Students, faculty, and staff always greeted one another with a hearty "hello" upon meeting on campus, giving the name "Hello Walk" to the pedestrian way in front of the Ad Building.

The "I Bench" was for years reserved only for seniors.

One of the school's oldest traditions required that students and staff say hello to one another when meeting, giving the name "Hello Walk" to the pedestrian way in front of the Administration Building.

By the Second World War, most of those traditions had been forgotten. At first, the *Argonaut* lamented the loss: "These . . . sacred traditions . . . went to make up college life in the good old days of seven or eight years ago. Most of the students on the campus today have never been a part of such frivolity, but we can hope that before too many years have passed, we will see . . . the return of the Idaho traditions." By 1967, however, a new generation of *Argonaut* reporters would have viewed such lighthearted activities as childish and irrelevant: "Even more disheartening than the static social system are the immature and non-intellectual issues which seem to occupy a good part of the student's non-academic existence." Revival of traditions in that atmosphere was out of the question.

Despite the loss of certain traditions, students attending the university during any period found numerous ways in which to spend extracurricular time. Students in the 1890s faced a more regimented campus than did most of those who followed. The faculty prohibited them from playing games on Sundays, and the university's first catalog warned men that "the frequenting of saloons and all questionable places of resort is not tolerated." Despite the restrictions, those early students had an active social life. Walking along railroad tracks and bicycling were popular weekend activities. Groups frequently serenaded one another or townspeople, and students organized a variety of clubs. Most prominent were the debating and literary groups, but musical organizations such as the Mandolin Club also gained popularity. The Young Men's and Young Women's Christian associations were active by the mid-1890s. And dances were very popular; the university hosted some in the corridors of the old Administration Building but held larger events in downtown buildings.

Mandolin and Guitar Club (1900).

Although the school's regulations became progressively less rigid, the university's first students in the new century still faced strict rules. As "fussing" became popular, for example, campus officials attempted to curb the activity, to the dismay of an *Argonaut* reporter:

> Like a bolt out of the blue there came last week a ukase from the powers that be at Ridenbaugh Hall absolutely and unqualifiedly forbidding—several things. To be specific, the inmates of Ridenbaugh are enjoined from loitering on the campus with any young man on week days; they are forbidden the privilege of receiving at the Hall any visitors of the male persuasion at any time from Monday to Friday evening, inclusive; in bold and simple terms the full effect of the mandate is to put the ban on fussing in any form in and around the dorm except on Friday evening, Saturday and Sunday.
>
> It is reported that indignation meetings are of nightly occurrence within the sacred precincts of what may properly now be called the nunnery.

Myrtle Hitt in her Ridenbaugh Hall room (1909).

Students attending the university in the ten years after 1900 not only were more numerous than those who preceded them, but had a wider range of organized extracurricular activities from which to choose. Musicians now had a few more options. In addition to the Mandolin Club they could join the University Band or the University Orchestra. Organized class activities

The University Orchestra (right, 1937), and men's clog and tap-dancing class (below, 1935).

A car caravan leaves campus for a picnic during Summer School (above, 1922), and Marie Cuddy, Professor Isaac Cogswell, and Robert McGregor in 1899 enjoying an outing near campus, a popular form of recreation at the turn of the century (left).

became more numerous. In the spring of 1906 all members of the senior class awoke at 4:30 one morning, piled into two four-horse wagons, packed picnic gear into another, and rode out of town for a day in the country. It was the school's first Senior Sneak. Every class held an annual spring picnic in those years—usually on Moscow Mountain. The sophomores began hosting their annual "Sophomore Frolic" dance, while the juniors started the "Junior Prom." Men and women also initiated special functions just for themselves. The "stag social," where men gathered for games and songs, gained popularity and a few years later women began the women's only "co-ed prom," which men attempted to infiltrate nearly every year.

Dances have always been a popular form of recreation at Idaho: Junior Prom (facing page, top, 1928); Publications Ball (facing page, bottom, 1936); Freshman Mixer (above, 1942); Nickel Hop (left, 1960).

One of the school's longest-lasting traditions also got its start in this decade. As early as 1906 student leaders attempted to organize a campus workday. The workday began around 1908 and, on May 23, 1910, Permeal French, Dean of Women, instigated the university's first Campus Day. During the day students, faculty, and townspeople cleaned the campus and planted shrubs and ivy. In the afternoon all gathered to sing songs and watch campus women participate in a May-pole dance. Over the years the event grew in popularity, although the workday aspect lost popularity as the university enlarged its maintenance crews. Eventually the day became

Student work crew constructing new steps at the School of Mines Building during Campus Day in 1923.

the May Fete, and the May-pole dance grew to be one of the school's most popular—and most photographed—events. Finally, the May Fete evolved into Parents Weekend.

Permeal French, dean of women from 1908 to 1936, perhaps influenced social life at the university more than any other person. In addition to establishing the Blue Bucket Inn, setting regulations concerning dress and behavior for women, and conceiving the idea of Campus Day, she organized another long-lasting university tradition in 1922: the singing of

The Campus Day May Pole dance was one of the school's most popular events: photographers gather (top, 1914); the dance begins (left, 1939).

The Blue Bucket

It is one of the most persistent mining legends in the West. Like most legends, it has several variants, but as most old-timers told it, a group of emigrants on the Oregon Trail in the 1840s claimed to have found a mine near the Snake River containing enough gold nuggets to have easily filled one of their blue water buckets. For some unexplained reason they chose not to pick up the riches. But they did tell people about their find, and their story spurred many unsuccessful searches for the elusive "blue bucket" mine. While it is doubtful the mine ever existed, its story fostered some tangible offspring on the University of Idaho campus.

Not surprisingly for a school located in a state with a rich mining heritage, several university entities take their name from mining lore. The student newspaper is the Argonaut; the yearbook the Gem of the Mountains. In March 1923 the university English Club published a literary magazine entitled The Blue Bucket, named for the mining legend. The magazine ran until 1940, featuring stories, articles, plays, and humor. But the "Blue Bucket" most fondly remembered by Idaho alumni is not something they read, but one of their most popular hangouts on campus.

For many years, Dean of Women Permeal French thought there should be a "suitable" recreation center near campus, and in 1924 she constructed a two-story brick structure at Deakin and Idaho avenues. The facility, with its ballroom complete with fireplace, became a frequent site for college dances. The structure also housed a tea room, a soda fountain, two dining rooms, and kitchen facilities. Under the wooden canopy over the

Christmas carols. The first organized caroling around a large, decorated tree on the Ad Building lawn took place in that year, and it became an annual event celebrated through the 1930s. The sophomore-sponsored Holly Week, which was climaxed by a semi-formal ball reigned over by the Holly Queen, was another traditional holiday activity for several decades.

In the 'teens and 'twenties, organized university activities reached a peak. The school scaled down or canceled many events during the depression and war years that followed, and postwar students increasingly preferred private parties to gala, highly structured events. But in those earlier years the campus buzzed with organized activities. The Argonaut's society-page editor outlined a few of the events students could anticipate during the 1916-17 school year: Sunday-afternoon calls at the sororities and Ridenbaugh Hall; YW and YMCA receptions; sorority pledge dances; Halloween Party; Athletic Ball; Sophomore Frolic; Junior Prom; Senior Ruff; Faculty Ladies Club afternoon parties for co-eds; Co-Ed Prom; smokers for men; plays; feeds and banquets; fraternity parties; Campus Day; living-group picnics in the spring; concerts; weekly dances; and comic operas presented by the Glee Club.

In the post-World War II era the campus became more susceptible to national fads, thanks largely to the influence of radio and television. Canasta parties swept the campus in the late 1940s, and in 1956 students participated in the school's first "panty raid"—incurring the wrath of the Argonaut's editor, who stormed against the "few renegade student leaders, encouraged by about ten per cent of the male population on campus, [who]

Backstage during make-up for "The Gondoliers" (1935).

Junior Week parade (1934).

succeeded in blacking Idaho's here-to-fore clean name in less than
an hour."

In 1961 the Twist dance fad hit Idaho, its strange movements at first taking
observers by surprise: "The dancers do not touch each other during the
dance and take hardly any steps, merely swaying the hips and using certain
gyrations. The partners synchronize their movements, working out their
own individual variations." That fad was followed by, among others,

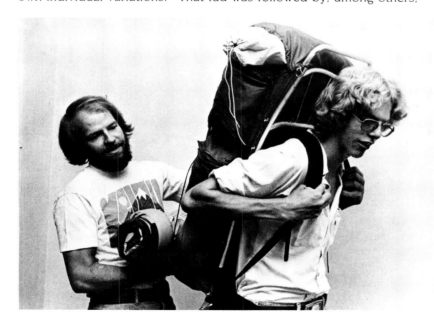

David Cockrell and Phillip Wichman prepare for an outdoor orientation backpacking
trip (1977).

front door a light covered by a blue leaded-glass shade gave the impression of a blue bucket. Fastened to the decorative scalloped molding highlighting the canopy was the building's name: The Blue Bucket Inn.

The Blue Bucket—or simply "Bucket"—quickly became the school's most popular recreation area. "Since school opened it has become a campus community house," noted the Argonaut in 1924. "To be in the best form is to take your lady friend to the Blue Bucket. The service is of the best. Pretty co-eds, and handsome eds are there to supply your wants, whether it be a fancy drink or a regular good home-cooked meal."

In addition to its attraction as a "drop-in" place, fraternities and sororities used the Blue Bucket for rushing parties, campus organizations held meetings, and groups sponsored banquets. For many years in the 1920s and 1930s there was even a Blue Bucket Orchestra. The Bucket also featured a giftshop with "a complete line of distinctive social stationery, and . . . appropriate and fancy articles." Perhaps the best-remembered part of the Bucket was its elegant Tea Room, where well-dressed waiters and waitresses served afternoon tea to students and faculty sitting at linen-covered tables adorned with fresh-cut flowers.

In 1928 Dean French and Bucket manager Bob Woods remodeled the building, enlarging the dance floor and covering the exterior with an "old English" motif. With the repeal of prohibition in 1933, faculty and students could purchase beer at the inn—a practice outlawed by the regents a few years later.

For several years university President Mervin Neale attempted to obtain federal Public Works Administration funds to construct a student union building. Recognizing the need for a student center, yet unwilling to wait longer for federal money, in 1936 the regents bought the Blue Bucket Inn from French. Over the course of the next year workmen extensively remodeled and enlarged the building. They added a new wing to the north and—attesting to the popularity of the Bucket's weekly dances—tripled the dance floor's space. The renovated structure opened in September 1937 as Idaho's first Student Union Building, and is shown below in 1941.

The regents authorized major renovation and expansion of the SUB in 1949 and again in the 1960s, but the building never completely severed its Blue Bucket roots. Throughout the latter 1930s, 1940s, and 1950s the SUB featured a Blue Bucket Cafe. In the early 1960s it housed a "Blue Bucket Inn Pancake House." Well into the 1970s "Blue Bucket" was the official name of the Union's snack bar. In the early 1980s university officials commissioned the remodeling of one room in the SUB into a tastefully designed luncheon area, where people could once again eat on linen-covered tables with cut

skateboarding or "sidewalk surfing"; Hootenanies; psychedelic light shows; macrame; streaking; an annual rock festival begun in the early 1970s that gained a regional reputation; and skateboarding again.

The trend through the 1960s and early 1970s was away from traditional activities, toward less structured functions accompanied by relaxed inhibitions. Where the Argonaut expressed indignation at panty raids in the 1950s, in the 1970s women spectators occasionally appeared topless at the annual Blue Mountain Rock Festival. By the late 1970s and into the 1980s the school again turned to more "traditional" values. Although the days of Senior Sneaks and Junior Proms did not return, the rock festival gradually evolved into a mellow folk-music concert before being discontinued altogether, and the Gem's editor received considerable student criticism when he included a nude section in the 1980 annual.

In many ways, however, students of the 1970s and 1980s were not all that different from their predecessors. While it is true that large campus affairs became less popular, students at Idaho have always created their own entertainment. The 1916 Argonaut article listing the wide variety of campus affairs concluded: "People will still flock to the picture shows and ice cream parlors with an ever new zest for an old mode of entertainment." The 1955 Gem stated: "Our fondest memories and lingering thoughts [include] . . . coffee in the Bucket, dancing in the Dipper, never-ceasing card games . . . rallies in the fall, dancing in the winter, picnics in the spring . . . the well-worn paths in the arboretum." These were images of college life that each generation of University of Idaho students could identify with—the intimate association of a few friends on campus and off, at places like Childers' Ice Cream Parlor, the Nest, the Perch, the Blue Bucket, and Biscuitroot Park.

"Here on this crested hill is the spot to which the entire State should look for intellectual leadership," President A. H. Upham noted in his 1921 inaugural address. "Every high school boy and girl should think first of a college education here. Every athlete should aspire to the privilege of representing Idaho in intercollegiate sports. Every debater should covet the chance to speak for Idaho from the University platform." As its reputation grew, the university appealed to an increasingly broad range of students, and university administrators sought ways to assist those who could not afford college. One method was to make scholarships available. The university offered its first scholarship in 1894, and in 1898 Moscow merchant William Kaufmann and his wife established the school's first continuing scholarship fund, to be awarded to students who had attained high scholastic standing and were "most needy." Over the years the wise investment of these and other donated funds enabled the school to award scholarships to thousands of deserving students.

flowers, reminiscent of Permeal French's Tea Room. The name chosen for the new establishment: The Blue Bucket.

The original blue bucket eventually became the student bookstore, as it is seen below, and in the mid-1960s the university

razed the original Blue Bucket Inn to create space for a student book store. But the name carried on and has become a University of Idaho legacy nearly as long-lived as the mining legend that spawned it.

"Our fondest memories," wrote someone in the 1953 *Gem of the Mountains*, include "coffee in the Bucket (facing page) . . . picnics in the spring . . . the well-worn paths in the arboretum (left)."

Co-ops

The United States Office of Education called them ''the outstanding achievement in student aid in the last five years . . . and a mark for other states to shoot at.'' By 1940, 18 percent of the University of Idaho's students lived in one, and the school was recognized as the national leader in a field mimicked by other universities from coast to coast. The object of all this praise was the university's highly successful cooperative-living system.

Land-grant institutions were established to make college educations accessible to people of all economic means, and at Idaho administration after administration sought ways to increase student aid and hold college expenses down. With the depression of the 1930s they were even further pressed to keep the campus open to all. But it was the students themselves who initiated a solution to the problem of high room and board expenses during this difficult period.

In 1932 a group of twenty-one men living at the Latter-day Saints' Institute met with George Tanner, director of the institute, and informed him that they could not afford their present housing. Tanner and the group came up with an idea to remodel the basement of the institute into cooperative living quarters, with the men sharing equally in household tasks. The experiment was so successful that the next year President Mervin Neale agreed to convert Senior Hall, an old building on Ash Street, into a cooperative for engineering students. Senior Hall, housing twenty-five men, was the first university-sanctioned living cooperative on an American campus. It was far from the last.

Still, not everyone qualified for scholarships and campus officials looked for other ways to help. A great number of students spent a good part of their time on campus working, and these outside jobs influenced much of student life. In 1914 President Brannon organized a faculty committee for the purpose of finding employment on campus and in town for needy students. Eventually, this committee grew into an employment bureau. As the 1921-22 biennial report stated, ''Many of the influential and highly respected students on the campus are earning every penny of their expenses and the only limit apparently to the number of partially self-supporting students is the comparatively small number of positions available in the town and about the campus.''

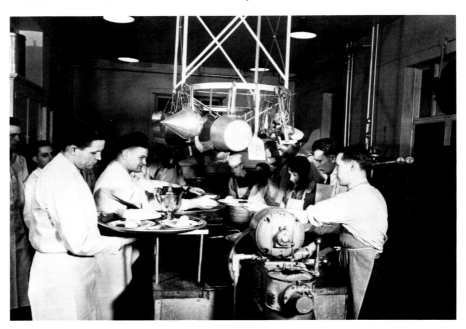

During the Great Depression, as many as 80 percent of the university's students held jobs on or off campus. Hays Hall kitchen crew (above, 1936); Student Civil Works Administration crew in the Arboretum (below, 1933).

Brothers Clement and Maurice March parked their "Depression Special" on campus in 1931. The portable home, built on an automobile chassis, was one of the ingenious ways students devised to make housing affordable during the depression.

The most difficult financial time for most students came during the depression of the 1930s. In an attempt to help, the regents lowered dorm rents during the worst years of the depression, while members of the Faculty Women's Club hired women students for housework. In 1932-33, approximately 80 percent of the student body held part-time jobs. Even more found employment under the New Deal. The Civil Works Administration provided employment for hundreds of Idaho students— cleaning grounds, repairing fences, improving the arboretum, working on drainage projects, widening and grading roads, mending library books, typing, and filing. The National Youth Administration also channeled thousands of dollars through the university for similar jobs. From the mid-1930s on, federal funds for student financial aid greatly assisted the university in its efforts to provide affordable educations.

One of the key components of assisting students has been providing inexpensive housing. Until the early 1900s, when Ridenbaugh Hall was constructed for women, all students lived off campus. Yet not all prospective students could afford to rent. Therefore the university added other dormitories for women and men and in the 1930s initiated its highly acclaimed program of cooperative living in an effort to further reduce expenses. Despite these efforts, the school could not provide all of the housing required—and many students wanted to live someplace besides a dorm or apartment. Consequently, the University of Idaho became home to an active fraternity and sorority system.

The university's "Greek" system began in the late 1890s with Kappa Phi Alpha fraternity. In 1901 it petitioned to join a national fraternity, and in

Requests for low-rent cooperative housing were so brisk that Neale appointed Tanner as director of cooperatives. In 1933 Tanner oversaw the conversion of Ridenbaugh Hall into a men's cooperative and established the College Girls' Club cooperative in an abandoned fraternity house. Ridenbaugh had only fifteen residents at the start of the 1933-34 school year, each paying $27 per semester for room rental and $20 per month for food. Once it was converted to a cooperative, the monthly cost dropped to $15 for both room and board, and the hall quickly filled.

Receiving increased requests for cooperative living quarters, the university expanded its program. In 1934 an old fraternity became the University Club. In 1935 Lewis Hall became a second women's co-op. In 1937 the university converted Lindley Hall from a dorm into a cooperative. Among the

many shaved duties at Lindley and the other co-ops was kitchen detail, such as that performed by Leonard Arrington. During this period the University of Idaho also became the first college in the nation to construct a new building specifically for cooperative

living. The one-story, wood-frame Idaho Club constructed in 1935 housed nearly 120 men and gained the attention of educators throughout the nation, many of whom came to inspect its operation. In 1938 President Harrison Dale authorized construction of another frame cooperative next to the Idaho Club—shown above—known as the Campus Club. The university's co-ops flourished throughout the depression. Students shared in maintenance tasks and lived under the supervision of faculty advisors. By the end of the 1930s, over 500 students resided in co-ops.

Most American universities dropped the cooperative idea with the return of prosperity after World War II. But at Idaho some co-ops remained. The Campus Club continued to provide inexpensive living for men for years after the war, while Ethel Steel House remained as a women's cooperative at the time the school celebrated its centennial observance. It serves as a reminder of the depression days, when university administrators throughout the nation sought ways to make college affordable and looked to Idaho for leadership.

1908 Phi Delta Theta admitted it to membership. Zeta Epsilon, begun at about the same time, did not succeed in becoming affiliated with a national group, Beta Theta Pi, until 1914. Kappa Sigma, the first national fraternity on campus, arrived in 1905; it grew out of a local group organized primarily by football players. The Kappa Sigma home, constructed in 1916, was the first fraternity house built in the state of Idaho. Beta Sigma organized in 1899 as the first local sorority, becoming affiliated with Delta Gamma in 1911. The first chapter of a national sorority, that of Gamma Phi Beta, was installed in 1910.

Founders dinner, Phi Delta Theta fraternity (top, 1908). Phi Delta Theta grew out of Kappa Phi Alpha, the school's first fraternity. Lambda Chi Alpha house (bottom, 1935).

At a "Squeal Day" in the 1960s, pledges react to the news that they have been accepted in Delta Gamma sorority (above); pledges in the 1970s (left).

Kappa Sigma house, the first fraternity house constructed in the State of Idaho.

The fraternities and sororities met in various locations in town and on campus until they constructed their own houses. In the late 1950s the university developed Nez Perce Drive and leased land to fraternities and sororities for a nominal fee. In 1960 Sigma Chi fraternity constructed a new house along this drive, the first of several that would follow. Other groups preferred the older houses closer to the campus core. As the university approached its centennial observance, it supported seventeen national fraternities and eight national sororities.

There have always been students at Idaho who have sought more than an education, a place to live, and entertaining activities. Some have found that religious teachings and associations helped, and the university has been a nationally recognized leader among state-supported colleges in molding religious and sectarian educational experiences.

In the university's early years, administrators worked to deflate the school's image as a Moscow or northern Idaho college. Early faculty members made regular trips to the southern part of the state recruiting students. Much of southern Idaho has always been heavily populated with members of the Church of Jesus Christ of Latter-day Saints, and many Mormons required some "evidence" that the state university was not an immoral institution before allowing their children to attend. The first solution to this dilemma was the establishment of strong YW- and YMCA chapters, two of the oldest organizations on campus. In the early years, Ys provided regular Bible study and devotional meetings. In 1928 the Latter-day Saints Church established a religious institute on campus—the first such institute ever established at an American public college. In 1930 local Protestant ministers organized the Idaho Institute of Christian Education, which was followed in 1946 by the Catholic Institute of Religious Education. All three— housed in handsome buildings on campus—continued to operate as the university approached its hundredth anniversary.

The university's charter restricts it from teaching sectarian religion or politics, but the school's administrators have been sympathetic to the efforts of various denominations to serve students' spiritual needs. "Religion is recognized as one of the greatest forces in the development of moral and ethical character, and is therefore an important factor in the lives of the students," President Jesse Buchanan stated in 1946. In an innovative program which captured the attention of educators around the country, the university allowed students to receive limited credit for the religious courses the three institutes offered. It also hosted a Religious Emphasis Week that, in the 1940s and 1950s, became extraordinarily popular and brought nationally recognized theologians to campus. Since its earliest

The university has been a national leader in molding both religious and sectarian educational experiences. Breaking ground for the Campus Christian Center (1950).

"The University's Saddest Hour"

It was a cold, autumn night. At 2:00 a.m. on October 19, 1956, an explosion awakened Tom McDevitt, a resident of Upham Hall. "I looked out my window," he later reported, "and saw flames shooting up the windows of the lounge of Gault Hall" (shown here

in 1955). McDevitt sounded a fire alarm. Harold Hunker, Gault Hall's proctor, also pulled an alarm handle, but none of the fire boxes in the new $500,000 "fireproof" dorm worked.

Shortly after two o'clock, 40 volunteer firemen, four fire trucks, and one ambulance arrived. Sheets of flame covered the building from the second through fourth floors as hundreds of students gathered to watch. Firemen extended an aerial ladder to the fourth floor, rescuing Virgil Young and Terry Murphy. Students Floyd Lydum and Lawrence LaRue climbed to the building's roof and lowered a rope, pulling Stephen Hinckley, Harold Jacobs, B. J. Schaffer, and J. D. Archer to safety.

There were many heroes that night, many potential victims saved. But rescuers arrived too late to help Paul Johnson of Davenport, Washington, John Knudson of Idaho Falls, and Clair Schuldberg of Terreton. "The University's saddest hour," President Donald Theophilus called it. Moscow Fire Chief Carl Smith also made a

statement: "This is a clear case
of arson."

Just a few days earlier, three
fires had swept through Sweet and
Chrisman halls, causing over
$3,000 in damage. University
officials placed the campus on alert
and posted student guards around
various dorms. As most concern
centered on older wooden structures,
no guards patrolled Gault Hall.
After the fatal fire the university
posted student, ROTC, and police
guards at all buildings on campus.
There were no more fires.

Investigators began probing
the ruins on the morning after the
blaze and launched "Operation
Arson." State and local officials,
arson experts, a score of police
investigators, technicians, volunteer
assistants, and polygraph experts
aided the operation. The
investigating team screened over
1,500 people. It sifted through
evidence for over a month.

On the day following the fire,
staff members at the Argonaut
held a meeting to decide how to
cover the event. Editor John
Hughes assigned freshman reporter
Paul Matovich of Wallace to the
story. "All the students . . . have
mixed emotions of grief, sorrow,
disbelief, and thankfulness for those
who were saved," Matovich wrote.
Hughes and other reporters used
Matovich's information in their own
coverage but did not publish the
freshman reporter's story. Instead,

years, the university has found creative ways to accommodate the spiritual
needs of students without threatening non-Christians, and without
overstepping the boundaries of required church/state separation.

As the Idaho student body grew, it required more structure and greater
communications to hold it together. During the school's first years, many
students knew all the other members of the student body. Naturally,
feelings of camaraderie were easier then, but the situation could not last.
"Idaho has a problem to face—the problem of the lonely student," the
Argonaut editorialized as early as 1917. "When this was a small school the
problem did not exist. . . . [But] as the student body grew, it inevitably split
up into groups."

One method of retaining unity has been through publications. The Blue
Bucket Magazine in the 1920s and 1930s and The Blot in the late 1940s and
early 1950s provided members of the student body with campus
information and humor. By far the most important student publications,
however, have been the Argonaut and the Gem of the Mountains.

The Argonaut began in 1898 as a vehicle to help pay off a debt incurred by
the football team. Student Guy Wolfe, who worked as a printer's devil at
the Moscow newspaper, volunteered to publish the paper if all students
would subscribe. The students agreed, but in the end many never paid their
subscriptions—leaving Wolfe with a substantial indebtedness to the Moscow
newspaper, which printed the Argonaut. The paper's publishers filed suit
against Wolfe, and the university threatened to withhold his degree unless
he settled the debt. Wolfe worked the entire summer of 1899 paying off the
Argonaut's bills.

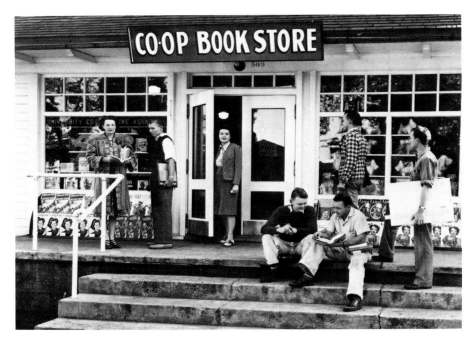

Co-op book store (1939).

Argonaut staff members in the 1970s. The student newspaper has reported campus activities since 1898.

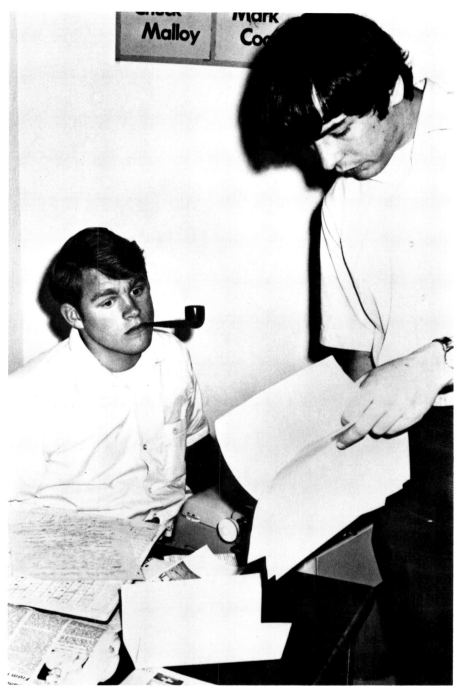

As a fundraising venture, that first *Argonaut*—which was then a monthly publication—dismally failed. But as a communication vehicle the paper met a vital need of the student body. The following year the students themselves underwrote publication expenses, and future United States Congressman Burton French served as editor. The *Argonaut* survived and

Hughes sent a copy of it to Latah County Prosecutor Lloyd Martinson, who headed the arson investigation.

The guards stayed on duty. Tensions remained high. The investigation dragged: one week, two, three, four. The university held a memorial service for the three students; over 800 people attended. The ASUI and Spurs hosted dances to raise money for a memorial scholarship fund. Still, things were far from normal. Then the break came. "Fourteen thousand sighs of relief were whispered and 14,000 residents of Moscow and students at the University closed both eyes Tuesday night for the first time in 33 days as word quickly filtered through news outlets that the 'University of Idaho arson case was solved,'" noted the Moscow newspaper. It was a few days before Thanksgiving. Paul Matovich, *Argonaut* student reporter, had been arrested for setting all the Idaho dormitory fires.

Matovich had been a suspect from the first. Editor Hughes felt he had shown an unusual interest in the fire cases, and assigned him to the investigation to see if he would slip some telling details into his stories. He did not. But investigators discovered that he had previously started a number of fires while at a California Air Force base. Still, Matovich was not the type one would accuse lightly. "I didn't figure he was any more likely to start a fire than anyone else," said his roommate, Robert Hill. Matovich had been editor of his high school yearbook and student body president. He took to extracurricular activities as soon as he landed in Moscow: *Argonaut* reporter; candidate for freshman class president. He also began lighting fires nearly as soon as he *arrived, for Paul Matovich was a pyromaniac.*

In April 1957 Paul Matovich stood trial in Moscow. There was never much question about his guilt—he confessed to the acts. Still, the jury "had difficulty" reaching a decision and appended to their final verdict of guilty a request that Matovich receive psychiatric treatment. State prosecutors had asked that he be hanged for first-degree murder, but Judge Hugh Baker agreed with the jury. He sentenced Paul Matovich to twenty-five years in prison at Boise and recommended that the penitentiary psychiatrist treat the young convict.

There were no pleas for more leniency; no clamors for a harsher sentence. All understood that Paul Matovich had mental problems. He deserved punishment, but he also deserved sympathy. He got both, and the university did its best to put its saddest hour behind it.

has been continually published—as a monthly, weekly, or biweekly—since November 1898.

The junior class began a yearbook known as the *Gem of the Mountains* in 1903, and in 1924 the Associated Students took over publication. Like the *Argonaut*, the *Gem* has operated largely independently of university administrative control or censorship throughout its history.

Changing times brought advances in communication media. On May 24, 1923, Bernadine Adair stood before a microphone, sang a few songs, and played the piano. It was the first program ever broadcast by a University of Idaho radio station. That first station, operating under the call letters KFAN, was largely a volunteer effort of a few radio buffs. The university did not have regular broadcasting until the 1940s, although it made efforts to

For several years, KUOI, begun in 1945, was the only student-operated radio station in the Pacific Northwest.

provide a permanent station before then. In the 1930s the regents considered the idea of cooperating with Washington State College—which had one of the oldest radio stations in the United States—to provide Idaho programming, but in those depression years they could not justify the extra expense. Finally, in 1945, a group of radio enthusiasts began station KUOI, which for many years was the only student-operated station in the Pacific Northwest. While students ran KUOI, the university later began KUID-FM, partially as a training station for communications majors. In 1984, Washington State University and University of Idaho officials finally agreed to merge their stations, this time primarily because of the cost savings to the University of Idaho. In that year KUID-FM became KRFA-FM, a branch of KWSU. In the 1950s, the university also began KUID-TV, a station that eventually became affiliated with the national Public Broadcasting System.

Print, audio, and visual media helped unite the campus, but the strongest unifying factor has been the students' own organizations. The Students'

University dinner following graduation ceremonies (1922).

Commencement exercises in Memorial Gymnasium (1939).

Athletic Association, formed in 1898, was the forerunner of the Associated Students of the University of Idaho. It began in an effort to pay off the indebtedness of the football team and was largely responsible for encouraging Guy Wolfe to begin publishing the *Argonaut*. In 1904 students organized a more formal "association" to oversee all student activities, but it was not yet greatly needed because the student body was still small and the association sputtered and died. In 1916, with student population steadily increasing, President Brannon encouraged the formation of both a men's and a women's union of students. Having taken this step, the students themselves pushed for a student council. After a few meetings, the council organized the Associated Student Body of the University of Idaho— later shortened to ASUI—which has overseen, organized, and financed many student activities since that time.

A university biennial report in the 1930s noted that the school's regents and administrators wholeheartedly accepted the theory that universities should provide, "in addition to intellectual training, what might be called the collegiate way of life, fully recognizing that the formative years of college constitute a period in which . . . desirable social and personal tastes and habits |are| developed." The university has adhered to that policy since the beginning.

Over the ten decades of its existence, students at the school have experienced great variety in their campus life. It has grown from a school with a handful of people to a community of over 9,000; from a time when everyone knew one another to a period when students and faculty found it necessary to begin an anonymous Crisis Line to assist students with their emotional and physical problems. It has evolved from a campus predominantly populated by single males to one approaching more equal numbers of men and women, many of them married, with children attending university-sponsored day-care centers and nursery schools. From the days when no students lived on campus because the school had no housing, through a time when most lived there, Idaho approached its hundredth year with over half its students again residing off campus.

Walking to commencement ceremonies (1975).

While students attending the university during its tenth decade might not recognize much were they transported back to the campus of the 1890s, they are the direct descendants of a process begun when pupils first arrived in October 1892. Over all the intervening years, several generations of Idaho students have shaped and molded campus activities to fit their needs. In the process they have developed the most vital, colorful, and memorable part of the university's history.

5

Athletics

Several generations of Moscow youth have made the trip up the hill to view university athletes in practice and competition. Awed, entertained, and inspired, they sometimes return home to try the same athletic feats themselves. In the 1890s, Alfred Carlton Gilbert was among those youngsters. "At the University of Idaho I saw my first pole-vaulting," he later wrote. "I thought it was wonderful, soaring so high in the air just by using a pole. . . . I made up my mind to try it." One evening after dark Gilbert walked out of town, stole a cedar fence rail, shaped it, sanded it, and began vaulting. "I suppose the farmer who owned that fence was angry at finding part of it missing," Gilbert speculated, "but he made an important contribution to a later world's record and an Olympic championship without knowing it."

In fact, A. C. Gilbert went on to set three world's records, win an Olympic gold medal in 1908, and revolutionize the sport: he was the first to use a bamboo pole and the first to vault by planting his pole in a box under the bar rather than using a spike on the end of his stick. He managed American Olympic teams in 1932 and 1936. In his spare time he invented a toy called the Erector Set.

Although Gilbert never competed for the University of Idaho, he reflects the impact of its athletic program upon the region. Indeed, not only children have watched, for athletics at Idaho have provided entertainment for all ages for nearly ten decades. It has been a program affecting those who played and coached as well as students, faculty, staff, alumni, and people with no formal connection to the school. It has grown from ragged, unorganized playing into a business with tremendous economic clout. And to many people outside the university today, the school is judged on only one basis: how well the Vandal teams compete.

Idaho's first intercollegiate athletic event occurred on June 9, 1893, when the school met Washington Agricultural College in a field day competition.

Despite its modern complexity and stature, the program began simply enough. The first officially recorded intercollegiate athletic event occurred in the first year of the school's existence. On June 9, 1893, students from Washington Agricultural College came to Moscow and competed with Idaho in a field day consisting of various track and field events. It was the beginning not only of sports at the university, but of a long, intense rivalry between Idaho and its nearby land-grant sister school, later named Washington State University.

In 1894 students petitioned the school to support intercollegiate football. They got a mixed reaction. The Board of Regents refused to appropriate $50 to equip a team, but the faculty did approve the constitution of an organization known as "the university football team." Untrained, with little practice, sporting uniforms assembled from any available clothing, the University of Idaho played its first football game that fall against a similarly equipped team from Washington Agricultural College and won 10-0. Gainford Mix, a student in the 1890s who played on the early Idaho teams, later recalled what they were like:

> We didn't have football suits. We wore baseball pants and old shirts; no nose-guards, no shin-guards, no padding. You see, the idea we had

Idaho's first football team (1893).

that padding kept you from hurting the other fellow. We figured the best way to save ourselves from getting banged up was to knock out our opponents, so we stripped for action. We played old style, mass formation, center rush, three downs to make five yards. The halves dropped back, the quarterback took the ball and passed it to the fullback. The halves grabbed the fullback, one on each side, the quarterback hooked him by the belt, the ends came around behind and pushed, and everybody took a running jump through center.

Grandstands were still in the future when Idaho played Washington State College in 1903.

Athletics at the university waned for a few years in the mid-1890s, and for a while there was no football. "Some of the more enthusiastic started a movement to organize a foot ball eleven, but were met with discouragement from every quarter," reported the first issue of the *Argonaut* in 1898. "Men that were willing to play were too light; those that had the weight positively refused to assist on the gridiron." But in that year the university's athletic program became considerably more organized. Idaho cooperated with Whitman College, in Walla Walla, and Washington Agricultural College in forming the "Inter-Collegiate Athletic Association," a pioneering athletic conference in the Pacific Northwest. For the first time Idaho competed in games conducted under supervision, adhering to established rules and regulations.

John Middleton quarterbacked Idaho teams in the early 1900s, then became a successful coach at the school, where he originated the "shotgun" formation.

As the university began to take athletics more seriously, the school hired coaches. Among the first was M. G. Arnold of Seattle, who organized a track squad in 1898. In those early years, football and track were the only intercollegiate sports. Baseball "did not receive much attention at Idaho," noted an early *Gem of the Mountains*, "partly because of the immense interest in football and track." And the school did not compete in basketball until 1906. But in the "big two" sports it often did well, its finest year coming in 1905 when "the slippery old bird of victory always hovered near." With Clarence "Hec" Edmundson winning two events, the three-member track team captured second place among all Pacific Northwest schools at the Lewis and Clark Exposition games in Portland. Adding to the glory, the football team went undefeated, scoring 113 points to its opponents' 2, and winning the Northwest championship. "This year's victories in football will do much toward advertising the University of Idaho to all prospective collegiate students," the *Argonaut* proudly predicted.

John Middleton quarterbacked some of the early-1900s teams, and in 1907 the school hired him as coach. He became one of football's great innovators, famous for opening up the game with his "Idaho Spread," which later became known as the "shotgun" formation widely used by collegiate and professional teams. The "spread" beat Washington State College during his first coaching season, 5-4.

Track and football continued to dominate the sports venue for several years. Idaho athlete John L. "Buck" Phillips set a new American collegiate javelin record in 1915, throwing 177 feet at the Penn Relays in Philadelphia, well past the old mark of 169, or—as the never-humble *Argonaut* announced—"Buck made 169 feet look like a shot of English brandy at a German beer bust." By then, however, basketball was replacing track as the second of the school's "big two" sports. Idaho played its first basketball game in January, 1906, and as with many sports at the school, it waged that initial contest against Washington State College. "We enter a new field to gain new victories and add new laurels," the student newspaper predicted hopefully. But the victories came slowly. Washington State won the first game 28-12, and it took nearly ten years before Idaho captured much attention. Then in 1916-17, under the coaching of former track star Hec Edmundson, the netters compiled the second-best record—behind WSC—in

Clarence S. "Hec" Edmundson, perhaps Idaho's finest ever track athlete, winning a race in 1908.

Shame of shames: The University of Washington has claimed an Idaho sports hero as its own. Go to Seattle and most people can tell you about Clarence "Hec" Edmundson. He was one of the Huskies' most successful basketball and track coaches. Many Husky cagers have played the game in Hec Edmundson Pavilion, one of the most prominent buildings on the Seattle campus. But in Moscow, only a few old-timers and some die-hard sports aficionados remember Edmundson as one of the university's most gifted athletes, teachers, and coaches. Still, it was Moscow and the University of Idaho that gave Hec Edmundson his start.

Clarence Sinclair Edmundson grew up in Moscow. His mother, Emma, operated a popular rooming house. Edmundson quite naturally matriculated to the university after high school—and there developed a remarkable talent as a distance runner.

the Northwest. The following year they were even better, going 10-2 and winning the Northwest conference championship.

Edmundson's 1917-18 team spurred the school's nickname, "Vandals." In those days, Idaho was the only school in the conference without a nickname. *Argonaut* sports reporter Harry Lloyd "Jazz" McCarty hoped to end that. During the football season he referred to the team as the "Wrecking Crew" and during the early part of the basketball schedule toyed with the phrase "Wrecking Crew" or "The Wreckers." Neither term appealed to editor-in-chief Frank Sutherland, nor to assistant editor and basketball player Ernest K. Lindley. Finally, McCarty tried a new appellation prior to Idaho's clash with conference powerhouse Whitman: "The opening game with Whitman will mark a new epoch in Idaho basketball history, for the present gang of 'Vandals' have the best material that has ever carried the 'I' into action."

McCarty used the word in a few more stories, but it did not catch on quickly. The newspaper's staff thought of changing it in favor of another marauding band, the "Huns"; but local patriots were already loudly criticizing the paper for its strong free-speech editorials during World War I, and "Huns" might further flame the controversy. Thus the season ended without a strong sentiment for "Vandals," but prior to the next basketball year regional reporters began using the name.

Still, some on campus hoped for something better. In 1920 the *Argonaut* sponsored a state-wide contest to develop a nickname for the football team, as "Vandals" was then applied only to basketball. The contest flopped completely. For a while that season the *Argonaut* referred to the

The University of Idaho has been graced with the presence of many athletes possessing more natural talent than Hec Edmundson, but it is doubtful it has had many who worked as hard. Hour upon hour, day upon day, Edmundson ran through the Palouse countryside—at a time when scientific training was unknown in distance-running circles. He developed fine endurance, the strength that allowed him to compete in several races during each meet. He also developed a gracefulness unusual among those who run distance races. Sports writers around the country frequently noted the beauty of his stride, a feature not missed by an Argonaut reporter who attended a track meet during Edmundson's last season of collegiate eligibility in 1908:

> *Captain Edmundson was Idaho's star. He took the 440, 880 and mile and ran a phenomenal lap in the relay. Edmundson was by far the prettiest performer of the day and even the most partisan spectator applauded his high class work. He simply toyed with his opponents in every race and . . . proved that he was in a class by himself as a distance runner. Edmundson is as graceful a runner as ever put on a shoe and his beautiful finish after a long hot pace arouses the keenest admiration.*

It was also in 1908 that Hec Edmundson organized the first University of Idaho cross-country club, a sport in which the school would eventually become a national power. And it was in 1908 that he became the university's first Olympic athlete, competing in the 800-meter run. Although Edmundson did not graduate until 1910, he exhausted his track eligiblity in 1908. During his years on the Idaho track team he lost only two races, even though he regularly ran in multiple events. His school marks lasted for years despite advances in training methods and equipment that made long-lived track records almost unheard of. In 1927 Don Cleaver—who would get second place in the two-mile run in nationals the following season—finally broke the last of Edmundson's school records, in the mile run.

Edmundson continued to train after completing his collegiate eligibility and between 1909 and 1912 became the nation's best half-miler. Once again in 1912 he made the American Olympic team in the 400 and 800 meters,

Felix Plastino, outfitted in the football gear typical of the 1920s.

football team as "The Huskies," but that name was already well established at the University of Washington. By 1921 reporters throughout the Northwest used "Vandals" to describe all Idaho sports teams. It was a name that "just happened," and there have been a number of people over the years who have felt something more dignified would be more suitable. But the name that casually rolled off the pen of Jazz McCarty in 1918 has remained.

The years of Idaho athletic dominance have often come in bunches. Periodically, several university teams seem to reach pinnacles of success at the same time. The first coincidence occurred in 1905; the second in the early 1920s.

The 1923 and 1924 football teams tore through most of their opponents in the Pacific Coast Intercollegiate Athletic Association with few defeats, much to the surprise of West Coast sportswriters and California coaches. The 1923 quarterback, Vernon Stivers, earned third-team All-American honors, an unusual feat for an athlete from such an isolated school away from media centers. Moscow businessmen were so proud of coach Robert Matthews that they bought him a new car. During those same years the

Idaho plays Oregon in the 1920s (top) and North Dakota in the 1930s (bottom).

making it to the finals in both events although he did not win a medal.

Upon graduating from Idaho in 1910 Edmundson became a teacher and coach at Coeur d'Alene High School, and in his first year his team won the Idaho interscholastic track and field meet. Administrators at Broadway High School in Seattle noticed that feat and hired him. He remained there only one successful season before his alma mater decided to lure him back to Moscow as principal of the School of Practical Agriculture and track coach.

Edmundson's gifts as a runner were matched by his talent as a coach, and throughout his long career he turned out winning teams, often against unfavorable odds. By 1914 he had molded the Idaho track squad into a regional contender. In 1915 Edmundson resigned over a salary dispute, much to the chagrin of the student body. `` 'Hec' has made a wonderful record at the University as a track coach and the country would have to be scoured from pole to pole before his equal could be found,'' stated the Argonaut. *Edmundson spent the next season coaching track at Whitman College in Walla Walla, but after receiving a petition from Idaho students asking that he be reinstated, the university rehired him in 1916 as both track and basketball coach.*

While continuing his successful track coaching, Edmundson also built the university's first powerful basketball teams. His 1916-17 squad finished second in the Northwest Conference, and his 1917-18 team went 10-2 and became conference champions. It remains one of the school's outstanding basketball units and is the one that inspired the university's nickname, the

Vandals, because of the way
Edmundson's players devastated
their opposition.

Clarence Edmundson
permanently left the University of
Idaho after that season although he

did briefly return in 1955 and
during a football game
acknowledged the introduction of a
new school trophy to be awarded
annually in his honor to the
university's most inspirational
football player. His string of
coaching successes had gained
national attention, and the
university was unable to offer a
large enough salary to keep him in
Moscow. In 1918 he coached track
at Texas A & M, and in 1919
went to the University of
Washington to head the track and
basketball programs. There he
became a Pacific Northwest
coaching legend. While his name
today is primarily associated with
the Seattle school, it was in
Moscow that he accomplished some
of his greatest athletic feats and
began one of the nation's most
successful college coaching careers.

In the 1960s the Vandals played in Neale Stadium (top). By the 1980s
they had moved inside to the Kibbie-ASUI Activity Center, better
known as "The Dome" (right).

Vandal cross-country team won consecutive Northwest championships. But the team gaining the most acclaim was again the basketball squad. Idaho had joined what later became known as the Pacific Coast Conference late in 1921 and immediately made an impact: its basketball team, led by senior Rich Fox—who later served as Idaho's basketball coach—and his brother Al,

Idaho joined what would later be known as the Pacific Coast Conference in 1921 and immediately made an impact. In both 1922 and 1923 (left), the Vandals won the Pacific Coast basketball championship. The university's first two basketball All-Americans, Al Fox (1923) and Fred Quinn (1946), are honored at halftime of a game, before their photographs are hung in Memorial Gymnasium (below).

Crowds packed Memorial Gymnasium to watch basketball games, especially when Gus Johnson (above) played for Idaho in the early 1960s.

a junior, won the coast championship and played in the national tournament at Indianapolis, the first such appearance for the Vandals. Unfortunately, Al Fox was too ill to play, and Idaho lost in the first round. The next year the conference hosted a championship playoff for the first time, and Idaho—the northern division champs—hosted the University of California, the southern division victors. Crowds filled the old gymnasium on campus well past overflowing as Idaho beat the Bears in two straight games. Guard Harold Telford and six-foot forward Al Fox were named to the All-Pacific Coast team, and Fox became Idaho's first All-American athlete.

While the 1927 football team tied for the conference championship, Idaho's major prowess in the late 1920s, 1930s, and early 1940s came in the less

Don Monson coached the finest men's basketball teams in the university's history in the 1980s.

Edmund Greenslet, George Leth, Earl Beck, and Lewis Bowman made up a championship 600-pound tug-of-war team in 1910–11.

Baseball (1937).

Tennis (above, 1937); fencing (left, 1939).

publicized sports of cross country and boxing. The Vandal harriers captured every Pacific Coast championship between 1937 and 1941, led by perennial individual winner Vic Dyrgall, who stormed onto the American running scene by capturing seventh in the national championships as a freshman in 1939. Dyrgall, one of the school's most talented distance runners—and it has had several—remains largely unrecognized in Idaho sports circles because he competed when the nation was preoccupied with war. After serving in the military, he returned to Idaho in 1946 to again win the Pacific Coast championship despite the hiatus in training and competition.

Vandal hurdlers compete against Washington State College (1936).

The Vandal powerhouse created by Dyrgall and coach Mike Ryan established Idaho as a cross-country force for many years. Between 1956 and 1962 the Vandals, featuring teams heavily dominated by students from England, regularly won Pacific Coast championships and fared very well nationally. They took third in the national finals in 1959 and ninth in 1962, when Paul Henden was named All-American. Idaho gradually de-emphasized cross country after that, but in 1980 Kyle Tonnemaker also earned All-American honors for the school.

It was boxing, though, that truly shone in the 1930s and 1940s, and the school has never had another athletic success to match that of its boxers in those years. Boxing started at Idaho in 1932 when Louie August, recently graduated from a Spokane high school, cajoled athletic officials into allowing him to teach a boxing class in return for a small monthly stipend to help pay his college expenses. His equipment consisted of two pair of gloves, two sets of headgear, and a punching bag. Thanks to August's enthusiastic boosterism, by the following spring Idaho had a boxing club with twenty-five members, a competition ring, and sophisticated equipment. The following year the "club" became a team, and Idaho began competing on the intercollegiate level.

Louie Denten became the first of many Pacific Coast boxing champions in 1934. By 1936 Idaho was a national power. Rolly Shumway won the school's first individual national championship that year, and the team finished fifth. In 1940 the Vandals won the national boxing championship, and they repeated the following season when Ted Kara became the first boxer in history to win three straight collegiate national titles. Laune Erickson won his second championship that year and would return for a third after the war in 1947, when Idaho tied for the national team title. That year also was the first of three national championships for Herb Carlson. Idaho won Pacific Coast championships in 1949, 1950, and 1951 and again tied for the national crown in 1950. By then, however, boxing was suffering a battering on two fronts. On the one hand, crowds no longer gathered to watch the team compete as they had in the 1930s, when boxing cards frequently drew more spectators than basketball games. At the same time, expenses steadily increased. In addition, boxing came under increasing attack for being physically harmful. As high schools around the nation dropped the sport, colleges soon followed since there was no pool of talent to draw upon. Idaho merely reflected a growing national trend when it eliminated the sport in 1954. Before then, however, the Vandal squads—under coaches Louie August, Ken Butler, and Frank Young—turned out individual and team champions with a consistency never matched by another Idaho sport.

In the 1930s, when Idaho was a national powerhouse, boxing matches frequently drew more spectators to Memorial Gymnasium than did basketball games.

By the time boxing exited, another minor sport brought Idaho considerable national attention. In 1949 Vandal skier Sverre Kongsgaard, an exchange student from Norway, set a new North American ski-jumping record. The feat brought Idaho publicity and helped encourage other Scandinavian students to follow Kongsgaard to Moscow. In 1956 two of them—Eirik Berggren and Reidar Ullevaalseter—earned All-American honors as the team finished fifth in the national championships. Berggren won his second national Nordic ski title that year, and he returned in 1957 to again become an All-American.

Ted Kara

Louis Vitus August surely orchestrated one of the university's greatest athletic recruiting coups in 1937. August had come to Idaho as a student in 1932 and, in return for a nominal monthly stipend, agreed to instruct boxers. After he graduated in 1936, the school hired him as a full-time boxing coach. If August was looking for job security, he could have done little better than convincing Theodore "Ted" Kara—shown above —to come to the school, for here was an athlete who could bring a program respectability in a hurry: Kara had already captained the United States Olympic boxing team even before setting foot in Moscow.

Kara's family liked to say they discovered Ted's pugilistic abilities one day in 1932 while living in Cleveland. It seemed the lad resorted to fisticuffs to settle an argument with a neighbor and handled himself quite competently in the exchange. There are athletes

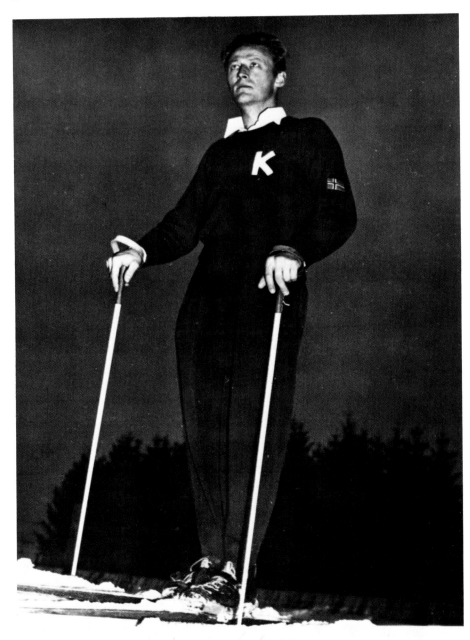

Minor sports carried the flame of Idaho athletic glory in these years as the "big two," basketball and football, floundered. There were a few bright spots. The 1945-46 basketball squad went 23-11, becoming northern division conference champions for the first time since the Al Fox years. Once again the Vandals played the California Bears for the league championship—this time in Berkeley—but lost, two games to one. Fred Quinn was named to the second-team All-American squad. After losing the league championship, the team suffered through many lackluster seasons, as did the football squad. When in the fourth game of the 1946 season the Vandal gridders scored their first touchdown of the year, the *Argonaut* sarcastically headlined: "Vandals Score!" Unfortunately, so did their opponents. Marquette won that game 46-6. Even the student newspaper proved hard-pressed to find anything positive to say: "It is indeed discouraging to be sports editor of the Argonaut during the football season. Without fail, the editor always gets the feeling of being first cousin to an undertaker." One bright spot in the late 1940s was the play of tackle Carl Kiilsgaard, who was named to several all-conference teams and played in the East-West Shrine game and with the college all-stars against the professional champion Philadelphia Eagles.

By the mid-1950s, though, the school entered another of those periods when several sports reached high levels of success at the same time. In addition to strong cross-country and ski squads, football and basketball

In 1949 Sverre Kongsgaard (facing page) set a North American ski-jumping record. The publicity lured several other outstanding Scandinavian skiers to campus and helped transform Idaho into a collegiate skiing power. Donald LeRoy Johnson puts the shot (above, 1936).

who are born with natural talent, and Ted Kara was surely one of these. Within a few months of his neighborhood scrap, and after only a brief stint at "training," Kara won Cleveland's all-city Amateur Athletic Union boxing tournament at 112 pounds. In 1933 he again won the all-city crown, this time at 118 pounds.

Kara dropped out of boxing for a couple of years but resurfaced in 1936 to win Golden Glove titles in both Cleveland and Chicago. Invited to that year's Olympic trials, he made the most of the opportunity, winning his division. His teammates elected him squad captain, and there at the Berlin Olympics—the one where Jesse Owens destroyed Adolf Hitler's super-race concept—young Ted Kara, not many years beyond his street-fighting days, represented the United States. He won his first two matches, including a historical-footnote bout in which he registered the first knockout of those games, and advanced to the semifinals in the 125-pound class before losing on a close decision.

The following year Ted Kara and brother Frank enrolled at the University of Idaho. "I don't like schools that are too large; you don't get acquainted," he said. "I liked what I knew of the Idaho coach and teams and I wanted to get out west—away from home." Coach August could not have been happier. Ted and Frank Kara devastated their freshman competition that year. In fact, it was a little lopsided for Ted to even fight freshmen—he never had a close match.

It did not make much difference when he moved up to varsity competition the next season. Ted Kara never lost a collegiate bout in four years. In 1939 he won the Pacific Coast Conference and national titles at 127 pounds. In 1940 he won the same championships at 120 pounds. In 1941 Idaho skipped the PCC contest in favor of a match against the University of Wisconsin, but Kara again won the national title at 120 pounds. He became the first boxer ever to win three NCAA championships, and tournament officials awarded him the John S. LaRowe trophy, given to the meet's outstanding fighter.

Kara's victories in 1940 and 1941 led the University of Idaho to national team championships. In the latter season the Kara brothers created collegiate boxing history. In addition to Ted's third consecutive title, Frank won the national championship at 127 pounds, the first time brothers had ever won titles.

After that season both coach and athlete joined the Army Air Corps. Louie August, who led the Vandals to two national championships, returned from his service stint and became a successful businessman in Spokane. Ted Kara was not so lucky. He died while on a mission in the South Pacific. Today a plaque hangs in Memorial Gym listing all of Idaho's national boxing champions. It is dedicated to the memory of Ted Kara.

Collegiate boxing ended in the 1950s, a victim of dwindling fan interest and increasing concern over injuries. Before the sport left the college ranks, however, the University of Idaho established itself as one of the nation's premier boxing schools. It turned out many outstanding champions, including two—Laune Erickson and Herb Carlson—who matched Ted Kara's record of three national titles. But those who remember Idaho's boxing teams will tell you there was no one better than Kara. And it was

Soccer (1970s).

finally came to life. In 1957 the Vandal football defensive line gained national attention, anchored by Jerry Kramer and Wayne Walker, both later to be professional stars. Kramer, Walker, and Larry Aldrich were named to the East-West Shrine game, the first time Idaho ever placed three players on the prestigious post-season squad. Kramer also earned All-American honors. In the same year the basketball team went 17-9 for its best showing in over a decade. It was led by the Pacific Coast Conference's leading scorer, All-American Gary Simmons, who once scored 38 points against Southern California at a time when tallies that high were almost unheard of. By the mid-1950s the first black athletes began playing for Idaho teams, and in 1959-60 one, Joe King, gained honorable mention All-American honors and received an invitation to try out for the 1960 Olympic basketball squad.

Two other black athletes would head another athletic resurgence in the 1960s and become among the best ever to play their sports at the school. Memorial Gym, completed in 1929, had seemed spacious to most Idaho basketball fans, especially when compared to the cramped facilities in the old gym. During the 1962 basketball season, however, the accommodations proved woefully inadequate. School kids ran to the gym immediately after the sound of the day's last bell. Later their parents, university students, faculty, and staff crowded into the small pavilion, all waiting to watch the basketball acrobatics of one player: Gus Johnson. "Seats at Memorial Gym were as scarce as snowballs in July," reported the student yearbook. "It was a common sight to see the Gym all but filled at 6:00 p.m. with long lines of people waiting for tickets."

The team won twenty games and lost six with Johnson averaging nineteen points a game. Most people, though, came to see him grab a rebound, turn, and throw an outlet pass, all seemingly in one motion. Johnson averaged over twenty rebounds a game that year, the second best in the nation. After this one brilliant season, Johnson went to the National Basketball Association where he became a perennial all-star. Idaho lost its coach at the same time, as Joe Cipriano moved to the University of Nebraska.

The school's athletic attention then focused on another player and another team. Ray McDonald followed his high school coach from New Mexico to Caldwell High School in the early 1960s and became an All-Idaho fullback, heavily recruited nationally. He chose to attend the University of Idaho, where football coach Dee Andros was building a conference contender for the first time in many seasons. By his sophomore year, McDonald was receiving rave reviews. "No other sophomore in the West is so much the core of his team as McDonald," noted *Sports Illustrated*. "Little ripples of alarm have been emanating from every school Idaho plays in the next three years." And good years they turned out to be, with Idaho at last posting winning seasons, beating Washington State University twice in a row, and capturing the conference championship in 1965. McDonald became an All-American. But in a fashion that was to be an unfortunate Idaho tradition, the school proved unable to retain the coach who set these winning standards; like Cipriano in basketball, Dee Andros left Moscow in 1965, to gain acclaim as a coach and athletic director at Oregon State University.

While McDonald and Johnson brought respectability to Idaho football and basketball, other sports contributed to the athletic resurgence of the mid-1960s. The ski team finished eighth in nationals in 1965, the same year that the tennis squad began a remarkable string of victories, winning the conference title in thirteen out of fourteen seasons. The baseball team also perennially won the conference title in the mid-1960s, and Idaho high jumper Steve Brown in 1967 became the first person in the Pacific Northwest to clear seven feet.

The Idaho football squad of 1971 set two new school records by winning eight straight games and by winning eight in a season, two more than any other Idaho team. Receiver Jerry Hendren was named All-American. Five years later the school retired the jersey of perhaps its greatest collegiate lineman, John Yarno, who was the first Vandal football player named to the Associated Press first-team All-American squad and the first lineman ever named Big Sky Conference player of the year.

It was not until the 1980s, though, that Idaho experienced another multi-sport Renaissance, perhaps its finest. It began when the university hired Don Monson as basketball coach in 1978, the year after the team had won only four and lost twenty-two games. In his first year, Monson's team went 11-15. In his second they won seventeen and lost ten, the best record since the Gus Johnson years. The 1980-81 season began with eleven straight wins, and the team ended with a 24-4 record, played in the NCAA national tournament, and appeared for the first time in decades on national polls of top collegiate teams. The 1981-82 season was one of those magical years

not just local hype: many aficionados of the sport consider Ted Kara the outstanding collegiate boxer of all time. In those days, the Kara name could draw huge crowds, and boxing was Idaho's only sport that paid for itself, despite the fact that the boxers had to travel greater distances than any other team. Five thousand fans regularly filled Memorial Gym for matches; in the memorable meet at the University of Wisconsin in 1941, 14,500 spectators watched. Naturally, Ted Kara won. Boxing brought the University of Idaho national acclaim—and brought to the campus one of the most gifted natural athletes ever to stroll its grounds.

that had come only twice before for Idaho basketball fans—with the Al Fox teams of the 1920s and the Gus Johnson squad of the 1960s. Monson's team, with its tallest player registering only six feet six inches, captured the imagination of the town, the state, and to some extent the nation. The Vandals recorded a 26-2 regular-season mark, including several victories over much larger schools. Ranked as high as sixth in national basketball polls, the squad won the school's first-ever NCAA tournament game and made it to the final round of sixteen before losing. Monson was named the nation's outstanding collegiate basketball coach. The next year, Vandal basketballers had a 20-9 record and played in the National Invitational Tournament, their third national post-season tournament in three years. Following that season, Monson left Idaho for the University of Oregon.

Monson's winning teams spurred other squads onto outstanding records. The 1983 women's track team placed second in their national meet, while the women's tennis team captured sixth and the men's tennis squad went 23-9. In Dennis Erickson's first year at coaching Idaho football the 1982 team—led by future professionals Ken Hobart and Sam Merriman—won nine, lost four, and made the NCAA Division IAA playoffs. Erickson would have four consecutive successful years and, with a 32-15 record, become the school's winningest football coach before moving on to the University of Wyoming in 1986.

Rivaling Monson's squad for the outstanding team at the school, however, was the women's basketball team. During one 1986 home appearance the squad drew over 5,000 fans, reminding many spectators of the three extraordinary men's basketball teams that had captured so much attention in earlier years. It had been a long struggle before women's athletics at Idaho reached this level of respectability and interest, however. As early as

The university required women students to take physical-education classes as early as the 1890s, but it was years before they could compete in intercollegiate athletics.

Although intercollegiate competition was very limited, the Women's Recreation Association sponsored a wide variety of athletic contests on campus, such as tennis (above, 1933), basketball (left, 1949), and track and field (following page, top, 1960).

1898 the university required its women students to take at least one year of "physical culture." But there was no movement to form organized athletic teams. Perhaps the first encouragement came in 1907 when the *Argonaut* supported the concept of a women's basketball team, one year after men took up the sport at Idaho:

There are several girls in college who have been successful players

elsewhere; why not here? To have a good ladies' basket ball team, the girls must have a coach, and they must be allowed to have the Gym certain hours without molestation. . . . Athletics for the girls in this institution is sadly neglected. Let us remedy this by assisting in every way the girls in basket ball.

Not until 1919-20, though, did the school organize athletics for women. Then, in line with similar actions taken by other colleges following the women's suffrage movement, Idaho offered a variety of intramural sports for women, including basketball, tennis, hiking, field hockey, softball, and horseback riding. By 1926 the women's rifle team competed against students from other schools, but that remained their only intercollegiate sport for many years.

The rifle team (below) was the school's first intercollegiate women's squad, beginning competition in the 1920s. The second intercollegiate sport—field hockey—was not organized until the 1950's (facing page, top).

The university in 1923 formed a women's athletic association, which began awarding "I" letter sweaters—similar to those men athletes had donned for years—to women who accumulated a set number of points in athletic competition. A women's "I Club" was formed in 1928 to foster sportsmanship on campus and encourage women's high-school athletics around the state.

By the mid-1930s Idaho hosted an annual "inter-college play-day," featuring athletic competition between women from Idaho, Washington State College, and Lewiston Normal. By 1950 field hockey joined rifle as an intercollegiate

Women's I Club, 1932. The I Club for women began in 1928 and awarded letters for points gained in intramural athletic competition.

Women's volleyball teams in the 1970s and 1980s turned in consistent winning seasons.

sport. In the early 1970s, women's intercollegiate athletics finally took a firm hold, boosted when the school began awarding its first athletic scholarships to women in accordance with federal regulations prohibiting sexual discrimination in collegiate athletics. The school also began hiring professional coaches for women's teams.

Since the early 1920s "Joe Vandal" had been the caricature of University of Idaho athletic teams. In 1977 a female figure joined Joe in a new, streamlined logo. Some Vandal supporters, who still viewed Idaho athletics as a male domain, grumbled. But a number of winning women's teams in the late 1970s and early 1980s helped those with sensitive male egos accept the change, for within a few years Idaho women transformed the school into a national contender in several areas.

Women's volleyball teams turned in consistently high performances in the 1970s and 1980s, culminating in the 25-13 season of 1984-85 when Pam Bradetich was named conference coach of the year. The strong tennis squad of the early 1980s earned a sixth-place finish at the national championships in 1982-83. Led by hurdler Colleen Williams and distance runner Patsy Sharples—the first woman ever named the Inland Empire's Amateur Athlete of the Year—the Idaho track teams of the early 1980s also did well nationally, as did the cross-country team. Swimmer Nancy Bechtholdt won 18 All-American awards during her Idaho career in the late 1970s and early 1980s.

Most interest, however, focussed on the dominating women's basketball teams of that period. The women cagers got stronger with each year of competition. In 1978-79 they went 17-6, followed by seasons of 25-6 and 22-8. In 1981-82 the team finally began to attract attention, competing in the national tournament and gaining a ranking of fourteenth nationally. Unfortunately, it labored in the shadow of Don Monson's best men's squad.

Pat Dobratz coached that team, in her second year at Idaho. She would turn out consistently successful squads until she left the school after the 1985-86 season. Her best two years were her last. In 1984-85, featuring the "Twin Towers" of Mary Westerwelle and Mary Raese, each six feet four inches tall, the team again made the national rankings. It eventually lost to powerhouse University of Southern California in the national tournament, but not before compiling the best-ever record of any Idaho basketball team—men's or women's—at 28-2. Even those who previously thought women should not be on the athletic field had to take notice. The next year's squad still had the twin towers and played exciting ball, frequently viewed by more people than attended the men's games, including one contest watched by one of the largest crowds ever to see a women's basketball game west of the Rocky Mountains. Still, that team was not quite as successful as its predecessor, finishing the regular season with a 23-5 record. It missed an opportunity at another NCAA tournament appearance but did get an invitation to play in the National Invitational Tournament. The squad made the most of the opportunity by winning it all, becoming Idaho's first national championship basketball team of either sex.

The women's team brought Idaho its first national basketball title in 1986.

From the time of disorganized football games in the 1890s to a period in the 1980s when the school turned out nationally competitive teams in many sports for both men and women, the athletic program at the University of Idaho grew into a complex, expensive operation in which coaches and administrators worked in stress-filled jobs. It was an evolution not without its problems along the way.

Athletic controversies arose almost at the same time as athletic competition itself. In the 1890s the most pressing problem revolved around determining player eligibility. Colleges accused one another—justly—of using non-student "ringers" to win games. The University of Idaho joined its first athletic conference in 1898 primarily because the faculty was interested in "purifying athletics" by establishing rules concerning player eligibility.

By the early 1900s, with rules on eligibility fairly well established, the university's primary goal became recruitment of individuals who qualified as both good students and good athletes. Though full-fledged athletic recruiting at Idaho is largely a product of the post-World War II period, its beginnings date back much earlier. In 1910 Edward M. Hulme wrote of his experiences recruiting a prospective student from Boise: "I promised the boy a place at $20.00 a month, but I fear he had definitely committed himself to some financial arrangement with Oregon. . . . The boy is well worth fighting for, both as a student and as an athlete."

Over the years, as recruitment pressures increased, some observers accused Idaho and other colleges of unethical procedures. In 1922, news that two star football players had competed illegally jolted the campus. "Our desire to be athletic victors must never again . . . superceed [sic] the desire to play fair," editorialized the *Argonaut*. "Let us resolve that a repetition shall never occur." Despite this concern, the National Collegiate

Athletic Association penalized the 1977-78 Vandal men's basketball team for just such violations.

Just as the university very early began to recruit athletes, so too did it recognize that good teams helped lure students of all types to the school. "At present a school is looked on with disfavor if it does not compare favorably with other schools in athletics," noted the *Argonaut* in 1910. "If a school is winning in athletics it attracts the attention of every high school student who hears of the facts."

Yet there was always considerable controversy over just how much money should be spent in order to gain athletic renown. The *Argonaut* commented in 1911: "Athletics . . . are alright . . . but are they worth the price we are paying for them? Would it not be better to reduce inter-collegiate contests . . . to intra-collegiate activities." It was an opinion more than vaguely similar to that expressed by the newspaper in 1974 when university administrators decided to raise student fees in order to place a domed roof over the new athletic stadium ("Is a roof over our heads four Saturdays in the fall more important than classrooms 365 days a year"), and to the objections of student leaders in 1986 when President Richard Gibb again increased student fees to support intercollegiate athletics.

In order to attain a viable reputation, a school must have viable competition, which was a problem for a university relatively isolated in northern Idaho. Consequently, the school attempted to align itself with conferences. In 1921 Idaho joined the Pacific Coast Intercollegiate Athletic Association—later known as the Pacific Coast Conference—and enjoyed immediate success competing against much larger institutions in Washington, Oregon, and California. Undoubtedly the stunning victories of Vandal football and basketball teams in the early 1920s brought the school recognition it could not have attained in any other way. But participation in the conference also exacted a toll. In 1922 Idaho played virtually all of its football games away from home because the school's football stadium was small and the athletic department could recoup much more revenue by playing at larger facilities. "Membership in athletic conferences, while it is a recognition of worthiness, . . . entails some hardships, particularly for a school situated like Idaho," noted the university's biennial report in 1924. "To enjoy competition with representative colleges of the conference, Idaho teams must travel great distances and be absent from the campus unusual lengths of time. They must play their games with their eyes always on a possible championship. . . . They compete, too, with city institutions where crowds and consequent incomes are entirely beyond Idaho's possibilities."

As the years passed, Idaho was less and less able to compete with those larger schools—particularly in football. In 1934 conference officials voted to suspend the Vandals from PCC play in the sport. They reluctantly reinstated the school in 1942, but Idaho competed league-wide for only a few years more. It played its last league football game against a California squad in 1948. Some people harshly criticized this decision not to schedule

Intramurals have been a part of Idaho athletics longer than intercollegiate sports, and they have provided a recreational outlet for thousands (below, and facing page).

137

California teams. The Boise *Statesman* said: "Just when we were beginning to believe that the University of Idaho was on the threshold of football prominence, we are thrown back behind the goal posts by the announcement . . . that Idaho is hauling in its horns." President Jesse Buchanan preferred to believe the school was "simply rationalizing our football schedule with our present capabilities."

The Pacific Coast Conference folded after the 1958-59 school year. Big colleges were disenchanted with playing at smaller schools with small gate receipts. Smaller schools found it increasingly difficult to compete and to meet the conference's financial requirements. The larger schools in Washington, Oregon, and California formed a new league. Idaho remained an independent for a few years but found it difficult to schedule games. The school hoped to join a conference that would "afford the Vandals a chance to romp at the expense of the opposition," according to an *Argonaut* sports writer. It believed it found just such a league with the formation of the Big Sky Conference in 1963, a league Idaho has retained membership in since.

But entry into the Big Sky was no panacea. The pressure to succeed and the cost of competition continued to rise. Indeed, some critics have claimed that the University of Idaho's major sports suffer from a system of "musical coaches." Especially since the end of World War II, coaches have moved in and out of Moscow with disturbing regularity. The unsuccessful ones have been fired; the successful ones have moved on to larger schools that could offer better salaries. This transience has been perhaps the biggest difficulty facing the athletic department since the 1940s.

Athletics changed the appearance of campus. In the 1930s, an open field became Neale Stadium (facing page), which eventually gave way to the Kibbie-ASUI Activity Center in the 1970s (under construction, above).

He Loved Golf

Francis L. James was born in England and grew up playing cricket, eventually competing professionally. A short man who spoke with a thick accent, James emigrated to North America where he found another sport to his liking: golf. He approached his new love with a zeal, and while he never made a significant mark as a player, he gained international prestige as a designer of golf courses. Over one hundred golfing greens owe their plan to his ingenuity, including some of America's most famous courses.

Golfers in the Moscow area had struggled for years, playing their favorite game on any available patches of land. One avid golfer, George Morey Miller, joined the university's English department in 1909. When he discovered his new residence had no golf course, he immediately began campaigning for a place to play. Along with other Moscow golfers, he constructed a five-hole course in the area where Ghormley Park was later located. Moscow linksters soon formed a golf club and rented eighty acres north of town where they established a nine-hole regulation course. World War I interrupted their golfing activity, but after the war the club bought a farm east of Moscow and in 1926 decided to build a first-class course. Not surprisingly, they hired Francis L. James to design it. In the 1930s the golf club gave the property to the Moscow Elks to be kept in perpetuity as a golf course for Moscow residents.

While the new course served the town's golfers, it did not greatly benefit the university. "Idaho students have the golf bug again," noted the Argonaut *in 1928. "Followers of this sport are getting so numerous that flying golf balls*

Swimming and diving facilities changed from cramped (below) to first-class with the 1970s construction of the Physical Education Building and Swim Center (facing page).

Sports changed the university in many ways—not the least of which was in the appearance of the campus. Some of the school's most imposing structures were built for athletic competition—the first gymnasium, later known as the Women's Gymnasium, and still later as Art and Architecture South; Memorial Gym; the Kibbie-ASUI Activity Center; and the Physical Education Building and Swim Center. Less visibly, but no less dramatically, sporting contests have shaped much of student life, for fans are as important to athletic competition as the athletes themselves.

The very first issue of the *Argonaut* in 1898 urged students to rally behind the school's teams: "To become a student of a college which cannot, or will not support athletics is like clerking in a store which does not advertise, being literally buried alive." The *Argonaut* for decades viewed athletic support as something that should be of paramount student concern, and its encouragement of "pep" became somewhat redundant. 1905: "Spirit must be more marked. . . . Let's have more of it. It is only one more week until the big games commence so let us raise the roof next Wednesday and prepare for the coming battle." 1916: "The only good rooter is a fanatic and the only proper state of mind when the team is behind is one of frenzy." 1930: "A student from the East saw Idaho in action for the first time in the game last Saturday. . . . When asked what he thought of the game he did not answer that the boys had not taken the game. . . . No. He asked why the lack of spirit." 1965: "Students just aren't gung ho enough about their University. . . . There is a great lack of school spirit."

Determined to alleviate that problem, students demanded a more suitable location. In 1930 they began voluntarily developing a course during a campus work day, a project university workmen completed the following year. Still, the course proved inadequate, and in 1935 the school purchased seventy acres adjoining the campus southwest of the arboretum, added thirty previously acquired acres to the tract, and made plans to build the state's finest golf course. They turned to Frank James to lay it out.

James had returned to the Palouse once more after his work on the Moscow Golf Club project when he designed Washington State College's golf course in 1934. The University of Idaho course was completed in 1936. James's third look at the Palouse region convinced him to stay. "What I like about this country is the way things grow," he said. "I am never going to leave it. I am going to die here." University administrators hired him as

Nonetheless, many former students' most vivid memories revolve around athletic contests. In earlier years this enthusiasm manifested itself in the creation and memorization of school yells and songs. "Here it is, almost time for the big game with Utah, and the important question arises, do we know our songs?" the *Argonaut* editorialized in 1922. "Two of the most important points upon which the university's spirit and enthusiasm are judged are singing and yelling. Our yelling is good; but our singing could have far more volume and enthusiasm."

manager of the golf course, golf coach, and resident professional. He died on the job in 1952.

After his death the university named the course clubhouse after him. A plaque inside reads: "He loved golf, and was loved by all those who played the game." University President Jesse Buchanan said at the dedication ceremonies: "He saw golf course possibilities where others could not see. He could not look at a bit of landscape from a train window without mentally visioning a green here and a fairway there. A cow pasture was not a cow pasture to James. It was a splendid golf course."

Indeed, one of Frank James's most significant attributes was his uncanny ability to design "splendid golf courses" utilizing what nature provided. He did not mutilate the natural surroundings; rather he gently molded and adapted them to a new use. Residents of Moscow and Pullman are the fortunate recipients of three of his designs. They are utilitarian uses of the landscape, enjoyed not only by golfers but by joggers, skiers, hikers, and sledders, a tribute to the man who envisioned golf courses where others saw only pastures.

The school's first organized yell was born during the football season of 1894 when, on a ride to Pullman to attend a game between Idaho and WAC, students wrote some words on small slips of paper, distributed them, and shouted them during the game. By 1896, Idaho had its first official school yell:

> Rah! Rah! Rah!
> Rah! Rah! Rah!
> Idaho! Idaho!
> Boom! Ba! Bah!

By 1899, the school boasted a wide variety of yells. Though short on originality, they were repeated with gusto at athletic contests:

> Hobble Gobble, Razzle Dazzle
> Zip! Boom! Bah!
> Idaho! Idaho!
> Rah! Rah! Rah!

Some yells were reserved strictly for members of various classes:

> Rakety Hackety! Wah! Who! Wah!
> Rakety Hackety! Wah! Who! Wah!
> Zip Boom Bah! Zip Boom Bah!
> Senior Preparatory, Rah! Rah! Rah!

By the 1920s, students gathered for one hour every Wednesday afternoon by the I Bench to practice yells so they could be shouted in spirited unison at football games.

"We don't think it is necessary to assume a figure S as a preliminary to leading a college yell," complained the A*rgonaut* in 1923, but acrobatics and choreography assumed a progressively greater role in cheerleading routines (facing page).

Pep rallies in 1922 (above) and 1961 (left).

No less significant than the yells were school songs. The student body encouraged the writing of new songs by holding an annual songfest competition. A surprising number of tunes thus were written over the years. Most of them, like the yells, were stronger on spirit than on memorable lyrics. A couple, however, have lasted. Student J. Morris O'Donnell wrote a number of Idaho songs, but his most remembered, composed in 1930, became the school's fight song, *Go, Vandals, Go!*.

Idaho pep bands in the 1920s (above) and 1930s (facing page, top).

In 1917 MacKinley Helm and Alice Besse collaborated to write new words to a song entitled *The Garden of Paradise*, composed by Sallie Hume Douglas. After decades of negotiating with Douglas and her heirs for authority to use her melody, the university finally received permission in 1948. The result, with a few word changes over the years, was *Here We Have Idaho*, which has long served as the university's alma mater as well as the state's official song.

Members of the student body held pep rallies before games and organized cheering sections at the contests. The students' enthusiasm made an impact. In 1897, after a game with the Spokane Amateur Athletic Club, a Spokane newspaper commented on the university's vocal "rooters," a word unfamiliar to President Gault. Believing the paper had insulted his students, Gault asked for an apology. Before long, however, "rooting sections" were well accepted. Leading them were yell leaders, traditionally an all-male group until the 1950s, although the university did have a rare woman yell

Yell leaders (1935).

leader before then. The yell leaders did precisely as their name implied and bore little resemblance to the well-choreographed cheerleading squads of the post-1960 period. In 1923 the *Argonaut* even protested the rudimentary routines that were then beginning to infiltrate the yell squads:

The recent basketball games have brought to light some male students who would do well in a Russian ballet, but who seem out of place leading red blooded men and women in stirring Idaho yells and songs. We don't think it is necessary to assume a figure S position as a preliminary to leading a college yell. If a little more attention were paid to the business of instilling enthusiasm into the crowd during the actual yelling, instead of wondering what the girls thought of graceful exhibition, better results might be obtained.

Still, "graceful exhibition" continued to creep into cheerleading. By the end of the 1920s, the school selected yell leaders as much for their acrobatic abilities as for their cheerleading attributes. The two male yell leaders of 1928-29 had a repertoire of stunts that included imaginary tight-rope walking, mock football plays, resuscitation efforts, and "the time-worn Tunney long count."

The Harvard yell contest, a stunt competition during the annual WSC-UI game in the 1920s, always prompted novel routines.

In 1954 the ASUI approved a squad of "pom pon girls" to accompany the three male yell leaders. The women became so popular that they soon dominated yell-leading squads, and their routines became more intricate. In 1961 Idaho cheerleaders introduced short skirts amid considerable campus discussion. "In case any near sighted males or baffled females wondered about the slightly glazed but very pleased look on most of the masculine faces at the Homecoming game," reported the *Argonaut*, "then it might be due to the new outfits of our pom pon girls, on which the skirts are short, short, short." A new era of cheerleading had begun.

Cheerleaders—their routines and their outfits—changed considerably over the years.

The fall Homecoming game was the biggest athletic event of the year, when student pep reached its peak. In 1909 the university began promoting Homecoming as an occasion for alumni to return to campus. The events changed some over time, but Homecoming activities traditionally included a rally, pajama serpentine, queen competition, living-group decoration

House-decorating contests (right), pajama serpentines (below), and Main Street parades (facing page) marked Homecoming festivities for many years.

Voice of the Vandals

Bob Curtis wanted to be the Voice of the Cougars. Washington State University's loss was Idaho's gain.

In the late 1950s Bob Curtis hoped to strike a deal to broadcast all Washington State athletic contests, but he could not agree on financial terms with the school. Curtis then met with University of Idaho Sports Information Director Kenneth Hunter and signed a contract. He intended to work a year for Idaho, and then move across the border again to Washington State. Things did not work out that way. After signing on as the Voice of the Vandals, he broadcast every Idaho football game and nearly every basketball game for over thirty years. He was named Idaho Sportscaster of the Year more than twenty times. He did confess to some mixed loyalties when he first began broadcasting Idaho–Washington State games, but that did not last long. While he was a Cougar graduate, Curtis became a Vandal loyalist.

Bob Curtis grew up on the family farm near Garfield, Washington. His father purchased the land in 1929—a tough time to start farming. Things were not much easier after Curtis took over the place. He became, as he said, "a full-time farmer and a part-time broadcaster." But broadcasting provided a good diversion from the pressures of farming.

After high school, Curtis attended Washington State College.

contest, and gala Main Street parade. The annual bonfire, however, was perhaps the event most remembered and publicized. Members of the freshman class gathered wood and other burnable material from around Moscow, painstakingly made a huge pile, doused it with oil, and set it ablaze during the big Homecoming rally. Just as traditionally, the university received complaints and bills from Moscow residents and merchants over the loss of flammable personal property. In the 1930s the freshmen voted to eliminate the bonfire and thus end one of Idaho's greatest traditions.

Homecomings were until the 1940s generally played against WSC, and one of the most difficult tasks for the freshmen after gathering fuel was guarding the pyre from Washington State College marauders bent on burning it before the big rally. The Cougars' methods were ingenious, if somewhat dangerous. Once, WSC students standing in the arboretum shot flaming arrows in the direction of the stack, but did not hit their mark. In 1924, some enterprising Washingtonians dropped phosphorous bombs from an airplane, but again did not succeed in setting the fire before being chased away by shotgun blasts. A more traditional method was to infiltrate a WSC student into the group building the pile. The Cougar would then try to light it and hope to escape from the angry Idahoans. Despite their many efforts, WSC never succeeded in setting the fire.

Washington State University and the University of Idaho are each other's longest-standing sports rivals. As the 1922 *Gem* stated: "The Pullman game is never a milk and water affair—it is a battle to the finish and brings out everything that a school stands for." The football Battle of the Palouse always drew huge crowds. Special spectator trains frequently ran from the

A high school basketball player, he tried out for the Cougar team, but because of an appendectomy he could not play. He hoped to find some way to stay close to sports, and when Washington State auditioned students to find broadcasters, Curtis won and began his radio career. As a WSC student he broadcast football, basketball, and baseball contests.

In 1946 Tidewater Associated Oil, which had the rights to broadcast all Pacific Coast Conference contests, hired Curtis to do home games for the University of Idaho and Washington State. He was the only student broadcaster employed by the oil company, and nearly 50 stations on the ABC network received his program. He worked with Associated Oil for ten years, until television began claiming the radio audience, forcing the oil company to discontinue its programming. That was when Bob Curtis hired on with the University of Idaho, intending at first only to stay a year, but instead remaining for a career.

It was a career filled with a variety of memories. Curtis remembered many of his broadcasts more for their weather conditions than for the games themselves. He recalled one contest between the Vandals and Utah State in Logan that he dubbed the "Snow Bowl" because snow blew so hard he could not see the field, making it difficult to call the game. He nicknamed a memorable game against Washington State the "Mud Bowl" because jerseys got so muddy that players, coaches, and broadcasters could not distinguish numbers. That was the game when the Cougars' star end, Hugh Campbell, lined up opposite his usual place, a move that went unnoticed because his number was

"away" to the "home" town. Through the mid-1920s, the contest was always competitive, but as WSC grew at a much faster pace than Idaho, the competition became one-sided. Although Idaho won dramatic games in the 1950s and 1960s, the "Battle" was discontinued as an annual event in the 1970s, though the two schools continued to compete regularly in other sports. Before then, however, several generations of Washington and Idaho students had lived in anticipation of "the big game."

Hijinks always accompanied that game. Usually these were harmless affairs: attempting to light the other's bonfire; stealing the clapper off the WSC victory bell; "borrowing" Butch, the Cougar mascot; painting crimson "W"'s on Idaho's "I" tank. At times, however, the pranks became more serious. "Every athletic contest between Idaho and WSC, held in Pullman, has been marked by rowdyism and discourtesies which have made it dangerous for a lady to attend the contest with out an escort," complained the *Argonaut* in 1906. After the 1957 game, firemen and police had to break up a riot with tear gas, hoses, and night sticks. More common was vandalism prior to the game. Frequently, buildings and walkways on either campus were painted, and occasionally the other school's letters were carved or burned into the football turf.

As these acts cost the schools considerable money, administrators and student leaders devised methods to prevent them. The most successful was the "loser's walk," when representatives of the losing student body walked ten miles to the victorious school following the game, took a good-natured

The freshman homecoming bonfire was a campus tradition for nearly two decades (facing page and below).

ribbing, and had their feet ceremoniously washed. The walk began in 1939 after a wager between sports writers for the WSU and Idaho student newspapers. By the mid-1940s the losing student body president and other campus leaders participated in the trek. In the 1950s the event became even bigger, with hundreds of students taking part. The most memorable walk—at least as far as Idaho fans are concerned—came in 1954. Idaho had not defeated WSC since 1925, and things did not look promising in 1954 as the Vandals had lost five straight games. But against WSC the "team

mud-covered. He caught a crucial scoring pass on the next play, and Washington State won the game, even though Idaho had led the entire way. Curtis was as much relieved as were players and coaches when Idaho's home football games were moved indoors to the Kibbie-ASUI Dome.

Over the years, Curtis enjoyed the friendship of some outstanding Idaho athletes: Wayne Walker and Jerry Kramer on the fine Vandal football team of the late 1950s; Brian Kellerman, guard on the Don Monson basketball teams of the early 1980s. He recalled basketball star Gus Johnson as a free spirit of incredible talent, and fondly remembered the musical as well as athletic abilities of footballer Ray McDonald. And there were memorable coaches, like "Big Stuff" Dee Andros, football coach of the 1960s; basketball mentor Joe Cipriano, whose recruiting coup got Johnson to Moscow; and Don Monson, who brought an athletic resurgence to Vandal sports.

There is a special relationship that develops between college broadcasters and players, a relationship unknown to most who follow sports. The broadcasters are for several months each year almost a part of the team—they travel with the team, eat with the players, relax with them. Coaches at Idaho encouraged this special relationship, believing Curtis would do a better job if he knew the players well. There is also a close relationship that develops between the broadcaster and his other crew members, such as the "color" people who worked with Curtis during his thirty years as Voice of the Vandals: Gene Hamblin, Gary Ball, Rick Nelson, Jerry Geidt, Jeff Brude, Wayne Anderson, and Tom Morris.

Another thing most people do not realize is the amount of work that goes into a sports broadcast. Broadcasters like Curtis must read all major sporting journals, receive mailings from sports information offices of the schools to be played each season, and subscribe to the hometown newspapers of opposing schools. The week before a game, these broadcasters study the particular team to be played, spending eight to ten hours preparing for each game. Afterwards, they replay the broadcasts, listening for cliches and trying to find other ways to improve.

To Bob Curtis, preparation and knowledge of the sport have always been the keys to success. Too many broadcasters possess only one of those key elements. They might be former players with a strong knowledge of the game. Or they might be well prepared, but not have the keen knowledge of the sport required for superior broadcasting.

Bob Curtis would not say so himself, but he was one of the rare ones who combined both knowledge and preparation, as evidenced in his unprecedented success at winning Idaho Sportscaster of the Year honors. He held a virtual deadlock on that title while serving as the Voice of the Vandals. Becoming the Vandals' voice was nearly an accident. But, after more than thirty years, Bob Curtis became as familiar to Idaho sports followers as any athletic director, coach, or player. He might have graduated as a Cougar, but he became as loyal as any Vandal around. And Idaho athletic followers who listened to his broadcasts spanning four decades were glad that his alma mater did not hire him back in the 1950s. It would have been hard for them to imagine Bob Curtis as the Voice of the Cougars.

Students in 1948 repaint the "I Tank" to remove WSC's "W"'s.

suddenly caught fire," as *Life* reported, and beat the Cougars 10-0. President Theophilus gave the students Monday off. "It's a little bonus, something I've been waiting 29 years for," he announced. The town hosted a large parade, and even WSC students joined in the spirit, over one thousand of them marching from Pullman to Moscow, the largest loser's walk ever. The event brought national publicity with a large photo layout in *Life*. Two other times—in 1964 and 1965, the Ray McDonald years—the Cougars walked. When the event was disbanded after 1969, the Cougars had walked only three times, but they were three memorable occasions for Vandal rooters.

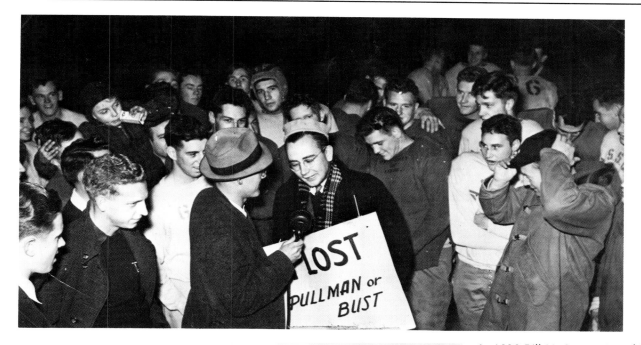

In 1938 Bill McGowan (speaking into microphone, above), *Argonaut* sports editor, initiated the idea of a loser's walk between Pullman and Moscow following the annual UI-WSC football game. The walk gained in popularity, and the tradition lasted for over thirty years. Vandal fans prepare to bury the cougar during the annual Idaho-Washington State football game in 1960 (left).

From football games played on muddy fields with improvised uniforms to a vast, multi-million-dollar, multi-sport operation supported by sophisticated equipment and a modern building complex, athletics at Idaho have grown into a significant aspect of university life. They help shape many people's opinions of the school and provide perhaps the dominating focal point for students' extracurricular activities. Athletic competition is nearly as old as the school itself and, like the school, in the 1980s bore faint resemblance to its predecessor of the 1890s.

6

The University and
the Military

It is May 1970, the time of Cambodia, Jackson State, Kent State, student strikes, Vietnam, teach-ins. True, there are college campuses where tensions are higher than at the University of Idaho. But the anti-war protests of the 1960s and 1970s have not bypassed Moscow.

May 5, 1970: two firebombs explode in the university's Naval Reserve Officers' Training Corps building, extensively damaging classrooms and storage areas.

May 6, 1970: over 500 people participate in a university assembly on the Administration lawn, debating President Richard Nixon's decision to invade Cambodia. Some students support the move; others oppose it, urging a boycott of classes. The ASUI Senate refuses to condemn the boycott and passes a resolution asserting that the decision to boycott rests with each individual. The resolution is not as strong as some student activists would prefer, but it is a statement the normally conservative senate most certainly would not have made a few years earlier.

May 8, 1970: differences between townspeople and university students have probably never been stronger. In an effort to cool tempers the ASUI sponsors a community forum downtown—an opportunity for Moscow residents to exchange views with students.

Land-grant colleges like the University of Idaho have long served the nation by training men and women for the armed services.

Relations between elements of the university's student body and campus branches of the United States armed services—the Army, Navy, and Air Force ROTCs—were poor in 1970. The *Gem of the Mountains* commented about that year's annual Tri-Service Military Review:

> "The Military marched,
> The Protestors protested,
> And Everybody had a flag."

Such tensions have not always been present. The University of Idaho grew in part from the idea that land-grant colleges should provide the nation with a ready fighting force, a body of responsible citizen soldiers. All Idaho men were required to take classes in military training, which they did without much complaint. A military uniform was as respected as the American flag.

By 1970 this had changed. Seeing their country embroiled too long in a misunderstood war, university students often vented their frustrations upon the embodiment of the military closest to home—the ROTC and its training facilities. Alumni from earlier years could not understand this protest: the military and the university had always co-existed, had matured together. Neither graying alum nor youthful freshman in 1970 completely understood the other. And few fully appreciated the long symbiotic relationship between the University of Idaho and the American military establishment.

The Morrill Act, signed into law by Abraham Lincoln during the Civil War, required each able-bodied man enrolled in a land-grant college to undertake military training. Accordingly, in 1894, Lieutenant Edward R. Chrisman became the University of Idaho's first military commandant. The National Defense Act of 1916 established an infantry unit of the Reserve

Some of the university's earliest cadets in 1897. Left to right: Winslow Howland; Lt. Edward R. Chrisman, campus commandant; Gilbert Hogue; Charles Simpson; and Paul Draper, one of two university men who died during the Spanish-American War.

Officers' Training Corps at the university, but this did not change the basic military training requirements. All men were still compelled to undertake two years of military training, but now a student could qualify for a commission with an optional two years of additional work. The Army ROTC remained the only military branch on campus until 1945, when a Navy ROTC unit formed. Two years later the Air Force established an ROTC detachment, and the university became one of the few colleges in the nation to have ROTC units from three branches of the armed services.

Student trainees generally took a regular university class-load, supplemented with some specific military courses and a certain amount of drill time. During the summers they received more specialized instruction and training. This training regimen remained mandatory at the University of Idaho until 1963.

Regiment in review (above, c. 1914); cadet field exercises on campus (right, c. 1914).

The school quickly assimilated its military role into its other functions. Students and staff often lined walkways to watch cadets pass in parade. The military band was well known for producing rousing martial airs at dances. The cadets held sham battles that drew crowds of spectators. The annual Military Ball, begun in 1905, was for many years the university's largest annual social function.

The best-remembered of the Military Department's activities during its first thirty years were its encampments. At times the encampments were on campus—such as that in 1909 when cadets pitched tents on the lawn directly in front of the gymnasium and armory. This week-long bivouac featured dress reviews, sham battles, dances, a parade through downtown Moscow, and the pleasant task of eating "pies, cakes and fruit sent in by the ladies of Moscow." At other times the cadets left campus and set up quarters in other Idaho communities like Genesee, Coeur d'Alene, Boise, and Lewiston. Genesee boys attempted to run the guards and sneak into the encampment there in 1901, but all were caught and "court-martialed within an inch of their lives." Genesee's young women, however, proved to be models of hospitality, hosting an ice cream social for the cadets where "the remarkable capacity of those Genesee girls for ice cream was discovered."

One of the most colorful of the military department's activities was its annual encampment, such as this one on the campus in the early 1900s.

159

The Argonaut's Finest Hour

*The 1917-18 Argonaut staff
was truly impressive. Ernest K.
Lindley, son of the university's
president, later became a reporter for
the* New York World, *the* New
York Herald Tribune, *and*
Newsweek. *He was also a radio
and television news broadcaster and
served as official biographer for
Franklin Roosevelt, and State
Department consultant for John
Kennedy. Harry Lloyd ''Jazz''
McCarty, one of the paper's best
sports reporters, gave university
athletic teams the nickname
''Vandals.'' A. J. Priest would
become one of the nation's most
distinguished lawyers, attorney for
one of the country's largest holding
companies. And although Carol
Ryrie was not on the staff in 1917-
18, she had worked with many of
those reporters, having been the*
Argonaut's *society writer the year
before. She would gain fame under
her married name, Carol Brink, as
an author of over twenty books and
winner of the nation's most
prestigious award for children's
literature. Heading this talented crew
was Frank B. Sutherland, editor-in-
chief, shown below.*

*Sutherland arrived at the
university in 1915 from Coeur*

Generally, women's roles in military affairs were limited to supportive activities such as cooking for the cadets, helping to organize social functions, and observing parades and drills. In 1896, though, Lieutenant Chrisman suggested to a group of Idaho coeds that they form a drill team to entertain Moscow residents. A group of ten women responded to the invitation, electing Margaret McCallie as captain. The women, in their white dresses, flowing sashes, and Civil War caps, took the drilling more seriously than Chrisman had intended. Practicing under the tutelage of student Charles Armstrong, Company C of the University Cadets became a well-disciplined, precise drill team. The company lasted only three years—until the Spanish-American War—and never received official university or military sanction. It was not until the Vietnam era that the military allowed university women to officially enter the ROTC units.

The school's military-training program helped produce some well-known American service personnel. Robert L. Ghormley became a vice admiral and prominent South Pacific naval commander during World War II and later had a park in Moscow named after him. Ross E. Rowell attained the rank of lieutenant general. A pioneer of Marine Corps aviation in the 1920s and 1930s, he became the first flyer to lead an organized dive-bombing attack in combat, the first Marine to receive the Distinguished Flying Cross, and the first Marine aviator to become a general. Reginald T. Myers received the Congressional Medal of Honor for action during the Korean War.

By far the most revered military figure at the university, however, was Idaho's ''grand old man,'' Edward R. Chrisman, whose life on campus spanned virtually the entire first half-century of the school's history. Born in

Company C, University Cadets, in 1897. Although started in jest, this first women's company gained a reputation for its precise drills.

Cadet exercises (top, 1922); ROTC band (bottom, 1923).

d'Alene. While at Idaho he was a member of the Glee Club, served as vice president of the Associated Engineers, and edited both the Argonaut and the Gem during his junior year. He dropped out of school in March 1918 because he was failing chemistry, a course he disliked. A university ruling prohibited students with failing grades from serving as editor of the Argonaut so, as Sutherland noted years later, "I checked out." Before he left, however, he set new standards for Argonaut editorial policy.

The most pressing editorial concerns in the paper's twenty years before Sutherland had been the perennial debates over whether the student body demonstrated enough pep at athletic and drama events. Sutherland was not opposed to school spirit, but as editor of the university's paper during wartime he encouraged students to keep their social life in perspective:

> Several days ago a red-haired gunner . . . fired a gun which announced to the world that the United States of America was at last on the fighting line in France. About that time 200 or so Idaho students were . . . cavorting around the gymnasium to the tune of "Broken Doll." And on the day that Germany drew first blood . . . the chief worries of the greater portion of the University of Idaho was "Are you going to lick WSC."

> We do not wish to belittle too much the importance of social life or of athletic games in war time, but there is a greater game going on . . . which should gauge everything that we do.

Many college editors around the country were beginning to encourage a more serious life view *among students suddenly thrust into a world war. What distinguished Sutherland from most of his colleagues—and indeed from many American journalists much more experienced than he who quickly buckled under government pleas for various forms of censorship—was his unwillingness to allow the war to dictate journalistic standards. Certainly the conflict should force citizens to think more seriously, but there were some American rights that must remain inviolate—especially freedom of the press.*

When attorney Edward Rosenheim spoke on campus in October 1917 about the need to curtail free speech Sutherland lashed out:

> *Of the many varieties of idiotic utterances for which war "patriotism" is responsible, none are more silly than the outbursts against free speech, such as was heard at assembly last Wednesday. To follow the policy advocated, to refrain from all criticism of governmental policy, would be absolute folly. The "my country—right-or-wrong" attitude . . . is far more inimical to freedom and liberty than all the anarchists and kaisers who ever existed. Graft and inefficiency thrive in this atmosphere of secrecy.*

Older members of the community did not know how to react to this unprecedented outspokenness in the Argonaut. Some responded that the proper role for a student newspaper was to report on student activities, not national issues. Rosenheim believed Sutherland was too immature to challenge the ideas of his elders: "I realized I was addressing a group of 'intellectually independent' but

Indiana, Chrisman graduated from West Point in 1888 and served in the so-called "Ghost Dance" Indian war in the Dakotas. University of Idaho President Franklin Gault hired him in 1894 to teach military tactics and mathematics. In those early days, when faculty were not overly specialized, Chrisman also coached and counseled students.

Lieutenant and Mrs. Chrisman arrived on campus in March 1894 and found the place a little bleak, with no trees in sight, mud everywhere, and a few patches of dirty snow still clinging to hillsides. Within a few months they were actively participating in university and community affairs, and the lieutenant became one of the college's most popular professors. When he left Idaho in 1898 to lead troops in Cuba during the Spanish-American War, students declared a holiday, and "Chrisman Day" was thereafter celebrated as an annual event for several years. When he returned to Moscow in 1902 to assume his teaching duties, the *Argonaut* proclaimed " 'Captain Chrisman is here. Yes, Chrisman is going to be with us again.' What a world of expectancy and enthusiasm those words created when they first echoed through the hall. A thrill of life leaped into one and all."

Chrisman's second tour on campus lasted until 1905. He then served in a variety of places, won a number of military honors, and was promoted to brigadier general during World War I. Following that conflict he could have requested a station almost anywhere; he chose to return to Moscow, where he became one of the few generals to serve as a commandant of student cadets.

General Edward Chrisman inspects cadet batallion in 1936, the year Congress took the unprecedented action of naming him Commandant of Cadets and Professor of Military Science Emeritus.

University officials dedicated the new Chrisman Hall to the school's "grand old man," General E. R. Chrisman, in 1939.

Chrisman remained at Moscow the rest of his life. When he retired from active army duty in 1932 he continued as a military instructor with the university. By the mid-1930s he had spent more time as a college military instructor than any other American officer. In 1936 the United States Congress took the unprecedented action of passing a bill naming Chrisman "Commandant of Cadets and Professor of Military Science and Tactics Emeritus" at the University of Idaho. President Franklin Roosevelt signed the act into law.

Edward Chrisman died in Moscow three years later—just a few days before university officials dedicated a new men's dormitory in his honor. In accordance with his wishes, an airplane scattered his ashes over the university's grounds, which by then contained handsome gardens and large trees, a considerable contrast to the barren campus the Chrismans first viewed in 1894.

The military has played a constant role in the university's history, but during America's five wars since the school was founded the connection between the University of Idaho and the nation's armed services has been even more pronounced. Following the lead of their popular commandant, Lieutenant Chrisman's university cadets volunteered for service during the Spanish-American War in extraordinary numbers. Thirty-nine of them joined Idaho Company D—producing the highest ratio of volunteers to students of any college in the United States—and served in Manila for a year. The university did not forget its volunteers. Faculty and students sent them books and a 200-pound Christmas box. When the war ended, Moscow and the university welcomed them home with a gala parade and celebration in September 1899.

what I overlooked was an editor who although probably hardly out of his teens would have the temerity to state . . . conclusions fraught with such tremendous two edge possibilities."

But Sutherland would have none of the "immaturity" argument. "The reason that American students . . . are mental laggards on the vital questions of the hour is that all expressions of serious thought along those lines has been discouraged," he wrote. " 'Leave it for the older heads' is the phrase flung at all attempts to reason. . . . This has led inevitably to mental stagnation, with the result that when a man is turned out an A.B. he rarely possesses the power to think independently."

If Sutherland's elders thought they could dull his sharp pen, they were sadly mistaken. The hard-driving editorials continued, and Sutherland forcefully castigated members of the university community for their efforts to curb the Argonaut's freedom of press:

It is for the university, which should be the stronghold of liberal thought, to make a stand against this bigotry which dumps freedom of speech and independence of thought into the same pot with sedition and treason; which attempts to supplant reason and perspective with the hate and the rash plunging of the mob. We must check this lest by our zealotry we defeat our end.

Sutherland was not only an editor of spunk—a crisp, clear writer, and a mature student who steadfastly refused to compromise his basic beliefs—he also disarmed his critics because he simply loved a good fight. He openly invited criticism and took great joy in responding to it. "Bring on the brickbats,'' he wrote. ``The more numerous they are, and the harder they are thrown the more they will be appreciated.''

In March 1918, overworked as editor of his college's two major publications and failing a class he did not enjoy, Sutherland resigned from the Argonaut. To the end, he retained his firm policy of advocacy. His parting editorial was perhaps his best:

> Mental discipline is right and necessary, insofar as it aids in the establishment of right mental habits, but when it attempts to dictate what a student shall or shall not think, it has overstepped its bounds. . . . This . . . rigid discipline . . . reduces all to a dead level of mediocrity. The exception, the one who does not conform is ejected. The professor does not understand him, wherefore the student must go. ``How beautiful,'' the professor then exclaims. ``What a unity in their mental processes.'' Yes. The unity of the treadmill, of the chain gang. . . .
>
> The fear of change must go. Change is the sign of progress, and of life. If there had been no radicals, no one to step out from the mass of contented conservatives, man would never have progressed beyond the cave-man stage.

When Frank Sutherland ``checked out'' of the University of Idaho, some among the faculty were no doubt pleased to see him and his acid pen leave. Years later, however, Sutherland stated that he received no pressure from the university administration to tone down his editorials—a credit to President Ernest Lindley, whose son took Sutherland's place.

Student cadets and townspeople hang the King of Spain in effigy (1898).

Sutherland later received a degree in mechanical engineering from the University of Pennsylvania and worked for the Pennsylvania Railroad and the Atlantic Refining Company. Not until the 1960s did Argonaut editors again consistently speak out as strongly and independently as Sutherland had. No one then would even remember the editor of the paper during its finest hour. Yet, whether they realized it or not, all later editors owed a debt to Frank Sutherland and similar strong-willed, often criticized college writers around the nation who helped push university journalism ``beyond the cave-man stage.''

Idaho cadets leave Moscow for duty in the Philippines during the Spanish-American War in 1898 (above). A parade in Moscow sends them off (facing page, bottom). Students prepare to send a box to university cadets serving overseas (left).

One of the Company D volunteers did not return. Ole G. Hagberg, born in Norway and the school's first international student, died of typhoid fever in the Philippines. A former university student, Paul Draper, who attended the school until 1897, served with the regular army in Cuba and in the

Philippines, where he died while attempting to rescue some of his men from drowning. University President Joseph Blanton ordered a bronze tablet honoring all University of Idaho volunteers placed in the Administration Building. The 1906 fire destroyed the plaque, but campus officials had a replica fabricated, and it now hangs in Memorial Gym. Blanton also spearheaded a fundraising drive to construct a statue honoring Hagberg and Draper. The memorial on the Administration Building lawn depicting a soldier standing at ease became the school's most photographed landmark.

World War I did not come as suddenly to the campus as had the Spanish-American conflict. Battles raged in Europe for nearly three years before the United States became involved. By early 1917, however, President Woodrow Wilson ordered the Idaho National Guard to mobilize, and several university students entered the service. Despite this advance call, the nation's declaration of war in April 1917 threw the school into confusion as students left for training camps or returned to family farms. Indeed, rumors abounded that the college would be closed, since every available person would be needed on farms, in industry, or in the military. But by early May the State Board of Education had decided against closing Idaho's colleges. Nonetheless, the state asked university officials to help minimize disruption to Idaho's agricultural production. In response, the College of Agriculture began an effort that lasted throughout the war of devising ways to stimulate greater production, and the entire university remained closed from June until early October in both 1917 and 1918 to allow students to work on harvesting crews.

The war drastically altered college life. Military recruitment reduced the number of men on campus, leading one writer in the *Gem* to lament: "Gradually the men began to disappear from our campus until, when school closed in June 1917, we resembled a young ladies' select seminary." In fact, for the first time, a woman became President of the Associated Students when Secretary Velma Spaulding automatically filled that position upon the departure of the president and vice president.

It was an altogether different school when classes resumed the following October. "There were no upperclassmen," reported the *Gem*, "and a University without upperclassmen is usually regarded as a ship without a rudder. The older University men were gone, as were the younger faculty." Other changes were apparent. Flags flew from living groups, and every day students raised a large flag on a new sixty-foot white-pine pole planted in the Administration Building lawn. Some athletic activities ceased while others were greatly curtailed. Social functions became less elegant and less expensive, and the home economics department began preparing "young women of the University to take an intelligent part in the struggle before us" by teaching first aid, home nursing, dietetics, and canning. The Department of Electrical Engineering taught courses in wireless telegraphy and radio operation, and both the Faculty Women's Club and Delta Gamma sorority adopted war orphans. Many university women volunteered for Red Cross service, making bandages and other medical supplies. Like other Americans, the university community largely did without sugar and observed meatless and wheatless days. A flag was hung in the main entrance of the Administration Building with hundreds of blue stars representing all university servicemen, surrounding a growing number of white stars representing all the men who died in the conflict. By war's end there would be thirty-two white stars.

In the spring of 1918 the federal government selected the university to provide vocational, mechanical, and engineering training to soldiers. The first vocational trainees arrived in June, and the university instructed over 200 soldiers during the summer. In October—at about the same time regular students returned—the Students' Army Training Corps (SATC) established a unit on campus. The nearly 700 SATC members who arrived that fall were divided into two groups: a collegiate section to train men as army officers, and a vocational section. By the fall of 1918 the University of

At Home During the War

Esther Thomas lived with her parents in Moscow and—like many of the town's young people—attended the University of Idaho after high school. Nicknamed "Tommy," she enrolled in 1915 and spent most of her college years as a typical coed. She majored in home economics, served in the Home Ec Club, DeSmet Club, Women's League, and Commerce and Economics Club. When asked for a quotation for her senior-year annual, she responded: "Civilized man cannot live without cooks." Her hobbies, she wrote, were "Going to movies. . . . And cutting classes—something I never had enough nerve to do when I was in the grades—so I make up for valuable time lost." She could not have cut many, for she received "A's" in most classes.

Esther Thomas kept a diary of her time on campus, and the brief entries provide an interesting glimpse of the University of Idaho during the closing days of World War I.

October 18, 1918
Mary, Mercedes, Bess and I go serenading barracks.

In early October, 450 men—members of the Student Army Training Corps—arrived on *campus. The army organized the SATC to prepare young men between ages 18 and 21 to become officers. Corps enrollees received training in such fields as engineering, chemistry, and vocational skills. Barracks on campus were set up in the gym, as well as the Sigma Nu, Kappa Sigma, Delta Theta, Beta Theta Pi, and Zeta Chi Alpha houses. Other SATC men quartered on North Main Street at the former Idaho National Harvester plant.*

October 20, 1918
Churches and schools closed on account of flu.

By October 19 the State Board of Health had imposed many restrictions upon the university to prevent the spread of a flu virus then raging across the country. Although the university as yet had no reported cases, most town and school activities were cancelled, including—much to Esther's dismay—all movies.

October 24, 1918
I take some flowers and apples to the ''flu'' boys. They start me in as a nurse. Needed!

By the end of October, three SATC men had died of the flu. That number would reach a dozen before the epidemic ended. Doctors at Moscow's Inland Empire Hospital turned their facility over to the exclusive use of army authorities. Townspeople established temporary hospitals in the Elks Temple, the Episcopal church, and a fraternity house. Many Moscow and university women risked their own health to volunteer as nurses.

October 31, 1918
Private secretary am I. Write the boys letters.

Corpsmen arrived on campus from throughout the West.

Idaho resembled a military camp. The administration published notice of new campus procedures in the *Argonaut*:

> From Reveille at 6 A.M. to Taps at 10 P.M., the University of Idaho is devoted to war service. This does not mean that the colleges of letters and science, agriculture, engineering, and law or the schools of mines and forestry have ceased to exist, . . . but it does mean that each of these organizations is enlisted for the war as well as for service in the reconstruction that must inevitably follow it.

Since most fraternity houses were nearly empty, many SATC men were quartered there; others stayed in the gym, which was fitted with long rows of cots. The men built their own mess hall behind the Administration Building. When the University took over the buildings of the Idaho National Harvester plant on North Main Street, the trainees equipped another large mess hall, remodeled a brick livery into a barracks, and constructed a frame building for additional housing.

Though hectic, the fall of 1918 was a period of brief intensity: warring nations signed a peace armistice on November 11, 1918, barely a month after SATC men had first arrived. But as bells chimed, whistles blew, and the community hosted a gala parade, Moscow faced a health crisis. The last group of SATC arrivals brought the Spanish influenza with them. The entire town and campus halted public gatherings, and health officials quarantined students. Student corpsmen wore flu masks made by university women, and everyone slept with windows open, believing the flu ''bug'' could not survive in cold temperatures. Despite the precautions, twelve SATC men died during the epidemic.

Students' Army Training Corpsmen constructed a mess hall behind the Administration Building during World War I.

Armistice Day in Moscow (1918).

By early December, with the Students' Army Training Corps demobilized, the university began a slow and difficult return to normal operations. Postwar inflation accompanied a rapid increase in student enrollment. Many faculty left, frustrated by increased workloads and no corresponding pay raises. "The number of resignations of both heads of departments and those in less important positions . . . have been entirely too high for efficient management," university administrators noted in their biennial report.

Despite the economic difficulties, the university gradually changed its wartime posture. By May 1921 the *Argonaut* complained that the flagpole placed on the university lawn during the patriotic fervor of the war had not been used once during the preceding school year. Other residents of Moscow and employees of the university also worried that people might soon forget the sacrifice of university personnel during the war and made provisions to prevent that oversight. When an American Legion organization formed in Moscow it named its post for Dudley Loomis, one of the first of the thirty-two university students to die during the war. University officials planted a memorial grove of thirty-two trees south of the Administration Building. In the early 1920s university faculty, students, alumni, and friends—including the Idaho American Legion—began raising money to build a much-needed gymnasium on campus as a memorial to the university's and the state's World War I dead. For years they struggled to raise the money necessary. The fundraising campaign even became the butt of campus jokes. The 1928 *Gem* featured a humor section centering on "Helen" and her campus adventures. In one episode "Helen and her roommate went walking. They went past the new gymnasium, which had been started fifteen years before. Progress had been rapid, and already the

Bedridden with the flu, many dictated letters to anxious family members who worried about their health. At nearby Washington State College, flu deaths were among the highest in the nation. Families had good reason to be concerned about men stationed in the Palouse.

November 2, 1918
Still at the nursing job. I can do almost anything that has to do with the "flu" now.

November 5, 1918
My last day of nursing.

Isolated cases of the flu continued to appear for another three months, but by early November the worst was over. The deaths occurred primarily within a two-week period.

November 6, 1918
Go into quarantine so I can go to school. Also had to get a health certificate.

During the epidemic, classes went on as usual for those SATC men able to attend. But in order to prevent the disease's spread, other students and townspeople stayed isolated as much as possible from the servicemen. The women living in Ridenbaugh Hall, for example, faced the frustration of quarantine by knitting, crocheting, and publishing a weekly newspaper entitled the Ridenbaugh Peek-a-boo, consisting primarily of dorm gossip.

November 8, 1918
I arrive at Ridenbaugh Hall. Dance with the officers.

Early in the war, Dean of Women Permeal French worried about the dangers of the university's women students mixing with the many soldiers on campus. She decided that the mingling was

169

bound to occur, but ''dangers'' could be minimized by providing ''wholesome supervised amusement'' such as dances. As university officials gradually lifted the quarantines, Dean French again allowed ''supervised amusements.''

November 11, 1918
Peace is declared!!! We have a parade.

Though some restrictions were gradually being lifted, the university's women students still technically remained under quarantine at the time of the armistice. Nonetheless, officials allowed all campus women and SATC men to participate in Moscow's armistice-day parade, provided they agreed not to break ranks and mingle.

November 12, 1918
Spend most of the day cooking for the flu boys.

In mid-November another outbreak of the epidemic hit, and another person died. While placed under stricter quarantine, women students did what they could to help. Most cooked. By November 12 the university's home economics department prepared food for forty patients each meal.

November 13, 1918
Ora and I make candy for Section B Barracks.

The SATC program was divided into two sections: those in Section A undertook collegiate training, while those in Section B, quartered in town, took vocational classes. Though the war was over, the men could not leave Moscow until the flu epidemic ended, and the servicemen enjoyed the favors Moscow's women did for them.

November 16, 1918
Go over to the girls hospital to help nurse those with the flu.

foundations were dug.'' Despite the delays, builders finally completed Memorial Gym in 1929. In the 1970s the federal government placed the building on the National Register of Historic Places, and it remains a permanent reminder of sacrifices made during the First World War.

Construction was slow, but in 1929 Memorial Gymnasium was finally completed and dedicated to the memory of Idahoans killed during World War I.

The university's involvement during World War II in some ways resembled that of the First World War. The National Guard's increased training activities as early as 1939 involved many faculty and students. By the fall of 1941 the school's enrollment had fallen by 8 percent, even though women entered in record numbers. But the increase in women did not offset the

The flagpole placed on the Administration Building lawn during World War I fell into disuse following the war, to the disappointment of some.

loss of men who either were drafted for military service or sought high wages in West Coast defense industries. The library began stocking a "Background for War" section in the late 1930s, and in the spring of 1941 University students raised $150 for the "Bundles for Britain" effort. "Please . . . greet the Students from me," wrote Mrs. Winston Churchill to the fund drive's chairman when hearing of the Idaho gift, "and tell them how much their activities are appreciated and how their thought of us warms our hearts."

Despite the preliminary preparations, many Idaho students proved unwilling to march unthinking into conflict. In 1940 some students—for the first time ever—protested "militarism at Idaho," and seriously questioned the

Despite the precautions, many women caught the flu, though none died.

November 17, 1918
My B-day dinner. War is over and there sure was no Hooverizing.

Like other Americans, Esther Thomas had suffered through the food restrictions placed upon the country by U.S. Food Administrator Herbert Hoover. The government lifted meatless, wheatless, sugarless, and other "less" days with the signing of the armistice.

December 3, 1918
No final exams to be given this quarter. HURRAH!!!!!!!

Moscow and university officials lifted the town and campus quarantines on November 25, but because classes had been severely disrupted university administrators dispensed with exams.

December 27, 1918
The whole bunch go coasting on first street.

January 5, 1919
The town is in quarantine again.

February 14, 1919
U of I versus Whitman 45-16. I would like to see a real basketball game once more.

June 10, 1919
Senior Day—Farewell to buildings.

June 11, 1919
Senior meeting. I was elected corresponding secretary for 5 years. Graduation exercises. Lunch at Mrs. Al Morgans for senior girls.

For a time, campus and town returned to normal. Early in January, when health officials reported an increasing number of flu cases in Moscow and surrounding communities, they

again temporarily closed many public meeting places. Moscow developed few flu cases, however, and life gradually returned to normal. It would take another year, though, before enough men returned to college campuses to produce "real" athletic contests again. But for the women of the university, school work continued as usual through the spring, and on June 11, 1919, Esther Thomas received her degree.

Background for War exhibit, University Library (1939).

school's compulsory military training. Conversely, some members of the faculty and administration criticized the student body for its meager support of war-bond drives and questioned the students' patriotism. The *Argonaut's* editor responded:

> Not a few are worried about student apathy as regards the present World war, the absence of patriotic fervor, the shunning of emotional display. . . .
>
> Those worried leaders shake their heads, and declare the remedy lies in the creation of more patriotism on the campus; the need for music and inspirational addresses.
>
> But students are baffled, too, by this reversal of form. . . . We were taught to hate war; . . . we read in books, heard in school and saw in veterans' hospitals, the ugly realities of modern fighting; . . . we were warned of emotional hysteria. . . .
>
> Forgive us our hesitation. You taught us well.

Still, when the Japanese attacked Pearl Harbor all questioning ceased, and the campus quickly organized for the war effort. The day after the attack, students and staff listened to President Roosevelt's war address over the public address system in the Administration Building auditorium. The federal government ordered immediate twenty-four-hour guards around the school's armory, heating plant, and engineering shops.

In the two weeks between Pearl Harbor and Christmas vacation, men left school in rapid numbers. Those students who remained participated in a wide array of war-related activities: fundraising drives for the Red Cross, war-bond rallies, campaigns to collect paper and metal, book drives for servicemen. Within a month, university administrators announced that the campus would begin operating on a twelve-month basis so that recent high school graduates could accelerate their education and receive their degrees

Draft registration on campus (above, 1940). Women students greatly outnumbered men during World War II and took over many campus activities, including the band (left).

before reaching draft age, which at that time was twenty-one. By early spring, campus residents practiced blackout drills, and school officials hung a service flag—similar to the one displayed during World War I—in the Administration Building, showing the number of university students and staff serving in the military and the number who died.

From May 1942 until January 1945 the university operated a training school for naval radio operators. Over four thousand operators attended courses ranging from sixteen to twenty-three weeks. With several hundred military men on campus, the university again became overcrowded. Most of the Navy trainees lived in Sweet and Chrisman halls, designed for 325 residents but now housing twice that number. The University Classroom, Forestry Laboratory, Agronomy, and Ridenbaugh Annex buildings were all used for classrooms, and two additional frame structures—which later became the Naval ROTC building and the Faculty Club/Satellite SUB—were also constructed for the radio trainees.

Over 4,000 Naval radio operators received training on campus during World War II, and some joined students in the 1943 commencement exercises after undergoing their training regimen (facing page, bottom). Chow lines were prevalent during the wartime period (facing page, top).

The University Cannon

Old Bertha has been around campus nearly as long as there has been a campus, though she gained the name rather late in life. Originally, Old Bertha had a companion—an unnamed one. The university acquired the two cannon, both Civil War veterans, in the 1890s, and for about ten years Idaho's cadets drilled with them regularly. In 1907 the United States Congress passed a bill officially presenting the cannon to the university, but by then the military department no longer used them. The new congressional gifts were relegated to a role as campus ornaments, gracing either side of the Spanish-American war memorial on the Administration Building lawn.

Though their days of utility had passed, the cannon became prominent university landmarks, photographed frequently, reminders of the significance of military training at this land-grant college. They remained on the campus green until about 1930. At one point during that period some raiders from Washington State College stole one and placed it prominently on one of the Pullman campus lawns—where it was also often photographed. Conveniently overlooking the fact that the cannon had been donated to the university, Idaho officials demanded its return on the grounds that the gun was federal property. Back it came, ceremoniously pulled the ten miles by a full WSC military honor guard. For a few more years both cannon decorated the lawn, but in the early 1930s officials relegated the deteriorating guns to the university's boneyard of outdated equipment.

Some enterprising members of Tau Kappa Epsilon fraternity requisitioned one

Army trainees arrived in July 1943, and the university served as a training facility until the end of the war in August 1945. Army men were divided into two units, Student Training and Reclassification (STAR) and the Army Specialized Training Program (ASTP). Approximately 3,500 men passed through the STAR program, their numbers ranging from 100 to 900 at any given time. They lived in Hays, Forney, and Lindley halls. The men received refresher courses in mathematics, languages, physics, chemistry, and other disciplines and were then sent to schools for ASTP training. The Army Specialized Training Program trained men for three months, primarily in engineering and foreign languages. These men lived in several fraternities and dorms, as well as in the Campus and Idaho clubs.

The presence of hundreds of military men on campus caused some friction between the trainees and regular students, who by this time were predominantly women. Before the war, enrollment had hovered around 3,000, men outnumbering women by three to one. By 1943 enrollment had dropped to about 1,200, with women outnumbering men about two to one. The Argonaut commented in that year that "you can't paste three distinct units together . . . and expect the rough spots to go away." The President of the Associated Women Students spoke more directly to the problem:

> Girls don't like . . . running the gauntlet of stares and remarks at the entrances of the various classroom buildings. The girls also aren't accustomed to being forced off the sidewalk by a group of passing men. . . .
>
> If that's the way you act in public, how can you expect the girls to be eager for a date with you? And remember these girls aren't here for the purpose of entertaining the service men. They are, believe it or not, here to get an education.

Army and navy trainees vastly outnumbered university students on campus during World War II.

A. Gerhard Wiens teaches Russian language class (1942).

In most areas, however, the students and trainees cooperated. The military men had a representative on the student activities board, participated in social functions, helped produce the *Gem* and *Argonaut*, and serenaded women's living groups. "Gee-Eyes Right," a 1944 production, was the

University production of "Gee Eyes Right" (1944).

of the barrels, acquired new wheels, set the refurbished gun on their lawn, and christened her "Old Bertha." The other cannon never made it out of the bone-yard and was no doubt scrapped. But Old Bertha went on to a more active life than she had known since the turn of the century. After every Idaho football victory, TKE members fired her off.

The TKE house in those days stood on Blake Avenue, and Old Bertha faced north. This caused no problem for many years as there was nothing north of the fraternity but a vacant field. In 1950, however, contractors began constructing a new music building.

After a particularly impressive victory over Utah that year, Tekes loaded Old Bertha with newspapers and golf balls and proudly lit her fuse. The discharge shattered the framework of the new building, causing the contractors a considerable delay—and costing the university a considerable amount of money. University President Jesse Buchanan ordered that the cannon be either removed or plugged with concrete so it could no longer be fired. The Tekes chose the latter.

On October 27, 1950, Tau Kappa Epsilon members draped a black cloth over Old Bertha, placed a large wreath over her muzzle,

played taps, and properly mourned the silencing of her big barrel. Ten years later, however, a new generation of Tekes decided that cannon are for firing. They hauled the gun to a nearby farm, drilled a hole in the concrete plug, poured in some powder, and lit the fuse, hoping to dislodge the plug. Instead, they only succeeded in splitting the barrel.

Once again Old Bertha seemed destined for the boneyard. But the Tekes, having once rescued her from that fate, decided otherwise. For two years the fraternity brothers—especially George Hirai—painstakingly repaired the barrel. By 1962 they again had the gun in presentable condition, freshly painted and cleaned, and rolled it back to their house. Today it still stands proudly in the yard of the Tekes' new home on Nez Perce Drive.

As the University of Idaho celebrates its centennial, Old Bertha is about ready to celebrate 100 years of association with the campus. Thanks to the efforts of Tau Kappa Epsilon, it remains one of the university's oldest landmarks.

biggest dramatic event of the war—a locally written and produced musical about humorous events at "Clearwater College" when the army and navy moved in. It received enthusiastic support from both servicemen and regular students.

Private First Class Henry Santiestevan, preparing to leave campus in the spring of 1944, summed up the feelings of many of his colleagues about their time in Moscow. "It won't be easy for us to leave," he wrote. "We have made friendships here, some of which will be lasting. . . . To some

University students and Moscow residents collected paper, scrap metal (above), and rubber (below) during the early years of World War II.

Harold Enquist, Otho Holms, and Glen Hunter, Army ROTC men, practice cooking for large groups (1941).

soldiers, Moscow, Idaho will be a part of them for the rest of their lives. Some fell in love here, some were married here, and, for a few of them, their first baby was born here.''

In addition to cooperation with the military personnel in their midst, there were other changes for regular students and staff. The campus observed meatless days, held farewell rallies for newly inducted troops, and experienced a marked decrease in campus social activities ''in tune with current economic trends.'' Women often wore corsages made of war stamps instead of flowers, both for economy and to support the war effort. The school de-emphasized liberal arts classes—which tried to teach ''humanity during a period of inhumanity''—in favor of technical courses. University personnel followed the war's progress by daily communiques and maps posted on the library bulletin board.

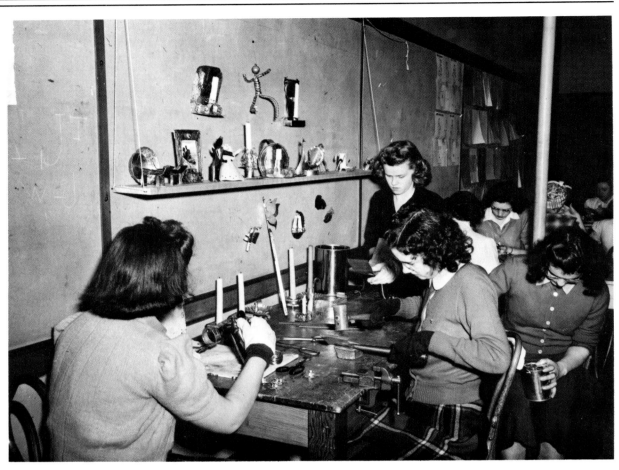

With copper and brass impossible to obtain, home economics arts and crafts classes substituted discarded metal cans during the Second World War (above). A women's automobile mechanics course (right, 1940s).

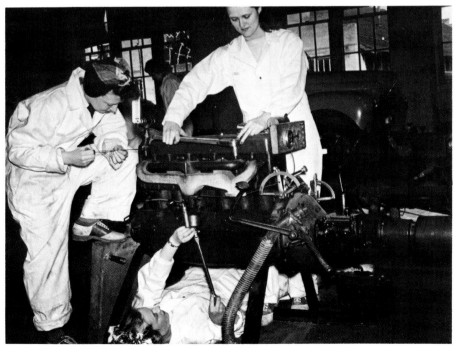

Because of the shortage of men, university women took over many of the school's essential services. For the first time, coeds worked in large numbers in dormitory cafeterias and at campus hang-outs like the Nest and Blue Bucket. Both faculty and student women sewed thousands of bandages and dressings, and the Faculty Women's Club sent money for Russian relief. Perhaps the university women's most prominent role was as Minute Maids, a group devoted to increasing the sales of war bonds. This group, which was founded in Boise with the second branch located on the Idaho campus, eventually spread throughout the nation during the war.

Home economics students rolling bandages during World War II (above). Minute Maids, a women's service organization founded in Idaho, sold war stamps and bonds on campus during the war (left).

In May 1945 the campus celebrated VE Day, and in August, VJ Day. Barely had the celebrations quieted when the university faced one of its most difficult tasks in more than fifty years of operation, finding room for all of the returning servicemen who took advantage of the GI Bill.

Faced with severe overcrowding, the Board of Regents in 1946 voted not to admit new out-of-state students. University administrators also warned many women—who were required to live on campus—not to come, as there were insufficient dormitory and sorority spaces. Even with these

Additional housing and cafeteria facilities were required in the rush of veterans and their families to campus following World War II: veterans housing under construction on Sixth Street (top, 1946); trailer village (right, 1950); Park Village at Third and Line Streets (facing page, top, 1946); Pine Hall cafeteria (facing page, bottom, 1947).

precautions President Harrison Dale was forced to apply to the federal government for surplus temporary housing units and trailers. By the end of 1946 the university had "Vet Villages" consisting of over 200 frame huts, 100 trailers, and a quonset-hut cafeteria. Around 100 students brought their own trailers with them, and at the beginning of the 1946 semester 300 men bunked temporarily in Memorial Gym.

Even with campus administrators scrambling to furnish housing for the rush of students arriving after World War II, some—like Jeane and Glenn Johnson—were forced to live in off-campus makeshift housing, such as that at the Valley View School.

Also for the first time in the university's history, officials faced a different type of housing problem: meeting the needs of a large number of married students. Before the war, the school had approximately fifty married students. By the early 1950s nearly 20 percent of its total enrollment were married. At first the university met this demand with temporary housing, but the increasing trend toward large numbers of married students forced the school to find a permanent solution. University officials replaced the temporary trailer village with married-student apartments and in later years continued to add units.

While the University of Idaho was still coping with the aftermath of World War II, the nation entered another conflict. But the Korean War brought little of the disruption of its three predecessors. The most visible change was a series of highly successful and well-publicized blood drives. During the 1950-51 school year the Associated Students sponsored what was reputed to be the first campus-wide blood drive in the nation. The drive gained considerable national attention, and in succeeding years various other universities challenged Idaho for bragging rights as the country's "bloodiest campus." But the Moscow school turned back all challenges, including one from Harvard.

With the war waning in 1953, the university and Moscow co-sponsored a May Day celebration designed to contrast with workers' celebrations held annually on May 1 in Moscow, Russia. Movie stars headed a large parade viewed by 15,000 people. There were speeches and fireworks; the community and campus donated 1,672 pints of blood and purchased nearly $400,000 in savings bonds. "When May Day was over," wrote a reporter for *Time*, "the men in charge . . . mull[ed] things over. . . . They had satisfactorily fulfilled, they decided, what they had come to regard as Moscow's destiny: the perennial challenge to show the world the difference between there and here.'' That May Day proved to be the grand finale of campus organizational efforts during the Korean War, but annual University of Idaho blood drives continued.

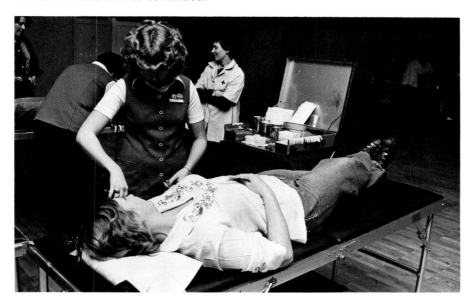

The university organized what was reputed to be the first campus-wide blood drive in the United States during the Korean War, and the drive became an annual event from that time on.

The Vietnam War was different from any that came before. Few citizens were concerned when the United States got involved in the conflict in the early 1960s. But in the ensuing years, Americans became increasingly critical of their country's actions in Southeast Asia. On the University of Idaho campus the Vietnam War kindled the most serious schisms in the school's history, although the unrest developed slowly.

By the spring of 1965 several American campuses had actively engaged in anti-war and civil-rights protests. But not the University of Idaho. This apathy concerned the *Argonaut*'s editor:

> All too few Idaho students have expressed an active interest in finding out and trying to do something about the Negro right to vote movement. All too few Idaho students have cared enough to take a stand one way or the other on American policy in Viet Nam. Panel discussions and forums of national and international affairs and academic problems here at Idaho have, with few exceptions, been poorly attended.
> It would be wrong to say that Idaho is just a party school. . . .
> But the problem is, just where do the interests of Idaho students lie?

Until the late 1960s, campus "teach-ins" were unheard of, but they then became regular university sights (below). So did student demonstrations, such as the one in support of President Ernest Hartung's policies in 1969 (right).

Just two years later, things had changed dramatically. The 1967-68 session began a period of anti-war activism that would last for more than seven years, bringing changes to the university's structure. Probably the first glimmer of these changes was a soggy anti-war protest march by forty-six people from campus to Moscow's National Guard Armory in October 1967. Most university students and townspeople did not quite know how to react. A passenger in a passing car threw eggs; a male student tossed a water balloon from Chrisman Hall; another threw a tomato from Sweet Hall; a Moscow resident shouted: "Send them all to Vietnam." The divisiveness of

The Naval ROTC building, constructed in 1942 (left), was firebombed in 1970 at the height of campus unrest over the Vietnam War (below).

the Vietnam conflict had finally reached the quiet northern Idaho town. During that same year Idaho students attended forums on the "Hippie Movement"; protested the presence on campus of recruiters from the Dow Chemical Company, the main suppliers of napalm in Vietnam; listened to that year's Borah Symposium, dedicated to discussing the issues of the war in Vietnam; boycotted classes to attend peace demonstrations on the

Administration Building lawn; and began the process of passing a students' bill of rights.

The various forms of student activism intensified in the following years, spearheaded by the Coalition for Peace and Survival. There were marches, teach-ins, moratoriums, boycotts, vigils, and leafleting. The tensions peaked with the Cambodian invasion in the spring of 1970, when a protestor burned the Naval ROTC building. University administrators struggled to maintain campus order during the days that followed. At nearby Washington State University, anti-Cambodian protests gradually evolved into a nine-day student strike against racism on campus. The more militant actions of the Washington students greatly concerned Idaho officials. In his annual address to faculty the following fall, President Ernest Hartung warned that student activism in Moscow would surely accelerate, spurred by "a rapidly increasing pace in . . . activism . . . at our sister institution across the state line." His fears proved unfounded as both campuses cooled, and conflict did not again reach the same fervor. Hartung himself had much to do with the calming influence, encouraging faculty and staff to listen closely to student demands and concerns.

While radicalism died down, it influenced the university's ROTC programs for years. Enrollments sagged in all three service training programs in the early 1970s, although the air force suffered less than the others partially because AFROTC began admitting women in 1971, something the Army did not do until 1973. With the end of the Vietnam War and the beginning of an all-volunteer army, all three services struggled to readjust to new circumstances. They could no longer rely on students to enroll merely to avoid the draft. "The . . . ROTC program at the University of Idaho has been revised to make it more competitive and intellectually stimulating to quality students," noted one biennial report during this period. These changes helped ensure the survival of a military training department that had matured with the university.

In the Chrisman Room of Memorial Gymnasium, dedicated in 1986, a life-size portrait of the old general looks down upon a trophy case containing his memorabilia. Lining the walls of the room are photographs of each of the university's Army commandants. Placed in chronological order, they represent a continuous chain of military presence on the campus for nearly a century. The Spanish-American war statue, vandalized in subsequent years, was restored in the 1980s to pristine condition. The Navy Building, firebombed in 1970, again holds offices and classrooms. A new generation of Idaho students walks by the building every day, unaware of the anti-military atmosphere on campus in those earlier times. The armed forces have once again been incorporated into the mainstream of campus activities, where they have been for nearly the school's entire history—through five wars and the intervening times of peace.

7

"We Want . . . a Just and Equal Treatment"

Minorities at Idaho

"What, then, is it that we want? Simply a just and equal treatment. . . . We wish to be recognized as bona fide ASUI members and as real students of Idaho and not as charming and pleasant but useless members of a young ladies seminary or finishing school situated next door."

UI Student Jeannette Orr, 1918

June 1896: the date of the University of Idaho's first commencement, marking the end of its fourth year. Fighting a seemingly unceasing battle for recognition, respect, and money, President Franklin B. Gault decides to turn the event into an extravaganza, a classy and showy affair. The biggest room he can find is the unfinished Administration Building auditorium. He orders bunting to wrap around the exposed rafters. It adds a touch of gaiety but cannot hide the fact that this is still only a shell of a building. "Although a rough unfurnished room, it answered the purpose," he would write later, "except that it was cold, and brick and mortar dust rattled down at times from the . . . walls."

A minor inconvenience, according to those who attended. This was the biggest occasion in the history of the school, perhaps in the history of Moscow. People flocked in from both town and countryside to what turned out to be a multi-day event, culminating on Thursday, June 11, when the graduates received their degrees. Florence May Corbett, Stella Maude Allen, Arthur Prentiss Adair, and Charles Luther Kirtley made up that first graduating group. It was one of the few times in the university's history when a class had equal numbers of men and women. Not only were Idaho's women a minority from nearly the beginning, they also received different treatment.

The first graduating class, 1896: Stella Allen, Florence Corbett, Charles Kirtley, and Arthur Adair. It was one of the few times when the university had as many women as men graduates.

For either sex, life at the university was sheltered in the 1890s. But women's lives were even more structured then men's, largely because university administrators found it necessary to assure parents that their daughters would be protected. The university's first *Catalog* noted that Preceptress (the title predating "Dean of Women") Harriet E. Cushman's

Hays Hall residents in the 1930s. In order to reassure parents that the university was a suitable place in which to entrust their daughters, officials required all women to live on campus in dormitories or sororities.

relations to the lady students will be largely influential and advisory. She will advise with the young ladies as to their boarding plans and surroundings, as to their studies, health and recreation, as to their companions, as to their attendance upon entertainments and other public gatherings, as to their deportment in school and elsewhere, and thus by wise and skilful direction seek to foster and confirm correct ideals of womanhood, duty and social grace.

In those years, women were approximately equal with men in terms of numbers, both on the faculty and in the student body. But there the equality ended. The first faculty consisted of two men—Gault and John E. Ostrander—and two women, Annette Bowman and Nellie G. Brown. Gault incurred the wrath of some members of the Board of Regents when he deigned to hire women, but the president insisted that a coeducational institution required women instructors. Even so, the regents' opposition proved strong enough to prevent "placing lady teachers in the same rank with the gentlemen." As a result, Gault divided the faculty into two classes—voting and non-voting. Women could not vote. Later, after women faculty members complained, the regents allowed some—such as Preceptress Cushman—to vote. Even so, most women instructors were disenfranchised from faculty policy matters until the turn of the century.

The university's treatment of women was not atypical of times when equality between sexes was but a dream in the minds of a minority. Nonetheless, the University of Idaho was in some ways a progressive leader in providing opportunities for women, and no better example can be found than the school's innovative domestic science—or home economics—program.

The idea of teaching home economics at the university level grew out of the new notion of education for all fostered by the Morrill Act of 1862. Kansas State University became the first college in the United States to offer credit for clothing and food courses. In 1902 the University of Idaho established a Department of Domestic Science, the first university in the Pacific Northwest to do so. Mary E. Young, the new department's first director, stated: "The fact that civilization has waited until the twentieth century to make domestic economy scientific, illustrates the old general truth that at the first we are interested in that which is of least value to us, while the most important is left till last."

Young held a joint appointment as preceptress and director of domestic science. She and Dora Porter, "demonstrator for the cookery course," met their classes in the twelve-foot-square Ridenbaugh Hall kitchen. They placed emphasis upon such matters as laying a kitchen fire and correctly breaking an egg. Eventually they added sewing instruction. The university at first required all freshmen and sophomore women to enroll in domestic science classes and offered electives in the department for upperclassmen and preparatory students. By 1903 the two-year program Young and Porter offered included classwork in the study of combustion, classification of food principles, bread making, food preservation, waitress and laundry work, cultivating vegetables, home nursing, and hygiene.

The first class in household science in 1895 (above) was given under the auspices of the Department of Agriculture. Seven years later, Idaho became the first university in the Pacific Northwest to establish a Department of Domestic Science. Evening cooking class in Ridenbaugh Hall in the early 1900s (left). This was one of the first classes offered by the new department.

A Case for Women's Rights

This is a story about an event on the university campus in the spring of 1918. But before the tale is told, it needs to be put in perspective. The Rocky Mountain states were the first to grant women the right to vote. In fact, Idaho was among the earliest states in the Union to adopt women's suffrage. In recognition of the vital role women had played in settling Idaho, Emma Edwards designed a state seal dominated by the figure of a woman. By the spring of 1918 America had been at war for one year. Women students greatly outnumbered men on campus during those war months, and women performed many important services formerly undertaken by male students. In fact, just a year earlier, the school had had its first woman student body president— and the student government had not collapsed.

But when women in 1918 asked for representation on the University of Idaho Athletic Board—

shown here in 1902—they ignited a stormy controversy. It seems, in retrospect, a simple and just request. After all, women paid fees to support athletics, just as men did. Women believed they had a right to compete in sports, just as men did.

Over forty-five women had enrolled in the classes by the end of the first year, greatly taxing the small Ridenbaugh facilities. Over the years the department—which changed its name to domestic economy in 1905 and home economics in 1911—grew with the introduction of new courses designed to meet women's changing needs, classes such as textiles, nutrition, institution management, art, housing, home furnishings, weaving, home management, consumer economics, child development, family relations, and training of home economists in business and journalism.

Jessie M. Hoover, who became director of home economics in 1912, immediately began impressing upon the predominantly male Board of Regents the need for a suitable facility to teach "women to do women's work." At the time, instructors held classes in rooms scattered throughout campus. It was no way to run a department, and Jessie Hoover let the administration and regents know about it—repeatedly.

Hoover's diligence paid off when, in 1916, workers completed construction of the Administration Building's south wing and home economics moved into the third floor of the older north wing—complete with a foods laboratory, dining room, art laboratory, two clothing laboratories, lecture room, and offices. Even so, by 1920 Katherine Jensen, Hoover's replacement, began presenting a case for even larger facilities. Finally in 1952 wreckers destroyed the school's beautiful—but long condemned—Engineering Building and erected in its place a new Home Economics Building. For the first time in the university's long history of teaching domestic science, the department finally had adequate space for long-term growth.

Home Economics students in cooking class in the 1940s (above), and practicing cooking for large groups at the Wallace dormitory cafeteria in 1976 (facing page).

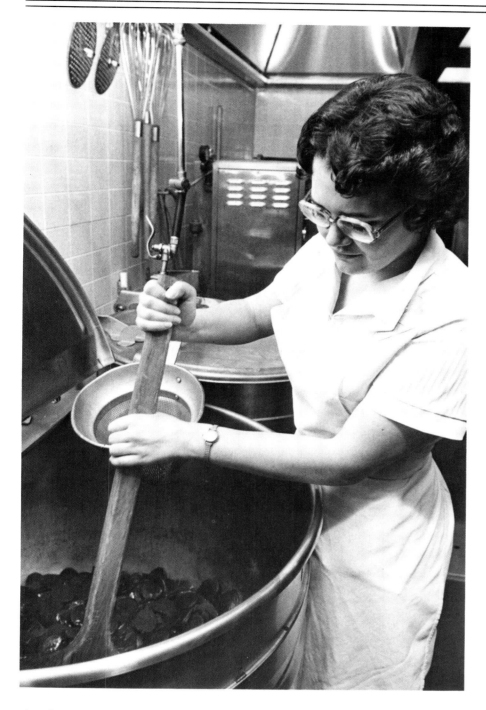

The department continued to experiment with ways to provide a broad range of experience for women completing home-economics degrees. In 1920 it required that every woman graduating from the department spend a period of time in a "home management house" or "practice cottage." There the women did regular household work and prepared family meals. In 1974 William Jasper became the first University of Idaho man to receive a degree in home economics. That same year the Department of Home

Furthermore, women represented at this time a vast majority of the school's student population.

But some men of fragile ego refused to be part of a movement that would allow women a choice in how the masculine activity of athletics should be governed. Some were so indignant that they published a tabloid at their own expense entitled Old Idaho Spirit. It stated simply that it was printed by "The Men of the University of Idaho." Among other things, the "Men of the University of Idaho" wrote:

A disgraceful scene took place yesterday morning in the ASUI meeting called for the purpose of nominating officers for the student body. Nominations of women for the athletic board and of men for May Queen are but indications of the utterly demoralized Idaho spirit. . . .

Men and women of Idaho, it is not a matter of representation that is being demanded. That is a mere subterfuge—an appeal to sympathy and not to reason. Publicity is the thing being sought by a few persons here and they do not seem to realize that their desires are magnified in an evil manner as concerns the fair name of Idaho.

It is doubtful that Jeannette Orr considered herself to be damaging the fair name of Idaho. Rather, she was motivated by a desire for equal treatment. Orr was a campus activist but had hardly shown any pretensions of being a "radical." She served on the Argonaut's staff and was president of Ridenbaugh Hall, secretary of the Women's Association, vice president of the English Club, secretary of the

Commerce and Economics Club. In the spring of 1918 she answered the frail complaints of the "Men of Idaho" with one of the strongest appeals for women's rights ever made by an Idaho student. Her letter to the editor appeared in the Argonaut.

This movement is a student movement entirely. It is a protest against purely local injustices and has for its aims the improvement of certain conditions that concern the students of Idaho. . . .

Most people, I believe, think that the sole desire of the insurgents is for participation in athletics. This is not the chief aim, but only a phase of the main issue, although an important phase. Almost no person who pretends to be modern in his ideas, will deny the right and the need of athletics for girls as well as for men. . . . But how many of the men would care for athletics that were class work and for which they [only] received grades and credits? Where would be the joy, the zest and the glory of the thing?

If girls athletics are right and necessary, why should they be denied recognition and the stimulus of applause and interest? Why should not the girl athlete receive an insignia? Why should not courts be kept up for them and the use of the gym granted them? . . .

That which seemed most to shock our opponents was the nomination of women for the athletic board. . . .

The nominations were as it were, the brick through the plate glass window, calling attention to our grievance. . . .

Economics became the School of Home Economics, in recognition of its growing importance to the university and the citizens of the state. The pioneering department of seventy-two years before had indeed prospered, sometimes against difficult odds.

In other ways, too, the university was quite progressive in enhancing the education of its women students. By the 1920s, for example, the school had three active women's student organizations, the Women's Council,

The Department of Home Economics home-management house in the 1930s (top), and the new house constructed on campus in 1965 (bottom).

Inter-Sorority Council, and Associated Women's Students. The college bragged that it was the only university in the country with three such groups.

Because of the generosity of several individuals and organizations, the school has also long been able to award scholarships to women students. In 1902 Sarah Headington, a Latah County educator, donated $5,000 to establish one of the university's early scholarship funds. The endowment was used to assist "young women of more than extraordinary ability." Mary Hall received the Headington scholarship in 1906. She graduated in 1908 and, after teaching in the Sandpoint schools for two years, married

Mary Hall Niccolls, university alumna, who left nearly $450,000 to the school for home economics scholarships.

In athletics the women students have no chance to participate and the $3.30 which each contributes every semester, must go down in their accounts as "spent for amusement." . . .

What, then, is it that we want? Simply a just and equal treatment in the ASUI, more use of our money, the recognition of the right of every woman to hold any office in the ASUI for which she personally is fitted. . . . Chiefly we wish to be recognized as bona fide ASUI members and as real students of Idaho and not as charming and pleasant but useless members of a young ladies seminary or finishing school situated next door. . . .

The early Victorian attitude of the men seem particularly incomprehensible when one considers that the state of Idaho had settled the equal suffrage question before most of the present students of Idaho were born.

Our movement is, we feel, essentially patriotic. When we are daily being told how the war is more and more putting on women the burden of social service and leadership, it would seem our duty to prepare by taking responsibilities in college.

If a person could vote on style and forcefulness, clearly Jeannette Orr had trounced the "Men of the University of Idaho" in this exchange. But issues often are not settled on merit. Jeannette Orr was graduated long before her demands were implemented. Women did form a separate athletic association in the 1920s and began awarding insignia. But athletics for women remained predominantly intramural *until the 1960s. Not until 1968 did the university pass a Students' Bill of Rights—over the objection of some influential men students—prohibiting discrimination on the basis of sex. Not until the 1970s did federal policy, combined with a legal suit filed by the Women's Caucus, force the university to grant women truly equal services in athletics and in the work place.*

Jeannette Orr was not an uncommon woman, but she was clearly one with ideas. Many other women had made similar statements for equality long before Orr was born. Still, she was in a minority, a pioneer in a struggle for campus equality lasting well over half a century. Her 1918 plea for just treatment remains one of the school's most eloquent statements in that long battle.

hydraulics engineer Calvin Niccolls. The two then moved away from Idaho, but Mary Hall Niccolls never forgot the university—or the scholarship that had helped finance her education. When she died in 1962 she left nearly $450,000 to the University of Idaho, "to be used for scholarships for young women in home economics." Headington and Niccolls are but two of several examples of generous beneficiaries who have donated money to assist women of the University of Idaho with their educations.

In an effort to convince parents around the state that the university was "safe," campus administrators early enforced a number of women's rules that were considerably different from those for men. Shortly after the construction of Ridenbaugh Hall, the university required that all unmarried, non-Moscow women students live on campus, in either dorms or sororities. This regulation against apartment living remained in effect until the 1960s. The state commissioner of Education commented in 1915: "A young woman housed in one of these dormitories is surrounded with every influence that will tend to make her a woman of the type that Idaho is proud to have."

Until the late 1960s the university's women students abided by rules that prohibited them from wearing shorts or pants on campus except when playing sports. As late as 1968 the Associated Women's Students *Handbook* informed new freshmen that " 'Grungies' or 'grubs' are the campus terms for very casual wear including cut-offs, sweatshirts, and cords. They are worn for study in the living groups, sports participation and some picnics. The times that this apparel may appear on campus are quite limited." Administrators even kept a close watch on women's formal attire. For example, 1920 rules forbade dancers from occupying the dark corners of a dance floor and asserted that "women wearing gowns with extremely low necks and no sleeves will be requested to leave."

Home economics sewing class (1920s).

The changing images of Idaho's women . . . plant science classes in the 1890s (top) and 1960s (left) . . .

Idaho Author

If I could tell it, as it really was! But I can only make a fiction of it, and write down how it seemed to me that it must have been. So any tale is a shadow of real life, and what we write an echo of a sound made far away.

Carol Ryrie Brink,
Snow in the River,
1964

Carol Ryrie Brink wrote beautiful fiction, much of it based upon her experiences in Moscow and at the University of Idaho. In the process she became perhaps the state's most gifted—though underrated—novelist.

Carol Ryrie was born in Moscow in December 1895 to Alex and Henrietta Watkins Ryrie. Hers was a family of leadership and prominence. Grandfather William W. Watkins, a "big, upstanding figure with fierce black eyes, bristling eyebrows and mutton chop sideburns," was an early Moscow physician and jovial town booster. He, as much as anyone, was responsible for landing the university for the burgeoning frontier community. He later served as secretary of the Board of

. . . May Queen (top, early 1900s), and students on the Hello Walk (bottom, 1920s) . . .

In addition to the dress codes, rules prohibited women students from smoking in most public places. "The University of Idaho has maintained a high moral standing," noted Dean of Women Permeal French in justifying the smoking ban in 1930. "In keeping with this I think it best that the girls do not become too flagrant with their cigarettes. It reflects upon us, and may be carried to a point where it will be harmful. When appropriations and building funds come before the legislature, it is curious but painfully true that such things as girls smoking have a direct bearing. A school is judged by its students." Other rules established the time of evening when women had to report to their rooms; limited the number of weeknight dates they could have; prohibited them from leaving Moscow without permission, and from visiting men's rooms; and forced them to sign out every time they left a dorm or sorority in the evening, stating where they were going, and with whom.

Both men and women students occasionally protested these restrictive

. . . Miss University of Idaho (top, 1969) and commencement (bottom, 1976).

Regents and gave money for the university's first student award, the Watkins Medal for Oratory. Carol's father was a Scottish emigrant who surveyed and named many of Moscow's streets and served as the town's mayor. Her mother was a talented musician. Her grandmother was a never-tiring storyteller. Young Carol Ryrie truly seemed born to good fortune.

Yet her life suddenly shattered. Alex Ryrie, her father, died of consumption in 1900. One year later a deranged young man assassinated her grandfather in what remains Moscow's most notorious murder. Her mother hastily remarried but committed suicide in 1904—in despair over her unhappy union. Carol Ryrie was not yet nine years old. She went to live with her grandmother and aunt.

These tragedies fostered an independence and self-reliance in Carol Ryrie. She yearned for brothers, sisters, and youthful parents but had to make do with self-amusement. She took long pony rides into the countryside. She carefully noted details of the local landscape. She spent hours listening to tales of her grandmother's Wisconsin childhood. Carol began keeping a diary and writing poetry, but her extreme shyness prevented her from sharing these with anyone. Once, at age thirteen, she submitted a poem to a Spokane newspaper, and to her surprise and embarrassment the newspaper printed it. Carol did not know how to accept the compliments people gave her. She later wrote in one of her novels—a fictionalized autobiographical account—that she "felt as if she would sink into the ground."

Frustrated and unhappy in Moscow schools, Carol transferred to the Portland Academy, where

she finally overcame her shyness. Here she truly began her writing career, publishing regularly in the school's monthly magazine. She attended parties and dances and came home triumphantly to Moscow after graduation to attend the University of Idaho.

She seemed a woman transformed. She was extremely popular on campus, joined many clubs, belonged to a sorority, wrote materials for student plays. "I was happy to be in the swim at last after being lonely and shy for so many years," she later recalled. The formerly unsociable girl became the Argonaut's society editor. She also appeared on campus during May Fete with her pony, cart, and friends. She is seen at the right in the photo below.

After her junior year, feeling Moscow was too small, Carol transferred to the University of California at Berkeley where she graduated in 1918. That same year she married Raymond Brink, whom she had met while he was a young mathematics professor at the University of Idaho. The Brinks would never return to live in Moscow, but Carol fondly remembered the town.

Raymond and Carol spent most of their adult lives in St. Paul and Minneapolis, where Raymond

covenants. Editorials in the *Argonaut* over a period of more than thirty years give a sense of the ongoing debate.

> College men are given complete freedom. . . .
> Why should not women be given a modification of the same opportunity? A complete absence of rules is, of course, out of the question, but extended hours, depending perhaps on the woman's academic standing, would leave the matter to her discretion.　(1937)

> The more observant among you have probably noticed there aren't very many coeds going to school here. . . . There remains the question "why?". . .
> The answer . . . is . . . plain. . . .
> Women do not like it here. . . .
> Why should they? Read those squirrelly female regulations they have written up for this place and you'll find out why they don't.　(1959)

> Frightening as it may seem to some, the sooner our little coeds grow up and accept the responsibilities that go along with being women instead of girls, the better.　(1968)

Finally, in 1968 the university passed a students' bill of rights that—over the objections of some male student leaders—prohibited regulations discriminating on the basis of sex. Gradually, the university administration dropped its long-standing policy of treating women differently than it did men. Still, the crusade for women's equality did not move quickly enough for some. At the insistence of concerned staff and students, President Ernest Hartung in 1971 appointed a committee to study the high attrition rate among Idaho's women students. This committee eventually became the Women's Caucus, which dramatically changed the relationship between the university and all women associated with it. The caucus spearheaded the drive for a Women's Center as

By the 1960s, the university provided nursery and day-care facilities so both men and women parents could attend classes.

well as a women's studies program. In 1973 the caucus filed a sex-discrimination complaint against the school with the Idaho Human Rights Commission. The commission ruled that the university had violated provisions of the federal Civil Rights and Equal Opportunity acts. As a result of this ruling, the university hired a full-time affirmative action officer, gave some employees retroactive salary adjustments, undertook a comprehensive study of staff salaries, and agreed to publish and maintain job descriptions for each position opening on campus. It was not the final battle, but it was perhaps the apex in a long struggle at the University of Idaho for women's equality.

The changes in women's status in the 1960s and 1970s reflected a growing national movement for equal rights for all women, just as the seemingly strict restrictions placed upon women students in an earlier time reflected the thinking of that era that women should be protected. More than any other person, Dean of Women Permeal French was responsible for instituting those rules. She set parameters of behavior for Idaho women that lasted until the late 1960s, over thirty years after she had retired—a tribute to her lasting influence.

Labels are usually grounded in some element of truth, and Dick d'Easum chose one with a certain amount of accuracy when he entitled his biography of French *Dowager of Discipline*. Surely, Permeal French was a disciplinarian. But an overemphasis on this aspect of her life distorts the fact that, for her time, she was also an ardent feminist who worked to improve the lives of Idaho's women.

When she arrived at the University of Idaho in 1908, Permeal French was the first person to bear the title Dean of Women. While some students disliked her disciplinary bent, most appreciated her feminist ideals. She frequently chastised the university's president, the regents, and state legislators for not treating women as well as they did men. Appropriations for women's academic and vocational courses must "be made equal" to men, she wrote in 1916. Women needed more living space, better and more instructors, and a proper "women's building." She was an expert in-fighter, and though she fostered an image of remaining aloof from campus politics, she knew the campus and state political systems well and used that knowledge to her advantage.

French encouraged the construction of both dormitories and sororities as a means of providing adequate and diverse housing for all women students. She organized Mortar Board, an honor society for senior women, as well as Daleth Teth Gimel, an honorary group for women who lived with their families in town. Daleth Teth Gimel was the first such town women's association in the United States, and soon other Pacific Northwest colleges organized chapters. French was a prime motivator behind the organization of the Associated Women's Students, the Inter-Sorority Council, the Women's Athletic Association, and other groups.

Technically, a "dowager" is "an elderly lady of imposing appearance." More commonly, the word connotes a certain prudishness. Permeal French

became chairman of the mathematics department at the University of Minnesota and wrote nearly as many books as his wife. Carol's first duties were raising her family, but she wrote incessantly—on the end of the ironing board, at the kitchen sink, and when her two children were asleep. Finally in 1936 she submitted a manuscript to the Macmillan Company based upon the Wisconsin stories her grandmother told her as a child. Caddie Woodlawn brought Carol Brink instant acclaim. It was awarded the nation's most prestigious prize for children's literature, the Newbery Medal. Between 1936 and 1977 Brink wrote nearly thirty books for children and adults, mostly fiction. Seven of them—three children's and four adults'—deal with accounts of life in and around Moscow. All Over Town, Louly, and Two Are Better Than One are happy children's books of her days in Moscow. Louly is based upon the adventures of Carol and Beth Soulen. Two Are Better Than One relives the adventures of Carol and Charlotte Lewis. Both Lewis and Soulen attended the University of Idaho.

Her trilogy of adult fiction based on Moscow history is darker, containing as it does the accounts of her family's tragedies. Buffalo Coat, published in 1944, details, among other episodes of early Moscow, the efforts of Dr. Watkins to establish the University of Idaho:

So The Golden West Academy started. . . . All . . . summer the brickyard had been busy turning out piles of brilliantly red brick for such a new building as should shed glory on the town. At Doctor's urging they put the building on a hill across the railroad tracks where everyone *could see it and feel pride. It would be the first and last thing in town to be seen by travelers on the railroad. They had the Governor up from the South to lay the cornerstone; and Doctor in a high silk hat headed the delegation that received him. The building went up perpendicular and Gothic, and also very red, with an abundance of decoration in white limestone as if the builders had been over it with frosting in a pastry tube. There were many steps to climb to it; and, inside, more steps mounted and mounted to a final small observation in the tower.*

"Hitch your wagon to a star," was one of Doctor's favorite sayings, and something of this intention had gone into the building of the Golden West Academy. It was an achievement of which the town was proud.

In addition to recounting the Watkins murder, Buffalo Coat also deals with the suicide pact of a married doctor and the young daughter of a Methodist minister, an early Moscow scandal. In turn, Brink's novel, with its descriptions of human motives and violence, caused its own tumult upon publication. This surprised Brink, who thought that Moscow had quite forgotten her.

*The second Idaho novel—*Strangers in the Forest, *published in 1959—and Brink's last book—*Four Girls on a Homestead, *a work of non-fiction published in 1977—are based upon the experiences of Carol's aunt on her timber homestead in the white-pine forests near Clarkia.* Strangers *gained popular national acclaim and was condensed by* Readers Digest. *The last of*

fit the title in only one way: she was imposing. In fact, she was quite large. But when she arrived on campus she was only forty years old and, rather than being a prude, she loved parties. The campus had never seen such extravaganzas as those organized by Dean French. Students and instructors should have fun, she believed. When it occurred to her that the university had no way of marking the arrival of spring, she organized the Campus Day and May Fete tradition. When social activities sputtered in late October, she sponsored Halloween costume parties. When everyone rushed from campus over the holidays without having a chance to celebrate together, she started the university's Christmas caroling tradition. When there was no adequate place on campus to dance or sip tea, she built the Blue Bucket Inn.

Permeal French retired in 1936 after twenty-eight years of service. Later the school gave her an honorary doctorate—to complement the honorary master's degree it had granted in 1920. On October 9, 1954, President Theophilus, hearing Dean French was ill, wired her that the newest women's dormitory on campus would be named the Permeal French House. The following day she died. French had dedicated most of her adult life to the university and its women. Time gradually changed ideas about how a university should treat its women students. After all, most educational theories grow outdated with time. But no one should question the sincerity of the University of Idaho's first Dean of Women.

Permeal French, second from right, returned to campus in 1938 for a presentation of her portrait to the university (above). Home Economics Campus Day float (facing page, top, 1914); Co-ed Prom (facing page, bottom, 1932).

the Idaho trilogy, Snow in the River, appeared in 1964. It was the most difficult to write, for in it Brink recounts the events surrounding her mother's suicide. The book examines the town during its later history, when both it and the University of Idaho have matured considerably from the period of Buffalo Coat. Snow in the River was Carol Brink's last major work. After writing it she spent her remaining years painting, writing poetry, and remembering with great pleasure her deep Idaho roots. She died in San Diego in 1981, eight years after her husband's death.

In 1965 the University of Idaho recognized Carol Brink with an honorary doctorate of literature, one of the last of many awards she won for her numerous works. Shortly after her death, the school named its faculty building after her, at about the same time that the Moscow Public Library named its children's library for her. Both were acts of belated recognition for one of the state's outstanding writers. Unfortunately, most Idahoans still have not heard of Carol Brink. Ask them about famous Idaho authors and they will probably respond by telling you about Ezra Pound, who was born in Hailey but left as an infant and never returned; or Ernest Hemingway, who moved to Ketchum late in life. Neither wrote about Idaho. One of the state's best novelists, who grew up in Moscow and attended the University of Idaho, did.

It took several decades, but by the 1970s women had become full participants in the school's political system.

In 1947 Herbert E. Lattig, director of student affairs, noted that "at times the men students at Idaho have outnumbered the women three-to-one." He believed "a state university should strive to have a more even balance between men and women students." The school made some efforts to reach a balance, but only twice since the 1890s—during World Wars I and II—have women students equaled or outnumbered men. They are the university's oldest and largest minority, but not its only one.

Over the years, the university has provided an education for many international students. Ole Hagberg of Norway was the first. He died for his new country as a university volunteer in the Spanish-American War. Another

Ole Hagberg, the university's first international student, died during the Spanish-American War in 1898.

international student, impressed with "the spirit of friendship permeating . . . the campus," wrote a book about his experiences. Hardit Singh Dhillon of India attended Idaho in the late 1920s. His *American College Life: A Record of Personal Experiences and Impressions* well expresses the frustration, awe, and wonderment that many international students have experienced on the Moscow campus.

Concerning the nuances of American student slang, he wrote:

> When I was taking a walk with an Indian friend of mine, one of his class-fellows met us and greeted him, saying, "How do you do?" And my friend replied, "Oh, nothing, just walking around." When the American student was out of sight, said my friend to me rather scornfully: "You know, Mr. Dhillon, these American students, though born with English, can't speak grammatically correct English. Now, this friend should have asked me 'What do you do?' instead of 'How do you do?' But I got the point and answered him properly." "No, dear friend," said I to him, "you didn't get the point, but entirely missed it!" and then I explained that his friend did not ask him a question but greeted him. "What a queer greeting!" he said.

On American classrooms:

> At the beginning of the hour a bell rings and students go into their respective lecture-rooms. . . . Until the professor comes, the students keep up an animated buzz of conversation; they don't sit quiet. Nor does this conversation stop suddenly when the professor makes his appearance. . . . The professor comes in, sees if the lights are on and if they are not, he puts them on, opens the windows, and shuts the door—all these things he has to do like a janitor; he never orders the students: "Open the window" or "Shut the door," as an Indian professor would do. The American professor does not like to impose himself upon his students as a superior being or as though he were a ruler.

About the fraternity system:

> Winning membership in a fraternity, the student discovers, is fraught with many unpleasant tasks. First, he is honored with the duty of keeping the "house" clean—of being a sweeper! A careless and poor job brings punishment from the upper-class members of the house and he is awarded a paddling with wooden paddles. He is made to commit to memory the songs of the university and of the fraternity. . . .
>
> He is made to wear a special kind of cap, usually green, so that he may easily be identified by upper classmen who are always conscientiously seeking to subject him to their atrocities.

Concerning football games:

> American football, in spite of its name, is played mostly with hands—the players take the ball in hands and by means of throws towards each other try to carry it forward. When the ball is being carried, the opponents try to arrest the advance of the carrier by clinging to his feet, legs, arms or whatever part of his body they can hold. Sometimes a number of them fall on each other as they try to catch the carrier, the carrier being underneath all of them. It is a rough game. As they proceed towards the goal, they gain certain points on the basis of the number of yards they get farther from the centre and nearer the goal, the technique of which I have never been able to understand fully. . . .
>
> When the match is being played the "yell kings" perform various kinds of "stunts." The "yell kings" are students whose main function is to keep up . . . enthusiasm. They are so called because they yell to keep up the

Hardit Singh Dhillon, from India, wrote a book about his experiences as a student at Idaho. The photograph was taken in the 1970s.

interest. Their yelling proceeds in somewhat the following manner: Rah-Rah-Rah! Rah-Rah-Rah! repeating it several times while the |fans| . . . also join them in their yelling, . . . finally ending with a sound: Rrr-rrr-rrr-rrr! Then there follows a clapping of hands from all over. It certainly is an exciting scene for the strange visitor.

Dhillon grew very fond of such strange and mysterious scenes. He would later encourage one cousin, three nephews, a son, and a daughter to follow him to the Moscow campus. While there, they—like the hundreds of other

Chen-Kueh Tsan, student from China (1923).

International student performances of homeland music have served to broaden the educational experiences of all Idaho students.

international students who have received an education at Idaho—learned much about the United States and taught much to Moscow residents and university students about their homelands.

International students, as well as international instructors and staff, have greatly aided the university's development and, almost without exception, have been enthusiastically received on campus. A rare exception came during the early days of World War II—and the victims of that unfortunate action were actually American citizens.

International students, faculty, and staff have received training or assisted in the university's development since the 1890s (above and following page).

Jennie Hughes

She will always be something of an enigma. Like many people of her race and sex, Jennie Hughes, a black woman, left little in the way of a written legacy. Most of what we know about her comes from the memories of acquaintances, from family descendants, or from people of later generations who remember hearing stories about her. Yet at the time she died in 1939 she remained, as the Argonaut *stated, "The only colored student ever to receive a degree from the institution." Jennie Hughes had graduated from the University of Idaho exactly forty years earlier, a member of the school's fourth commencement class.*

Jennie Eva Hughes was born in Washington, D.C., on July 20, 1879. Some time later her mother, Louisa, married Lewis E. Chrisemon. The Crisemons had three children, born in Pennsylvania in 1884, Indian Territory (Oklahoma) in 1888, and Idaho in 1891, indicative of the family's gradual westward migration.

In the mid-1890s the Chrisemons arrived in Moscow, becoming the town's only black family. Lewis Chrisemon was a pioneering Moscow merchant, being either a restauranteer, a barber, or perhaps both. His stepdaughter Jennie Hughes graduated from Moscow High School in 1895.

We can only guess what it was like for the Chrisemons in those days. There were some businesses that refused to serve blacks; no doubt there were several people who did not wish to associate with them. On the other hand, many early black emigrants found life in small western towns less prejudiced than in the East or South. At the least, since blacks were such a tiny minority, they were frequently treated better than in other regions because white residents did not feel threatened.

The Chrisemons might well have been the second black family to have settled permanently in all of Latah County. Joe and Lou Wells had arrived a few years earlier and lived near Deary. Joe was a logger; Lou, a hostess and cook of extraordinary reputation, ran a lodging house for loggers and homesteaders. While they were no doubt excluded from some parts of local society, Joe and Lou Wells were well respected. In fact, Joe used to say he was the only white man around Deary—all the rest were Swedes.

The Chrisemons were probably also generally well received, for they lived in Moscow several years, and Lewis's business prospered. Still, it must have been difficult being the only blacks in a city of whites. That no doubt explains why they were so pleasantly surprised one day in the late 1890s when the Settle family mistakenly debarked from a train at the Moscow depot. Lewis Chrisemon was so happy to see another black family that he convinced the Settles to remain, and they became the town's second black residents.

The Settles had come from the deep South. Eugene Settle, one of the family's four boys, remembered Moscow as a tolerant place. He received a few stares from surprised classmates on his first day at school but was largely accepted. He was a young boy when the family arrived, but he remembered Lewis Chrisemon—a man who "drove a nice horse to a single buggy"—as being exceptionally kind and generous to his parents, helping them find a farm outside of town.

Lewis and Louisa Chrisemon sent Jennie to the university after she graduated from Moscow High,

On the day after Pearl Harbor, President Harrison Dale presented a calm, sincere message to the students of the university. It was a thoughtful statement that attracted considerable national attention and was copied by several other colleges. Dale concluded his communication with a warning against jingoism: "All native American citizens whether of German or Italian or Japanese ancestry are American citizens by birth, sharing with all of us the heritage of American democracy. With those who are proved unworthy of this heritage our government will deal promptly and with deserved severity. To all others, who, like ourselves, are Americans by birth we can show the spirit of true Americanism." Four months later, President Dale and Idaho Governor Chase Clark chose to refuse admission to six Japanese-American students who deserved a better version of the "spirit of true Americanism."

In April 1942 Seattle officials forced six American citizens of Japanese ancestry from their homes, as well as from their classes at the University of Washington, as part of the Japanese relocation during the hysteria of World War II. University of Idaho sociology instructor Paul Hatt went to Seattle, picked up the students—three men and three women—and brought them to Idaho. Clark and Dale then formulated a policy that refused admission to any out-of-state Japanese-American students. Hatt temporarily housed the six in Moscow, but they were chased from town by a group of local roughnecks who threatened violent action. In a rare front-page *Argonaut* editorial reminiscent of Frank Sutherland's indignant and hard-hitting journalism of World War I, managing editor Knox Craig blasted the administration, the governor, and the local hoodlums:

> It must come as a shock to all university students here on the hill that . . . in a university town—where of all places objectivity, liberalism, cool thinking should prevail—such ugly, violent racial antagonism would flare up. . . .
>
> When people begin taking citizenship in terms of race, they are borrowing from the handbook of fascist leaders. When a minority group begins shoving another smaller group of citizens around with no regard for their rights as citizens, they are using the tactics of Nazi storm troopers.

It was not a time of which the city and the university can be proud. Like all institutions in all parts of the country, the University of Idaho has experienced acts of racism. Seldom, however, have they been so overt. Jennie Hughes, who graduated from Idaho in 1899, was the school's first black graduate and would remain its only one for decades. There is no evidence that she received any overt racial slurs. But she was an anomaly for the university in a state that traditionally holds one of the nation's smallest black populations.

The University of Idaho, like many colleges, first became "integrated" primarily because of athletics. Following World War II, northern universities began to recruit black athletes heavily. While this caused some scheduling disruptions between northern integrated schools and their southern counterparts that refused to play against blacks, the idea of athletic integration caught on quickly. Noting the growing trend in 1946, the *Argonaut* editorialized that "some Negro youths are just as good football players as Caucasian athletes" and detailed one of the first experiences of a black player competing against Idaho: "A Negro played in Neale stadium last Saturday [for the University of Oregon]—he was not singled out as an

and there, too, she seems to have been well received. Margaret McCallie was a year ahead of Jennie and remembered her as "that lovely colored girl," who was one of the few women students not belonging to the YWCA, even though her classmates urged her to join. Jennie hesitated because she did not belong to a church.

Jennie Hughes joined nearly everything else she was eligible for, however, and accumulated an admirable academic record. In 1898 she won the Watkins Medal for Oratory, the university's most prestigious award. The following year she received her bachelor of science degree, and is shown— second from right in the bottom row—with some of her classmates.

Although the university had a black graduate as early as 1899, it really did not become integrated until the late 1950s, and then at first primarily because of the recruitment of black athletes.

Either during her last year in college or shortly after graduation, Jennie Hughes met George August Smith. The two married and moved to Wardner, in the heart of the Coeur d'Alene mining district. Smith was a railroad employee who had speculated in mining stock. He did quite well, and the family prospered. In 1912 they moved to Spokane with their four children— three boys and a girl. Jennie Hughes Smith lived in that city the rest of her life.

Jennie Smith apparently retained fond memories of Moscow

and the university, for she sent one of her sons, Berthol, to attend the school. He died in 1919 in Moscow before graduating, apparently only the second black student ever enrolled. His mother remained the only graduate. When the Crisemons had first arrived in town, the Hotel Moscow was segregated; when Jennie Smith returned in 1919 to take her son's body home, she stayed there. Times had changed. Friends and acquaintances stopped by to pay their respects. It seemed not to matter that she was black.

Jennie Hughes Smith died at a Spokane hospital on August 19, 1939, and was buried at Riverside Park Cemetery. She was sixty years and one month old. There are no streets in Spokane named for her or her family; no buildings on the University of Idaho campus. Though Jennie Hughes was a pioneer for her race, perhaps it is best that we remember her the way she would probably best like to be remembered: as a student who attended the university, did her job well, graduated, and lived a successful life—like thousands of "ordinary" students who have passed through the school's halls. But it is right that we remember, too, that the university must have treated Jennie Hughes well, or she would not have sent her son to its campus. That is something of which the institution can be proud.

object for calculated, cold-blooded carnage. We can recall how he was once helped from the ground after a tackle by the man who brought him down. Such displays of sportsmanship far outshadow the threats winding their way from the land of plantations."

Within a decade blacks had also integrated Idaho's athletic teams without any incidents of overt racism. Almost exactly ten years after the newspaper's story about the University of Oregon's black athlete, the *Argonaut* described the school's friendly treatment toward its own nine black students. One was elected freshman class vice president; most were athletes. "The Negro-white relationship at the University of Idaho is in sharp contrast to that of Alabama," the paper editorialized. "Here in Moscow, Negroes aren't run out of town on the end of a rail. Instead, often times, they are packed off the gridirons and basketball courts on the shoulders of their fellow team-mates—white in color. . . . Each has been accepted on his own individual merit."

The university had reason to be proud of its acceptance of blacks. On the other hand, from a black person's perspective, the white-black relationship was not as good as it could have been. Although white students generally treated their black colleagues cordially, blacks experienced subtle forms of racism. In 1959 some students circulated a petition protesting the university's lease of land to Sigma Chi fraternity, which practiced discrimination. The fraternity's charter stated that "no person shall be eligible to membership . . . who is not a white male." Later, during the times of rising black consciousness in the late 1960s and 1970s, Idaho students formed a Black Student Union. It was a place for blacks to gather, and served as a vehicle for increasing the awareness of Moscow residents and non-black university students concerning the black experience on campus and in American history.

Certainly, women, international students, and blacks are not the only minorities who have enrolled at Idaho. American Indians and Chicanos also formed active student societies on campus in the late 1960s and 1970s. Together with the Women's Caucus and Black Student Union, they brought permanent changes in people's perceptions toward minorities and substantial curriculum advancements. But the examples of blacks, international students, and women shed light on the minority experience on campus generally.

Overall, the University of Idaho can be proud of its record. Ignorance and lack of consciousness have been the usual causes of discrimination on campus. To a minority student that type of discrimination is uncomfortable—and inexcusable. But it is qualitatively different from overt, hostile action. The University of Idaho generally has opened its doors to a wide variety of minority groups. As those groups have made their problems and desires known, the school has attempted to respond in ways that have increased the educational experiences of minority and majority students alike.

8

Reaching Out to Community, State, and Nation

The university's threefold mission has remained unaltered since the 1890s: teaching, research, and service. The University of Idaho has always been more than just a single college campus. Few of Idaho's residents—even if they have never visited Moscow—are unaffected by the school's outreach and research efforts. And the impact of the school's teaching, research, and service does not stop at the state's boundaries.

Actually, the university was conceived through outreach. In 1887 the United States Congress passed the Hatch Act, which encouraged development of agricultural experiment stations at land-grant colleges. In February 1892 the university's regents organized the Idaho Agricultural Experiment Station—nearly eight months before the University of Idaho officially opened its doors. In so doing, they received a welcome check for $15,000 from the federal government.

In those early years, as first acting president J. H. Forney emphasized, "agriculture received our best attention because through the agricultural department we derived our principal sustenance." Thus the university's first official function provided residents of Idaho with agricultural outreach services. That has remained a vital aspect of the school's role since those days.

The regents placed the headquarters of the Idaho Agricultural Experiment

From its earliest years, the university's administrators sought innovative ways in which the school could extend its services to Idaho's farmers. One method devised was through exhibits at local and regional fairs.

Station in Moscow so professors in the agriculture department could serve dual roles, teaching college students and assisting the state's farmers. Robert Milliken became the station's first director and in the fall of 1892 issued the first two of what would become an important series of invaluable bulletins. The first outlined the role of the station. The second encouraged Idaho farmers experiencing problems with insects to "properly pack" and mail them "for one cent per ounce" to Moscow. Once the insects arrived, agricultural scientists would make every effort to "satisfactery [sic] answer any inquiries regarding their life history, or the best means of destroying them if they are injurious."

Infused with enthusiasm at having received $15,000 in federal funds merely by organizing an experiment station in Moscow—which was really a "station" in name only, since the school had no farm or land upon which to experiment—the regents decided they could assure themselves of further federal Hatch allotments by opening branch stations around the state. Consequently, in 1892 residents of Grangeville, Nampa, and Idaho Falls donated land for agricultural experiment substations. Town residents were excited. The Board of Regents was excited. Federal administrators of Hatch funds were pleased. The project was a dismal failure.

From the first, the stations were a source of irritation and expense. The Nampa station was 350 miles away; Idaho Falls, 600. Grangeville was a mere 100 miles distant, but accessible only by stagecoach.

With the failure of the school's first attempt to operate agricultural experiment substations around the state in the 1890s, Moscow residents donated land to the college for the University Farm, and much of the school's experimentation has since concentrated on work at the home farm (below and following page).

Communications were slow at best. The university sent assistants to each station, but they had problems. Local merchants would not accept university warrants for supplies, and administrative matters took up most of the assistants' time, leaving little for agricultural work. Local residents felt they had been duped into donating property. "Up to the present time," complained the Blackfoot *Register* in 1893, "the station at this place has been of no practical benefit to the town of Idaho Falls, to the people of Bingham County nor to the state."

Nobody was happy with the arrangement, least of all the federal government. Idaho was not alone in its difficulties with substations. In 1896 the Department of Agriculture prohibited the use of Hatch funds to pay for substation operations. The state refused to make up the difference, and in January 1897 the regents closed the substations in favor of a central farm on the university campus. Moscow residents purchased land for the new farm and donated it to the school.

School administrators then investigated other ways in which the university could reach the state's agricultural community. In 1898 the university began its popular program of offering "farmers' institutes" in remote locations. Faculty experts addressed audiences on state-of-the-art agricultural techniques. The state benefited, and so did its university. The institutes helped refute some of the bitter charges that the school was only a university for the north. Further, many young people who received their initial contact with the university through its institutes later enrolled. Over the years the institutes became increasingly elaborate, reaching thousands of Idahoans. In 1902 the university sponsored sessions in fourteen counties, attended by 5,000 people. In 1904 it hosted thirty sessions; five years later, 159.

Simply getting around the state with all of the equipment necessary to provide practical demonstrations became increasingly difficult, so the school leased rail cars. A 1912 *Argonaut* described the farmers' institute demonstration train:

> The train consists of a flat car arranged for a live stock demonstration and lectures, a large baggage car fitted for live stock, a second baggage car consists of horticultural, grain-growing, smut-treating and dairy exhibits and demonstrations. There are two day coaches for lectures, and a sleeping and dining car for the accomodation [sic] of the party.

These outreach efforts proved so popular that the university sought ways to increase its involvement with the state's agricultural communities. It retained the farmers' institutes and the demonstration trains into the 1920s and added other services as well. In 1910 the school began sponsoring what became widely known as "Moveable Schools of Agriculture," the forerunner of the university's agricultural extension service. While the institutes had provided a scattergun introduction to agricultural problems, the moveable schools were aimed at special areas of concern in particular parts of the state. Rather than giving demonstrations for a day or two and traveling on, the "schools" moved into an area during the winter and stayed for one or two weeks. "Students" attended classes for the entire session, learning from half a dozen or more agricultural experts.

As the extension schools immediately gained recognition and popularity, university administrators explored ways of providing state residents with

Agricultural engineering students inspect soil-erosion control works (1935).

localized service on a more permanent basis. They instituted a system of providing a few expert "field men" who would "go directly into the homes, the orchards, the fields and the stables on the farms, where requested, and demonstrate the best methods to be followed in the various lines of agricultural effort." This plan had obvious merit but one serious drawback: travel was difficult in Idaho, and the university was too far away from many agricultural regions to provide the kind of immediate help farmers often needed. In 1912 William Carlyle, dean of the College of Agriculture, suggested that an agricultural expert be headquartered in each county. Over the years, the "county agent" system became firmly established in virtually all of Idaho's forty-four counties. The university's various extension services, funded in a three-way partnership utilizing county, state, and federal money, have reached into every corner of Idaho, serving not only farm families but town and city residents as well.

As more money became available, the university reactivated its system of branch stations. The first of these second-phase stations was opened in Caldwell in 1906. By 1909 the university operated substations in four locations. Over the years the school abandoned some sites and added new ones, but the second incarnation of the branch station program proved to be permanent. University officials were more cautious in accepting bequests of land than they had been in the 1890s. Each substation had to fulfill a need of Idaho's farmers. Thus by the 1970s the college undertook fruit and vegetable research at Parma, bean experimentation at Kimberly, potato research in Aberdeen, livestock work at Caldwell, and special work on northern Idaho crops in Sandpoint. At perhaps the most unusual branch station, in Tetonia, the university ran nationally recognized experiments in high-altitude agriculture. University scientists also cooperated with federal agencies in operating other experiment stations, such as the United States Sheep Experiment Station in Dubois.

In addition to these specific outreach programs, research scientists at the University of Idaho—both within the College of Agriculture and in other departments—have aided the state's farmers in a myriad of other ways. Indeed, agriculture-related research in such areas as growing potatoes, sugarbeets, and wheat and raising sheep have improved yields and profits for farmers and stockmen throughout the nation. In its first one hundred years, the University of Idaho has truly fulfilled its mission under the Morrill, Hatch, and other federal acts to assist the agriculturalists of Idaho. It is doubtful that there is a farmer in the state—large or small, knowingly or unknowingly—who has not benefited from the university's agricultural outreach.

The university's extension services have also aided farm homemakers. A 1908 farmers' institute meeting in Caldwell attended by over 500 people marked the first time that members of the Department of Domestic Economy gave demonstrations. By 1913 the university boasted that ''the Home Economics work of the Extension Department touches vitally the entire life and development of every community. It is applicable in the home of every citizen of Idaho, no matter what may be his calling, occupation or business.''

Although the first effort failed, the university eventually developed a successful series of agricultural substations in the state, such as the one at Parma (left). DeLance Franklin, superintendent of the Parma branch station, displaying a new type of onion he developed there in 1963 (below).

For nearly 100 years, university student and faculty scientists have undertaken valuable research for the nation's agriculturalists (this and facing page).

In addition to providing programs at the farmers' institutes, home economists met with women's clubs, teachers, and youth groups to provide instruction in cooking, sewing, home management, and a wide variety of other areas. In 1926 Idaho became one of the first states to offer a vacation summer camp for farm women where, in addition to recreation, attendees received instruction in a variety of home economics disciplines. By 1927 over 1,000 women attended four vacation camps, and the idea continued to grow for several decades. At about the same time, the university began offering junior short courses in agriculture and home economics for Idaho youths, the beginning of the important extension services offered to thousands of 4-H members throughout the state in following years. As the idea of county agents became accepted throughout Idaho, the university added home demonstration agents to the staffs in many counties.

Home economics outreach adapted to changing times. For instance, in 1920 the department offered evening classes for women and in the early

The university has offered extension services to thousands of 4-H students in the state, including an annual summer camp at the Moscow campus: morning exercises (facing page, 1923); class in hog judging (above, 1923); tour of the University Farm (left, 1962).

1970s it placed 100 home economics aides in seventeen counties to improve the dietary standards of low-income people. The extension and outreach services of the School of Home Economics have benefited the lives of the state's urban and farm women in ways as diverse and important as the university's agricultural outreach programs.

At first, the university's primary outreach activities centered on agriculture and home economics. By the 1980s the school's services had grown tremendously in variety and impact. A university publication boasted about the school's diverse outreach program:

> A foreign language professor meets regularly with residents of a local nursing home to converse with them in their native tongue, German. A library in southeastern Idaho needs a reference book not available in the community and calls the University of Idaho for a book loan. The citizens of Hayden Lake are concerned that a proposed new sewer line and housing development will destroy archaeological artifacts so they call on the University of Idaho Laboratory of Anthropology to do a preliminary archaeological evaluation.
>
> The University of Idaho is a resource, a reference, a capability upon which the citizens of Idaho can draw.

Most of this outreach work began after World War II, but some predated that period. Two of the best pre-war examples are in the fields of mining and forestry. During World War I the School of Mines conducted a statewide geological survey of minerals that might prove helpful to the war effort. Recognizing the value of this activity, the state in 1919 established the Idaho Bureau of Mines and located it at the university, with the dean of the School of Mines also serving as the bureau's director. Over the years the bureau and the university have jointly undertaken research for Idaho's mining industry.

The School of Mines has offered research and outreach services to the state's mining industry since World War I. Students in training for rescue work in mine disasters (1922).

Students undertaking field work in a mine (1950s).

The School of Forestry, like Mines, conducted experiments from nearly its first days on campus to help both farmers and foresters. In 1911 the Potlatch Lumber Company engaged the school to run a series of experiments on its cutover lands to determine the best methods of removing stumps. As a result of this effort, the school published a bulletin entitled *Methods of Clearing Logged-Off Land* that was widely distributed in the

The university has been a national leader in forestry research and outreach since establishing a forestry department in 1909. Reforestation project with Harrison schoolchildren (1950s).

Slash fire research (above, 1950s); beam testing (right, 1960s).

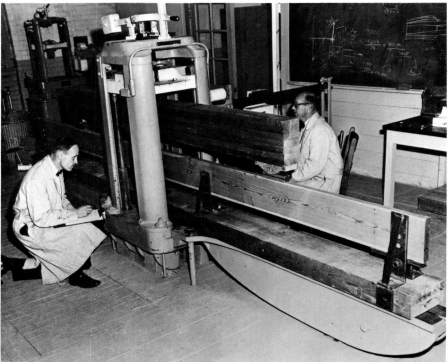

region, and in 1917 it cooperated with Washington State College in sending a "land-clearing" demonstration train through eastern Washington and northern Idaho. By the mid-1920s the school was cooperating with state and federal agencies in the control of white-pine blister rust and in studying woodlots and windbreaks. In 1927 the university named its first extension forester, and about this time, with financial assistance from the Potlatch Company, it began some of the country's earliest experiments on the potential uses of forestry byproducts. In 1928 it established the Idaho Forest Experimentation Station, the precursor to the Forest, Wildlife and Range Experiment Station organized in 1939 "to . . . conduct investigations and research into the forestry, wildlife and range problems of the forest lands of the state." That same year the university appointed its first extension conservationist.

Although a few other departments had outreach programs of varying levels of sophistication, this aspect of service really began to grow in the 1950s. Beginning with the 1949-50 school year, for example, the university started a service of renting films and audio-visual materials to schools and organizations. With the completion of the school's television center in 1955, it began producing a larger quantity of informational films. At the same time, television programming took on added significance, to the

Perry Allen, audio-visual instructor, inspects a film prior to sending it to a school (1959). The university loans audio-visual materials to groups throughout the state.

227

KUID-TV programming reached virtually every corner of the state in the 1970s and 1980s.

extent that KUID-TV programs in the 1970s and 1980s reached virtually every corner of the state. Other innovative outreach programs begun or enhanced in the 1950s included correspondence study; the Play Lending Library, serving schools and groups throughout the state; the annual Summer Institute for High School Teachers of Science and Mathematics; and the Engineering Experiment Station, which conducted research and provided short courses, seminars, and workshops for non-university students. Late in the decade the university established two additional research arms to help other segments of the state's population: the Bureau of Business and Economic Research; and the Bureau of Public Affairs Research.

The university's policy of reaching out to all parts of society perhaps grew more rapidly than any of its other functions in the 1960s, 1970s, and 1980s. Several departments trained high school teachers from throughout the Pacific Northwest to better serve the needs of rural disadvantaged children. The College of Education's Upward Bound program prepared economically and culturally deprived children for college educations. University students earned credit while working in community health and planning agencies throughout the state as part of the federal ACTION volunteer program. Videotaping projects coordinated by the Office of Continuing Education enabled the university to offer credit courses almost everywhere in the state. Continuing Ed also provided advisory services to the Nez Perce Indian tribe in connection with pre-school, youth, and adult programs. The Department of Drama and Speech scheduled annual drama tours, presenting shows at high schools around Idaho. The Department of

Journalism hosted annual high school journalism conferences and institutes. The College of Forestry, Wildlife and Range Sciences sponsored a variety of research efforts at its sixty-five-acre Wilderness Research Center in the heart of the Frank Church–River of No Return Wilderness area. The Idaho Water Resources Research Institute provided training and information. The campus was at times converted into an "Elderhostel" during summers as people over age sixty came to enjoy academic classes and university entertainment. In addition, during much of this period, the university maintained off-campus resident instructional centers in Coeur d'Alene, Boise, Twin Falls, and Idaho Falls with courses and programs in fields such as business, counseling, education, political science, vocational education, and nuclear engineering.

Much of the university's outreach programming has been enhanced by cooperative efforts between it and other colleges and universities. Generations of Idaho and Washington State University students recall relations between the two schools mainly in terms of athletic rivalry. Both of these land-grant schools opened their doors to students in 1892, and, although the Washington institution grew to be twice as large as its Idaho neighbor, they have developed similarly. Despite their proximity, however, the two schools did little in the way of formal cooperative programming until the 1960s, when they cross-listed certain graduate programs, making the unique class offerings of one institution accessible to students of the other. The number of graduate and undergraduate cross-listings accelerated

The Vandaleers have become one of the university's most popular forms of outreach, performing in all parts of Idaho and beyond--including trips in the 1970s to California (above) and South America. They provide the school with invaluable public relations.

The Borah Foundation

It was a most circuitous route, the one that led Salmon O. Levinson to donate $50,000 to the University of Idaho in 1929. Levinson was a wealthy Chicago lawyer, philanthropist, and social icon. He contributed heavily to Hull House, the educational and social improvement center established by his close friend, reformer Jane Addams. He discussed current affairs with another personal friend, philosopher and educator John Dewey. It is doubtful he ever thought much about Idaho. During most of his free time he put his nimble mind to use devising ways to prevent war.

After the concept of a League of Nations floundered in political controversy following World War I, Salmon Levinson began looking for other ways to unite nations against war. Because he spoke from a position of considerable influence, people listened. In fact, Levinson's idea that national governments should condemn war grew into a crusade. All popular movements eventually find politicians willing to help spearhead them, and Idaho's Senator William E. Borah proved very willing to move into this fray.

Borah had spoken out against war before he met Levinson, but by the time the two joined forces in the mid-1920s the senator brought considerable political clout to the union, having just been named chairman of the powerful Senate Foreign Relations Committee. With Borah hammering away from inside the government and Levinson from outside, the anti-war campaign gained such strength that eventually it forced President Calvin Coolidge to take note. So, too, did Secretary of State Frank Kellogg and French Foreign Minister Aristide Briand.

229

In August 1928 *fifteen nations met in Paris and endorsed a treaty renouncing war. Eventually, sixty-four countries signed the agreement, known as the Paris Peace Pact or, more commonly, the Kellogg-Briand Treaty. It was the most popular foreign relations act of the 1920s. Americans and others around the world rejoiced in the belief that nations had finally banished war. A few years later, the whole world learned it was one thing to sign a treaty, quite another to abide by it.*

In the flush of initial victory, however, Salmon O. Levinson sought other means of promoting peace. Less than a year after the Kellogg-Briand Treaty was signed, he donated $50,000 to the University of Idaho to establish the William E. Borah Outlawry of War Foundation. It was the largest endowment gift the university had ever received.

Levinson not only hoped to promote the cause of peace, he wanted to honor his friend and associate, Senator Borah. Borah was a long-time friend of the University of Idaho. His father-in-law, former governor William J. McConnell, was one of the school's founders; Borah himself had been the featured speaker at the first commencement, long before he became a senator. When Levinson searched for an institution in Idaho to house the foundation, the university seemed an obvious choice.

The foundation sponsored its first speaker in 1931 when Harvard University professor Manley Johnson delivered a series of lectures that were later published in a book entitled Progress in International Organization. *In 1938 the foundation brought Eleanor Roosevelt to campus. From these beginnings, the Borah Foundation has grown into one of*

Not only does the university reach out to other parts of the state, but it also provides an exciting setting for field trips. Earl Larrison shows Cub Scouts the mammal collections (1950s).

Cecil Bondurant leads a tour through the radio/television center (1960s).

Fraternities and sororities provide thousands of hours of community outreach service annually, such as landscape work at Moscow's McConnell Mansion (1970s).

the university's most acclaimed means of community and scholarly outreach.

In the late 1940s, the foundation switched to a symposium format. Since that time, dozens of nationally and internationally renowned scholars and statesmen have addressed local audiences and television viewers concerning current affairs of critical importance. Unfortunately, Salmon Levinson's proposal to outlaw war completely failed. Today we look back upon the Kellogg-Briand Treaty with the same sort of whimsical nostalgia that we apply to flappers, flivvers, flasks, and other reminders of that curious decade, the 1920s. But Levinson's endowment to the University of Idaho has flourished. Perhaps it has done little to prevent war, but the Borah Foundation has broadened the viewpoints of the thousands who have attended, listened to, or read about its sessions. Understanding always begins with knowledge. Surely Salmon Levinson and William Borah would be pleased were they here to view the result of their efforts.

through the 1970s and into the 1980s but attracted only limited student attention because the two universities had different academic calendars—Idaho beginning in August and Washington State in September. In the mid-1980s WSU changed its schedule to match Idaho's, and the idea of a "University of the Palouse" gained strength. There was no discussion of joint governing bodies, but laboratory, library, telecommunication, and

The University of Idaho held the first summer school ever sponsored in the Pacific Northwest in 1899. Since that time, the summer-school sessions have taught thousands of youngsters and adults.

other facilities have been increasingly shared in a venture of cooperation that has attracted national attention. At a considerable cost savings, and at no additional expense to students who now have access to two modern university campuses, the University of Idaho and Washington State University have found ways to bridge state borders to provide better educational training to thousands of college students.

At the same time, the university increased its cooperative efforts with Idaho schools. Idaho, Idaho State, and Boise State universities jointly sponsored workshops and conferences and shared in research projects. The university assisted North Idaho College by offering programs on its Coeur d'Alene campus. Lewis-Clark State College and Idaho cooperated in providing computer training for farmers. Together the university and the College of Southern Idaho presented courses on farm management. At the Idaho Falls off-campus center, Ricks College, Brigham Young University, and Idaho State University joined Idaho in providing instructional programs.

Agriculture, forestry, home economics, mining, drama, journalism, education, telecommunications—all these fields and more have been the recipients of the University of Idaho's outreach services. Of course, in many ways the school's strongest form of outreach has come with the placing of nearly 60,000 college graduates in positions throughout the world. Beyond this, however, the University of Idaho has always been an institution involved in providing services to isolated communities and families. It is unlikely that any other state institution has had a longer, more dynamic, or more important impact upon Idaho's people and economy.

A Note on Sources

This history was written in a twelve-month period in 1985 and 1986. The amount of time allowed for undertaking research, uncovering illustrations, and writing was of necessity short, as university officials wished to publish the book before the beginning of the school's centennial observance in January 1988. As a result of this time constraint, as well as the nature of this project as a popular history for the general public, no effort was made to undertake research in all of the rich primary resources available to scholars concerning the university, particularly at the University of Idaho Library's Special Collections and Archives. This brief essay, however, should provide future researchers with a starting point for understanding the school's history. Unless otherwise noted, all unpublished materials can be found in Special Collections. The letters "MG" following some citations refer to its manuscript group number. At the time research for this project was undertaken, many records in Special Collections were being reclassified, so MG numbers were not yet available for some of the following citations. Finding aids are available at Special Collections to assist future researchers. All published materials can be found in the university library's general collection or in Special Collections.

The most comprehensive history of Idaho is in the first two volumes of Merrill Beal and Merle Wells's *History of Idaho* (New York: Lewis Historical Publishing Co., 1959), which contains considerable information on the formation of the state's higher-education system. For background on Idaho State University and its history as a branch of the University of Idaho, see Beal's *History of Idaho State College* (Pocatello: Idaho State College, 1952).

The following provide helpful background on the Moscow and Latah County areas, as well as general information on the development of the university: W. G. Emery, "A History of Moscow, Idaho," an 1897 newspaper supplement available at the Latah County Historical Society; *An Illustrated History of North Idaho* (Chicago: Western Publishers, Inc., 1903); Charles J. Munson, *Westward to Paradise* (Moscow: Latah County Historical Society, 1978); Homer David, *Moscow at the Turn of the Century* (Moscow: Latah County Historical Society, 1979); and issues of *Latah Legacy, The Quarterly Journal of the Latah County Historical Society*.

Carol Ryrie Brink's novel of early Moscow, *Buffalo Coat* (New York: The Macmillan Co., 1944; rprnt, Latah County Historical Society, 1980), contains entertaining and largely accurate information on the founding of the university, as does her unpublished typescript "A Chain of Hands," available at the Latah County Historical Society. For the economic relationship between the university and the community in more recent times see Michael J. Bosch, "The Economic Impact of the On-Campus Research Effort of the University of Idaho on the Community of Moscow, Idaho," master's thesis, University of Idaho, 1976; and K. R. Stafford, et al., *The Economic Impact of the University of Idaho on the Community of Moscow, Idaho* (Moscow: Idaho Research Foundation, 1974).

The most accessible work for those interested in general background to the university's history is Rafe Gibbs, *Beacon for Mountain and Plain: Story of the*

University of Idaho (Moscow: University of Idaho, 1962). Also valuable are the Gibbs papers (MG 49), which contain materials Gibbs gathered for the writing of his book—including reminiscences of several people long associated with the institution. In 1936 Paris Martin wrote "History of the University of Idaho"; and in 1939 Cornelius J. Brosnan wrote "From Enabling Act to University: A Half Century of Advancement, University of Idaho, 1889-1939," followed in 1952 by his massive "History of the University of Idaho." All three are unpublished but invaluable sources of information. Also very helpful are Harrison C. Dale, *Statutes and Decisions Relating to the University of Idaho* (Moscow: University of Idaho, 1944); Jess D. Rhodes, "The Transition of the University of Idaho From a Pre-University to a University Organization: A Preliminary Survey of the First Quarter Century, 1889-1913," master's thesis, University of Idaho, 1952; and Michael G. Ryan, "The Historic Origins of the University of Idaho," master's thesis, University of Idaho, 1939.

Surprisingly, very little has yet been published in journals on the university's history. Among the useful articles to appear to date are Jesse Buchanan, "Higher Education in the Palouse Hills: Why Do Washington State University and Idaho Rub Shoulders?" *The Pacific Northwesterner* (Spring 1980): 17-27; and Lois A. Fisher, "The Role of Politics in the Organization and Development of Public Higher Education in Idaho and Washington," *History of Higher Education Annual* (1985): 111-132.

The Bookmark, a journal published by the university library, frequently carries articles relating to the school's history and in addition serves as a primary source detailing the growth of the library. More detail on the library's history can be found in Robert D. Hook and Richard J. Beck, "The University of Idaho Library: A History," typescript, 1986. For specifics about other university schools and colleges see Florence Aller, *75 Years to Remember: Home Economics at the University of Idaho, 1902-1977* (Moscow: University of Idaho School of Home Economics, 1977); George Savage, *The University of Idaho College of Forestry, Wildlife and Range Sciences: 1909-1984—An Album* (Moscow: University of Idaho College of Forestry, Wildlife and Range Sciences, 1985); "Highlights in the History of the College of Law," typescript, c. 1985, housed at the College of Law; J. H. Forney, "The First Steps Toward Establishing a Law School at the University of Idaho," typescript, 1908 (MG 5008); the papers of Robert Milliken, the first director of the Idaho Agricultural Experiment Stations (MG 5014); and the transcript of a 1939 radio broadcast relating the history of Idaho's agricultural outreach activities, available in collection SC/UNI-3 at the Latah County Historical Society.

The largest group of papers concerning the school's development are those from the Office of the President, University Group no. 12, which were still being processed as this project was undertaken and were therefore used only sparingly. University administrators naturally make regular reports of activities. Over the years these have been published in volumes with varying titles, including the *Annual Report of the University of Idaho to the Governor and the Board of Regents*; the university's section in the *Biennial Reports of the*

State Board of Education; and the *President's Annual Report*. These contain useful synopses of administrative history and campus development. Researchers should also see Blaine Stubblefield, ed., "History of the University of Idaho, 1889-1924," typescript, 1924 (MG 5143); Ronald Magden, "The Political Background of the Location of the University of Idaho," typescript, 1954 (MG 5009); the transcript of an interview with J. H. Forney by E. R. Chrisman in 1935; and the Edward M. Hulme scrapbooks of clippings relating to the university (MG 42). Special Collections also has many unprocessed small collections of publications and memorabilia placed in general files under the names of campus organizations, living groups, and departments.

The best sources on campus life are the various student publications, most particularly the student newspaper, *The Argonaut*, published since 1898, and the yearbook, *Gem of the Mountains*, published since 1903. The university library maintains an index to the *Argonaut*. Also very helpful are issues of two campus literary magazines published in the period from the 1920s to the 1950s: *The Idaho Blue Bucket* and *The Blot*. For historical background on these publications see Robert M. Finlayson, "The Idaho Blue Bucket: A Short History of Its Birth and Death," typescript, 1950; Orval Hansen, "History of the Idaho Argonaut," typescript, c. 1947; Frances Hanley, "History of the Idaho Argonaut," typescript, n.d.; and William D. Hansen, "A Short History of the Gem of the Mountains," typescript, 1950.

Among the faculty members who have left written accounts of their time at Idaho are Charles A. Peters, "The University of Idaho and Charles A. Peters," typescript, n.d.; Frederic C. Church, diaries; Jay Glover Eldridge, diaries; and Martin A. Larson, *Plaster Saint: A Novel of Heresy on the Campus* (New York: Exposition Press, 1953), a highly charged and entertaining novel by a disenchanted member of the English department in the 1920s. Minutes of faculty meetings dating from 1892 are in the registrar's office, while minutes of the Faculty Women's Club for selected years are in Special Collections.

Papers of the Women's Caucus (MG 109) provide insight into the affirmative action battles on campus in the 1970s. Materials relating to campus observances of Religious Emphasis Week can be found in MG 5106. Materials relating to the formation of a local chapter of the Phi Beta Kappa national honorary are in MG 61. Two helpful manuscripts about campus life during wartime are Howard C. Sarvis's "The Army and the University, 1918," typescript, 1984 (MG 5118); and Carla Rotert's "The University of Idaho During the World War II Years," typescript, 1968 (MG 5132). Also helpful are the materials in MG 5021 relating to the 1941 "Bundles for Britain" drive.

Information about other aspects of campus life can be found in a variety of places. Indispensable are the several student scrapbooks housed both at Special Collections and at the Latah County Historical Society in its manuscript collection on "University Student Life." Many of these scrapbooks contain diaries. Also available at the historical society are brochures, memorabilia, flyers, and the like in the University of Idaho Archives and the Gelwick Family Archives. Additionally, the society retains the papers and records of Tau Mem Aleph, an organization of university men not living in fraternities and sororities. The latter is in collection SC/TAU-1. The historical society's large oral history collection is also rich in interviews conducted with people associated with the university. Among the interviews utilized during this project—all of which have been transcribed—were those with the following individuals: Louis Boas, Carol Ryrie Brink, Gustav Carlson, Lola Gamble Clyde, Abe McGregor Goff, Della Beardsley Johnson, George "Hap" Moody, Theodore Sherman, Mi Lew, Lillian Woodworth Otness, Eugene Settle, and Margaret Wilson Schimke.

Special Collections maintains a complete file of student handbooks that delineate changes in campus norms over time. Also useful in understanding student life are the reminiscences of Hardit Singh Dhillon (MG 5103); Dhillon's *American College Life: A Record of Personal Experiences and Impressions* (Delhi, India: Uttar Chand Kapur and Sons, 1953[?]); Minnie Galbreath Marcy, *History of the Class of 1901, University of Idaho* (privately printed, 1951); J. Morris O'Donnell, compiler, *Songs of the Vandals* (Caldwell, Id.: The Caxton Printers, 1933); and the papers of Margaret McCallie Moore (MG 5159).

The outstanding reference on the history of the university's buildings and grounds is "University of Idaho Buildings History," typescript, 1953. Also invaluable is the section on the university in Lillian W. Otness, *A Great Good Country: A Guide to Historic Moscow and Latah County, Idaho* (Moscow: Latah County Historical Society, 1983). Information on university landscaping and plantings can be found in correspondence between Olmsted Brothers, Landscape Architects, Brookline, Massachusetts, and university officials for the years 1907-1920. Original copies of this correspondence are in the Olmsted Papers, Library of Congress, File 3275, container B 222. Photocopies are at the Idaho State Historical Society (MS 531). Also see *Shattuck Arboretum and Botanical Garden: Master Plan Report* (Boise: Richard Carothers Associates, 1980). For some specific buildings see the materials on the David Memorial Carillon in MG 5093; Keith C. Petersen and Carol Young, "Historic Structures Report: The Blue Bucket Inn," Latah County Historical Society collection SC/PET-6; and Mrs. S. P. Davis and Mrs. J. J. Anthony, "The Administration Building of 1892," Latah County Historical Society collection SC/DAV-2.

Information on some of the university's better-known personalities can be found in the following sources. The Latah County Historical Society's collection SC/BRI-3 contains a scrapbook of clippings and other materials relating to university founder John Warren Brigham. Leslie V. Brock's "Lawrence Henry Gipson, Historian: The Early Idaho Years," *Idaho Yesterdays* (Summer 1978): 2-9, 27-31; Evelyn Rodewald's "The Life of Frederic C. Church," *Latah Legacy, The Quarterly Journal of the Latah County Historical Society* (Spring 1982): 15-24; and William Ratigan's *Highways Over Broad Waters: Life and Times of David B. Steinman, Bridgebuilder* (Grand Rapids, Mi.: William B. Eerdmans Publishing Co., 1959) provide information on three of the school's most distinguished faculty members. Dick d'Easum's *Dowager of*

Discipline: The Life of Dean of Women Permeal French (Moscow: University Press of Idaho, 1981) is a popular biography. Material concerning long-time military commandant Edward R. Chrisman is in MG 5015. MG 5035 and MG 5095 contain biographical information on Salmon O. Levinson, founder of the Borah Foundation. Materials concerning university graduate—and long-time United States Congressman—Burton French can be found in MG 55 and in the Latah County Historical Society's collection SC/FRE-2. The historical society also maintains a considerable collection of materials relating to Carol Ryrie Brink in its Brink Archives, as well as copies of most of her published works. For additional information on Brink see the following writings by Mary E. Reed: "Carol Ryrie Brink, Our Idaho Author," *Latah Legacy, The Quarterly Journal of the Latah County Historical Society* (Spring 1982): 1-9; "Carol Ryrie Brink: Idaho Novelist," *Plainswoman* (Jan. 1983): 3-6; and "Folklore in Regional Literature: Carol Brink's *Buffalo Coat*," in Louie W. Attebery, ed., *Idaho Folklife: Homesteads to Headstones* (Salt Lake City: University of Utah Press; Boise: Idaho State Historical Society, 1985): 216-222. For Olympic champion Alfred C. Gilbert, who was inspired to take up pole vaulting after watching University of Idaho athletes, see A. C. Gilbert with Marshall McClintock, *The Man Who Lives in Paradise* (New York: Rinehart & Co., 1954), and Keith C. Petersen, "A. C. Gilbert: Millionaire with Moscow Roots," *Latah Legacy, The Quarterly Journal of the Latah County Historical Society* (Summer 1979): 22-28.

For further information on Idaho athletics see MG 5043, which contains a reminiscence by the university's first track coach, M. G. Arnold; MG 5072, which has background information on naming Idaho's teams the "Vandals"; MG 5080, which holds correspondence relating to the effort to have Vandal basketball star Al Fox admitted to the National Basketball Hall of Fame; and Don Theophilus, Jr., "Boxing at the University of Idaho," typescript, c. 1953.

Photograph Credits

In the following notations, the University of Idaho Library's Special Collections and Archives Department is abbreviated as UISC. The Latah County Historical Society is abbreviated as LCHS.

Page 1
UISC 1–52–51
Page 2
UISC 1–2–26
Page 3
UISC 1–128–17
Page 4
Left, UI Publications
Right, UISC 1–61–11
Page 5
Above, UISC 1–110–2
Below, UISC 1–99–8
Page 6
Left, UISC 1–100–2
Right, UISC 1–89–4
Page 7
Left, UISC 1–58–4
Right, UI Publications
Page 8
Above, UISC 1–6–3
Below, UISC 1–99–7
Page 9
UISC 1–52–20
Page 10
Above, UISC 1–52–13
Below, UISC 1–52–60
Page 11
Above, UISC 1–112–3
Below, UISC 1–112–4
Page 12
Above, UISC 1–52–22
Below, UISC 1–66–12
Page 13
Above, UISC 1–104–3
Below, UISC 1–74–32
Page 15
UISC 6–10–1

Page 16
Left, UISC 3–148b
Right, UISC 6–10–1
Page 17
Idaho State Historical Society
1148–5
Page 18
Above, LCHS 1–2–21
Below, LCHS 1–2–40
Page 19
UISC 3–8a
Page 20
UISC 3–8b
Page 21
UISC 1–75–8
Page 23
UISC 1–105–15
Page 24
UISC 1–105–15
Page 25
UISC 1–2–8
Page 26
Left, LCHS Individual File ''F''
Right, UISC 3–4e
Page 27
UISC 2–124–1
Page 28
UISC 1–51–9
Page 29
Idaho State Historical Society
78–2.96
Page 30
UISC 1–51–7
Page 31
Left, UISC 1–51–32
Sidebar, UISC 2–109–74
Page 32
Above, UISC 1–51–22
Below, UISC 1–201–28
Page 33
Above, UISC 1–55–1
Below, UISC 1–105–1
Page 34
Above, UISC 1–105–7
Below, UISC 1–94–14

Page 35
UISC 1–210–11a
Page 36
Above, UISC 1–58–7
Below, UISC 1–58–18
Page 37
UISC 1–56–24
Page 38
Above, UISC 1–214–6
Below, UISC 2–141–48e
Page 39
UISC 2–119–1
Page 40
UISC 2–76–1
Page 41
Left, UISC 2–76–26
Sidebar, UISC 6–187–1
Page 42
UISC, uncataloged
Page 43
LCHS 17–3–14
Page 44
UISC 1–51–24
Page 45
Above, UISC 1–51–31
Below, UISC 1–51–30a
Page 46
LCHS 1–3–40
Page 47
UISC Scrapbook LD/2327.7/
1911/P48
Page 48
UISC 1–54–4
Page 49
Above, LCHS 1–6–42
Below, UISC 1–54–6
Page 50
Above, UISC 1–66–11
Below, UISC 1–205–36
Page 51
Above, UISC 1–52–73
Below, UISC 1–52–4

Page 52
Sidebar, UISC Scrapbook LD/
2327.7/1911/P48
Above, UISC 1–52–8
Below, UISC 1–206–4
Page 53
Above, UISC 1–60–2
Below, UISC 1–60–12
Page 54
Sidebar, UISC 3–36a
Above, UISC 1–67–3
Below, UISC 1–67–11
Page 55
Above, UISC 1–70–1
Below, UISC 1–201–27
Page 56
Above, UISC 1–122–1
Below, UISC 1–222–20
Page 57
Above, UISC 1–74–21
Below, UISC 1–74–9
Page 58
Above, UISC 1–117–1
Below, UISC 1–89–2
Page 59
Above, UISC 2–143–16
Below, UISC 1–128–18
Page 60
Above, UISC 1–139–3
Below, UISC 1–139–2a
Page 61
UISC 1–147–13
Page 62
UISC 3–118a
Page 63
Above, UISC 2–88–6
Below, UISC 2–88–3
Page 64
Above, UISC 1–205–13
Below, UISC 2–86–3
Page 65
Left, UISC 1–219–1
Sidebar, LCHS Shattuck Glass
Negative Collection

Page 66
Sidebar, UISC 1–218–8
Page 67
UISC 1–241–36
Page 68
Left, UISC 3–2a
Right, UISC 3–21f
Page 69
Above, UISC 2–109–15
Below left, UISC 3–43f
Below right, UISC 3–5f
Page 70
UISC 3–36o
Page 71
Left, UI Alumni Center
Right, UISC 2–140–1
Page 72
Above, UISC 3–469l
Below, UISC 1–104–4
Page 73
Left, UISC 2–217–1
Right, UISC 3–758f
Page 74
Left, UISC 2–141–115b
Right, UISC 1–211–16
Page 75
UI Publications
Page 77
UISC 2–143–8
Page 78
UISC 2–88–19
Page 79
UISC 2–88–34
Page 80
Above, UI Publications
Below, UISC 2–78–18
Page 81
Left, UISC 2–78–11
Right, UI Publications
Page 82
UISC 2–149–1
Page 83
Left, UISC 1–112–1
Right, UISC 1–52–32
Page 84
UISC 2–89–1
Page 85
Above, UISC 1–101–3
Below, UISC 1–102–3
Page 86
UISC 2–144–1
Page 87
UISC 1–58–24b
Page 88
Above, UISC 2–81–9
Below, UISC 1–230–1

Page 89
Above, UISC 2–101–4
Below, UISC 1–142–4
Page 90
Above, UISC 2–97–1
Below, UISC 2–95–1
Page 91
Above, UISC 2–104–1
Below, UISC 2–44–2
Page 92
UISC 2–99–4
Page 93
Above, UISC 2–99–55c
Below, UISC 2–99–32
Page 94
UISC 2–141–131e
Page 95
Above, UISC 2–85–1
Below, UI Publications
Page 96
Sidebar, UISC 2–143–11
Right, UISC 2–143–8
Page 97
Left, UISC 1–6–8
Sidebar, UISC 2–143–15a
Page 98
Above, UISC 1–59–10
Below, UISC 6–8–2
Page 99
Left, UISC 2–119–2
Below, UISC 1–62–12
Page 100
Sidebar, UISC 1–71–7
Above right, UISC 1–214–6
Below right, UISC 2–13–2
Page 101
Above, UISC 2–48–5
Below, UI Publications
Page 102
UISC 2–12–8
Page 103
Left, UISC 2–83–1
Sidebar, UISC 1–95–5
Page 104
Sidebar, UISC 1–95–1
Right, UISC 1–170–2
Page 105
UI Publications
Page 106
UISC 2–106–1
Page 107
UISC 2–109–48
Page 108
UISC 2–109–33
Page 109
UISC 2–109–192

Page 111
UI Alumni Center
Page 112
UISC 2–118–1
Page 113
Above, UISC 2–115–2
Below, UISC 2–115–16
Page 114
UISC 3–537b
Page 115
LCHS Individual File "E"
Page 116
UISC 3–327d
Page 117
Above, UISC 2–115–30
Below, UISC 2–115–54
Page 118
Sidebar, UISC 2–115–123
Above right, UISC 2–115–136
Below right, UI Sports Information Office
Page 119
Above, UISC 2–116–59
Below, UISC 2–116–25
Page 120
Above, UISC 2–116–29
Below, UISC 2–116–26
Page 121
Left, UI Sports Information Office
Right, UI Sports Information Office
Page 122
Above, UISC 2–153–1
Below, UISC 2–117–1
Page 123
Above, UISC 2–127–2
Below, UISC 2–128–3
Page 124
UISC 2–118–6
Page 125
UISC 2–125–33
Page 126
Sidebar, UISC 2–125–3
Right, UISC 2–165–2
Page 127
UISC 3–264b
Page 128
UI Publications
Page 130
UISC 1–231–13
Page 131
Above, UISC 2–182–12
Below, UISC 1–231–11
Page 132
Above, UISC 2–182–5
Below, UISC 2–108–137

Page 133
Above, UISC 2–182–2
Below, UISC 2–193–1
Page 134
UI Sports Information Office
Page 135
UI Sports Information Office
Page 136
UISC 2–154–6
Page 137
Above, UISC 2–164–1
Below, UISC 2–164–4
Page 138
Above, UISC 1–85–1
Below, UISC 1–85–7
Page 139
UISC 1–147–11
Page 140
UISC 2–129–2
Page 141
Left, UISC 2–129–13
Sidebar, UI Publications
Page 142
Above, UISC 2–132–6
Sidebar, UI Publications
Page 143
Above, UISC 2–108–29
Below, UISC 2–84–71c
Page 144
UISC 2–108–3
Page 145
Above, UISC 2–108–25
Below, UISC 2–218–1
Page 146
UISC 2–133–8
Page 147
Above left, UISC 2–115–70
Below left, UISC 2–163–5
Below right, UI Publications
Page 148
Above, UISC 2–84–13
Below, UISC 2–84–4
Page 149
Left, UISC 2–84–1
Sidebar, UI Sports Information Office
Page 150
UISC 2–102–6b
Page 151
UISC 2–102–9
Page 152
UISC 1–88–6
Page 153
Above, Bill McGowan Photograph Collection
Below, UISC 2–115–153

Page 155
UISC 1–208–127
Page 156
UISC 1–208–47
Page 157
UISC 1–208–5
Page 158
Above, UISC 1–208–22
Below, UISC 1–208–21
Page 159
UISC 1–208–1
Page 160
Sidebar, 1919 *Gem of the Mountains*, p. 44
Right, UISC 1–208–8
Page 161
Above, UISC 1–208–25
Below, UISC 1–208–2
Page 162
UISC 3–47a
Page 163
UISC 1–76–5
Page 164
Above, UISC 6–5–5
Below, LCHS 1–2–62
Page 165
Above, UISC 6–5–2
Below, UISC 6–5–11
Page 166
UISC 1–99–2
Page 167
1920 *Gem of the Mountains*, p. 31
Page 168
UISC 6–3–1a
Page 169
LCHS 1–2–22
Page 170
Above, UISC 1–61–3
Below, UISC 1–61–9
Page 171
LCHS 1–6–33
Page 172
UISC 6–1–1
Page 173
Above, UISC 6–4–1
Below, UISC 2–107–1
Page 174
UISC 6–4–20b
Page 175
Above, UISC 6–4–18
Below, UISC 2–109–40

Page 176
LCHS Subject File "World War II"
Page 177
Above left, UISC 1–240–1
Below left, UISC 2–141–112d
Sidebar, UISC 1–117–19a
Page 178
Sidebar, UISC 2–19–4
Above right, LCHS Subject File "World War II"
Below right, LCHS Subject File "World War II"
Page 179
UISC 1–208–61
Page 180
Above, UISC 1–221–24
Below, UISC 1–224–22
Page 181
Above, UISC 1–221–31
Below, UISC 2–255–3
Page 182
Above, UISC 1–120–2
Below, UISC 1–120–3
Page 183
Above, UISC 1–90–2
Below, UISC 1–64–2
Page 184
UISC 2–119–4
Page 185
Above, UI Publications
Below, UISC 2–147–1
Page 186
Left, UI Publications
Right, UISC 2–216–3
Page 187
Above, UISC 1–83–2
Below, UISC 1–83–3a
Page 189
UI Publications
Page 190
UISC 2–122–1
Page 191
Above, UISC 1–59–1
Below, UISC 1–59–9
Page 193
Above, UISC 1–221–1
Below, UISC 1–221–2

Page 194
Sidebar, UISC 2–91–2
Right, UISC 1–221–53
Page 195
UI Publications
Page 196
Above, UISC 1–106–2
Below, UISC 1–153–1
Page 197
UI Alumni Center
Page 198
Sidebar, 1919 *Gem of the Mountains*, p. 33
Right, UISC 1–221–12
Page 199
Above, UISC 1–210–14a
Below, UISC 1–210–19
Page 200
Sidebar, LCHS Individual File "Brink"
Above right, UISC 2–99–56
Below right, UISC 2–142–3
Page 201
Above, UISC 2–151–2b
Below, UISC 2–109–197
Page 202
Sidebar, LCHS Individual File "Brink"
Right, UISC 1–221–76
Page 204
UISC 3–6b
Page 205
Above, UISC 2–99–48
Below, UISC 2–99–2
Page 206
Left, UI Publications
Right, UISC 3–22c
Page 207
UISC Manuscript Group 5903
Page 208
Left, UISC 3–241a
Above right, UISC 1–222–35
Below right, UISC 2–142–17
Page 209
UI Publications
Page 210
UISC 2–142–9

Page 211
Left, UI Publications
Sidebar, UISC 2–110–1
Page 213
UI Alumni Center
Page 214
UISC 6–2–1
Page 215
UISC 1–1–2
Page 216
Above, UISC 1–105–3
Below, UISC 1–105–13
Page 218
UISC 1–217–4
Page 219
Left, UISC 6–48–1
Right, UISC 3–1013a
Page 220
Above, UISC 1–212–5
Below, UISC 1–206–9
Page 221
Above, UISC 1–217–12
Below, UI Publications
Page 222
UISC 4–1–5
Page 223
Above, UISC 4–1–8
Below, UISC 4–1–32e
Page 224
UISC 1–223–1
Page 225
Above, UISC 1–223–21
Below, UISC 1–218–27
Page 226
Above, UISC 4–14–4
Below, UISC 1–218–41
Page 227
UISC 3–834a
Page 228
UI Publications
Page 229
UI Alumni Center
Page 230
Above, UISC 1–214–22
Below, UISC 3–968a
Page 231
UI Publications
Page 232
UISC 1–222–1

Index

Citations with an asterisk (*) refer to references within a sidebar. Citations in parentheses refer to photographs.

Academy of Idaho. See Idaho State University
Adair, Arthur Prentiss, 190, (190)
Adair, Bernadine, 106
Administration Building (first), (2), 7, 25, (25), 27, 28, (28), 29, (30), 31–33, (31), (32), 37, 43*, 44, (44), (45), 46, (46), 48, 49, 61, 166, 190
Administration Building (second), (1), 3, 7, 8–9, (9), (10), (11), (12), 46, 48, 49, 51, (51), 51–52*, (52), 59, 167, (171), 172, 174, (176), 194, (222)
Affirmative Action, 73, 203
Agricultural Experiment Stations, 29, 42, 214–219, (219). See also University Farm
Agricultural Extension Service, 217–219, 222, (222), (223)
Agriculture, College of, 33, 37, 39, 48–49, 61–62, 64*, 73, 167, 214, 218, 219
Agriculture Department. See Agriculture, College of
Aldrich, Larry, 128
Alexander, Moses, 65*, 67–68
Allen, Perry, (227)
Allen, Stella Maude, 190, (190)
Alumni Association, 64
American College Life (book), 207–208
Amphyctyon Literary Society, 82
Anderson, Wayne, 151*
Andros, Dee, 129, 151*
Annex Building, 33, (33), 35
Arboretum. See Shattuck Arboretum
Archer, J.D., 103*
Argonaut, 104-105, (105), 107–108, 160–165*, 177
Armstrong, Charles, 160

Army Specialized Training Program (World War II), 176
Arnold, M. G., 114
Arrington, Leonard, (99)
Art and Architecture South Building. See Gymnasium
Associated Students University of Idaho, 105*, 107–108, 156, 167, 184, 195*,197*
Associated Women Students, 176, 197, 198, 203
Athletic Board, 194–198*, (194)
August, Louis, 124, 125, 126*, 128*
Axtell, Harold, 48
Ayers, George, 68

Baker, Hugh, 106*
Ball, Gary, 151*
Baseball, 114, (122), 129
Basketball, 114–115, 117–118*, 119, (119), (120), 121, (121), 127–130, (131), 131–132, 134, (135), 135–136, 151*
Beck, Earl, (122)
Beta Sigma Sorority. See Delta Gamma Sorority
Bechtholdt, Nancy, 134
Berggren, Eirik, 126
Besse, Alice, 144
Beta Theta Pi Fraternity, 100
Big Sky Conference, 129, 139
Black Student Union, 212
Blake, Henry, 24
Blanton, Joseph P., 42, 166
The Blot (magazine), 104
Blue Bucket Inn, 14, 92, 94–97*, (96), 181, 204
Blue Bucket Magazine, 94*, 104
Blue Mountain Rock Festival, 96
Boise Junior College. See Boise State University
Boise State College. See Boise State University
Boise State University, 66, 232
Bondurant, Cecil, (230)

Bookstore, 14, (71), 97*, (97)
Borah Foundation, 54*, 229–231*
Borah, William E., 229–231*
Bowman, Annette, 28, 42*, 192
Bowman, Lewis, (122)
Boxing, 124–125, (125), 126–129*
Bradetich, Pam, 134
Brannon, Melvin A., 61, 65*, 67–68, (68), 98, 108
Brigham, John Warren, (19), 19–21*, 20, (20)
Brigham, Morton, 20*
Brigham, Nellie Wilson, 19–20*
Brink, Carol Ryrie, 160*, 200–205*, (200), (202)
Brink Hall, 205*
Brink, Raymond, 202–203*
Brown, Nellie, 28, 192
Brown, Steve, 129
Brude, Jeff, 151*
Buchanan, Jesse E., 71, (71), 103, 138, 142*, 177*
Business and Economic Research, Bureau of, 228
Butler, Ken, 125

Campus Club, 100*, 176
Campus Christian Center, 14, 103, (103)
Campus Day. See May Fete
Carlson, Herb, 125, 128*
Carlyle, William, 218
Carnegie Library (Moscow), 48, (49), 205*
Catholic Institute of Religious Education, 103
Chrisemon, Lewis E., 209–212*
Chrisman, Edward R., 156, (157), 160, (162), 162–163, 188
Chrisman Hall, 54, 104*, (163), 174, 186
Church, Frank, 54*
Cipriano, Joe, 129, 151*
Clark, Chase, 210
Cleaver, Don, 116*

Coalition for Peace and Survival, 188
Cockrell, David, (95)
Co-ed Prom, 91, 94, (205)
Cogswell, Isaac, (89)
College Girls' Club, 99*
College of Idaho, 29*, 30*
College of Southern Idaho, 232
Company C, University Cadets, 160 (160)
Continuing Education, Office of, 228
Cooperatives, 98–100*, 99
Corbett, Florence. See Johnson, Florence Corbett
Craig, Knox, 210–211
Crisis Line, 109
Crockett, R. M., 42*
Cross Country, 116*, 119, 124, 127
Cuddy, Marie, (89)
Curtis, Charles, 53*
Curtis, Robert, (149), 149–152*
Cushman, Harriet E., 191–192

David Family, 9
David, Homer, 33
Dale, Harrison C., 54*, 61, 70, (70), 100*, 183, 210
Daleth Teth Gimel (women's honorary), 203
Deakin, James, 24, 25
d'Easum, Dick, 203
Delta Gamma Sorority, 100, 167
Denten, Louie, 125
Dhillon, Hardit Singh, 207–208, (207)
Dobratz, Pat, 134
Domestic Economy Department. See Home Economics, School of
Domestic Science Department. See Home Economics, School of
Douglas, Sallie Hume, 144
Drama and Speech Department, 228

Draper, Paul, (157), 165–166
Dubois, Fred T., 17, (17), 19, 20, 21
Dyrgall, Vic, 124

Edmundson, Clarence S., 114–115, (115), 115–118*, (118)
Education Building, (60)
Education, College of, 228
Eldridge, Jay Glover, 14, 44
Electrical Engineering Department, 167
Engineering Building, 7, (25), (37), (92), 194
Engineering, College of, 71
Enquist, Harold (179)
Engineering Experiment Station, 228
Erickson, Dennis, 130
Erickson, Laurie, 125, 128*

Faculty Club Building. See Satellite Student Union Building
Faculty Women's Club, 99, 167, 181
Farmers' Institutes, 217
Field Hockey, (132), 133
Football, 112–113, (113), 114, 115–116, (116), 117, (117), (118), 121, 127–129, 135, 136, 149–152, 150–151*, 177*
Forest Experimentation Station. See Forest, Wildlife and Range Experiment Station
Forest, Wildlife and Range Experiment Station, 227
Forestry Department. See Forestry, Wildlife and Range Sciences, College of
Forestry, Wildlife and Range Sciences, College of, 62–65*, 224, 225-227, (225), (226), 229
Forney Hall, 53, (53), 176
Forney, James H., 26, (26), 27, 30–31, 214
Forney, Mrs. James H., 42*
Fox, Al, 119, (119), 121, 130
Fox, Richard, 119
Franklin, DeLance, (219)
Fraternities, 99–100, 102, 168, 168*, 176. See also names of specific fraternities
French, Burton, 8, (82), 105
French House, 204
French, Permeal, 14, 92, 94–97*, 169–170*, 200–201, 203–204, (204)

Gamma Phi Beta Sorority, 100
Gault, Franklin B., 26–28, (26), 30, 39–40, 41–42, 42*, 144, 162, 190, 192
Gault Hall, (103), 103–106*, (104)
Gee–Eyes Right (play), 177–178, (177)
Geidt, Jerry, 151*
Gem of the Mountains, 104, 106, 177
Ghormley, Robert L., 160
Gibb, Richard D., 73–74, (75), 136
Gibbs, Rafe, 2
Gibson, C. W., (82)
GI Bill, 65, 182
Gilbert, Alfred Carlton, 112
Gipson, Lawrence Henry, 28–31*, (29), (31)
Golf Course, 4, (5), 140–142*, (141), (142)
Gooding, Frank, 48
"Go, Vandals, Go" (song), 144
Great Depression, 69, 94, 98–100*, 99
Greenslet, Edmund, (122)
Gymnasium, 37, (48), (49), 121, 140, 168

Habib, Philip, 54*
Hagberg, Ole G., (157), 165–166, 206, (206)
Hall, Mary, see Niccolls, Mary Hall
Hamblin, Gene, 151*
Hartung, Ernest W., 61, (73), 73–74, 188, 202
Hatch Act, 29, 31, 39, 62, 214, 215, 217, 219
Hatt, Paul, 210
Hays Hall, (98), 176, (191)
Headington, Sarah, 197
Heating Plant Building, (55), 172
Hello Walk, 13, (13), 14, (72), 85, (85), (200)
Helm, MacKinley, 144
Henden, Paul, 124
Hendren, Jerry, 129
"Here We Have Idaho" (song), 144
Hill, Robert, 105*
Hinckley, Stephen, 103*
Hirai, George, 178*
Hitt, Myrtle, (87)
Hobart, Ken, 130
Hogue, Gilbert, (157)
Holly Week, 94
Holms, Otho, (179)
Homecoming, (148), 148–149, (149), (150), (151)

Home Economics Building, 7, 194
Home Economics, School of, (180), (181), 192, (193), 194-196, (194), (195), (196), 198, (205), 219, 222–223
Hoover, Jessie M., 194
Horticulture Building, 34, (34), (35)
Howland, Winslow, (157)
Hughes, Jennie Eva, 209–212*, 211, (211)
Hughes, John, 104–105*
Hulme Contest, 83–84, (84)
Hulme, Edward Maslin, 82, 84, 135
Hunker, Harold, 103*
Hunter, Glen, (179)
Hunter, Kenneth, 149*
Huntley, Frederick, 37–38

I Bench, 9, 85, (85), 142
I Club, 83, 133, (133)
Idaho Bureau of Mines, 224
Idaho Club, 99–100*, (100), 176
Idaho Institute of Christian Education. See Campus Christian Center
Idaho State University, 41, 62–66, 232
Idaho Technical College. See Idaho State University
Idaho Violet (cow), 37
Infirmary, 54, (57)
Inter-Collegiate Athletic Association, 114
Inter-Sorority Council, 197, 203
I Tank, 4, (5), 6, (6), (58), 150, (152)

Jacobs, Harold, 103*
James, Francis L., 4, 140–142*
Jasper, William, 195
Jensen, Katherine, 194
Johnson, Donald LeRoy, (127)
Johnson, Florence Corbett, 27, 190, (190)
Johnson, Glenn, (184)
Johnson, Gus, (120), 128–129, 130, 151*
Johnson, Jeane, (184)
Johnson, Manley, 230*
Johnson, Paul, 103*
Journalism Department, 228–229
Junior Prom, (90), 91, 94, 96

Kappa Phi Alpha Fraternity. See Phi Delta Theta Fraternity
Kappa Sigma Fraternity, 100, (102)
Kara, Frank, 127–128*

Kara, Theodore (Ted), 125, 126–129*, (126)
Kaufmann, William, 97
Kellerman, Brian, 151*
Kelly, Frederick J., 69, (69)
KFAN Radio, 106
Kibbie-ASUI Activity Center, 4, 60, (61), (118), (139), 140, 151*
Kiilsgaard, Carl, 127
King, Joe, 128
Kirtley, Charles Luther, 190, (190)
Knudson, John, 103*
Kongsgaard, Sverre, 126, (126)
Korean War, 160, 184–185
Kramer, Jerry, 128, 151*
KRFA Radio, 107
KUID Radio. See KRFA Radio
KUID Television, 107, 228, (228)
KUOI Radio, (106), 107

Laboratory of Anthropology, 224
Lake Huntley, 7, 37–38
Lambda Chi Alpha Fraternity, (100)
Land Grant Act. See Morrill Act
Larrison, Earl, (230)
LaRue, Lawrence, 103*
Latter-day Saints Institute, 98*, 103
Lattig, Herbert E., 206
Law, College of, 68
Leth, George (122)
Letters and Science, College of, 64*, 67–68
Levinson, Salmon O., 229–232*
Lewis, Charlotte, 203*
Lewis–Clark Normal School. See Lewis–Clark State College
Lewis–Clark State College, 66, 133, 232
Lewis Hall, 99*
Lewiston State Normal School. See Lewis–Clark State College
Library, 2, 3, (32), 41*, (49), 54, (55), (56), 171,(172)
Life Science Building, (54)
Lindley, Ernest H., 61, 68, (68), 164*
Lindley, Ernest K., 115, 160*
Lindley Hall, 53, 99*, (99), 176
Liszt Hall. See Horticulture Building
Loomis, Dudley, 169
Loser's Walk, 150–152, (153)
Lydum, Floyd, 103*

McCallie, Margaret, 160, 211*
McCarty, Harry Lloyd, 115, 116, 160*

McConnell, William J., 16, (16), 20, 21, 30, 42, 230*
McDevitt, Tom, 103*
McDonald, Ray, 129, 151*, 152
McGowan, Bill, (153)
McGregor, Robert, (89)
MacLean, James Alexander, 3, 7, 14, 29*, 31, 37, 42–44, 46, 48–49, 61–62, 64*, 66–67, (69), 82
Mandolin Club, 86, (86), 88
Marcellus, Hazel, 78–79
March, Clement, (99)
March, Maurice, (99)
Marshall, Thomas R., 53*
Martinson, Lloyd, 105*
Matovich, Paul, 104–106*
Matthews, Robert, 117
May Fete, 92, (93), (200), (202), 204, (205)
Memorial Gymnasium, 3, (4), 37, 53, 53*, (108), (120), (125),128, 128*, 129*, 169–170, (170), (175), 183, 188
Merriman, Sam, 130
Middleton, John, 114 (114)
Military Ball, 158
Miller, George Morey, (68), 140*
Milliken, Robert, 215
Mines Building. See Engineering Building
Mines, College of, 41, 224, (224), (225)
Mines, School of. See Mines, College of
Minute Maids, 181, (181)
Mix, Gainford, 112
Monson, Don, (121), 129–130, 134, 151*
Morrill Act, 29, 30, 31, 38, 39, 41, 62, 156, 192, 219
Morrill Hall, 48–49, (50), 63*
Morris, Tom, 151*
Mortar Board, 203
Moscow, Idaho, 4, 16, 17, (18), 19, 20, 21, 24, (24), 25, 30, 34, 35, 40, 42–44*, 48, 62*, 117, 140*, 149, 156, 159, 163, (164), 168, 168–172*, 169, (169), 184–185, 190, 200–205*, 209–211*, 210–211, 215, 217
Moscow Public Library. See Carnegie Library
Moveable Schools of Agriculture, 217

Murphy, Terry, 103*
Music Building, 14, (58), 177*, (177)
Music Hall. See Horticulture Building
Myers, Reginald T., 160

Naval Reserve Officers' Training Corps Building, 156, 174, (187), 188
Neale, Mervin G., 53*, (69), 69–70, 95–96*, 98–99*
Neale Stadium, 54, (118), (138), (153)
Nelson, Rick, 151*
Nez Perce Drive, 4, 6, 102, 178*
Niccolls, Mary Hall, 7, (197), 197–198
North Idaho College, 232
Northern Idaho College of Education. See Lewis–Clark State College

O'Donnell, J. Morris, 144
Old Bertha (cannon), 6, (6), 176–178*, (177), (178)
Old Steps Memorial, 7–8, (8)
Orr, Jeannette, 190, 195–198*, (198)
Ostrander, John Edwin, 27, 192

Pacific Coast Conference, 117, 119, 136, 138, 139
Pacific Coast Intercollegiate Athletic Association. See Pacific Coast Conference
Paradise Creek, 14, 37
Parents Weekend. See May Fete
Phi Delta Theta Fraternity, 99–100, (100)
Phillips, John L., 114
Physical Education Building and Swim Center, 140, (141)
Plastino, Felix, (116)
Porter, Dora, 192
Potlatch Lumber Company, 63*, 225, 227
Presidential Grove, 9, 51–54*
President's House, 4
Price, Clement L., 64–66*, (66)
Price Green, 4, 66*
Priest, A. J., 160*
Public Affairs Research, Bureau of, 228

Quinn, Fred, (119), 127

Raese, Mary, 134
Reed, Miles Frank, 62, (82)
Religious Emphasis Week, 103
Reserve Officers' Training Corps, 156–157, 160, 188
Retherford, Jesse, 62
Ricks College, 232
Ridenbaugh Hall, 6–7, (7), (25), 35, (36), 51–52*, 87, (87), 94, 99, 99*, 169*, 192, 194, 198
Ridenbaugh, Mary E., 35
Robins, C. A., 66
Roosevelt, Eleanor, 9, 53–54*, (54), (70), 230*
Roosevelt, Theodore, 9, 51–52*, (52), 53*
Rosenheim, Edward, 162*
Rowell, Ross E., 160
Rifle Team, 132, (132), 133
Ryan, Mike, 124
Ryrie, Alex, 200*, 201*
Ryrie, Carol. See Brink, Carol Ryrie
Ryrie, Henrietta Watkins, 200*, 201*

Santiestevan, Henry, 178–179
Satellite Student Union Building, 174
Schaffer, B. J., 103*
Schuldberg, Clair, 103*
Senior Hall, 98*
Senior Sneak, 91, 96
Settle, Eugene, 210*
Sharples, Patsy, 134
Shattuck Arboretum, 4, 64–66*, 96, (97), (98)
Shattuck, Charles Houston, (62), 62–66*, (65), 67–68
Shumway, Rolly, 125
Sigma Chi Fraternity, 102, 211
Silver and Gold Book, 41–44*, (42)
Simmons, Gary, 128
Simpson, Charles, (157)
Sisson, Edward, 68
Skiing, 126, 127, 129
Smith, Berthol, 211–212*
Smith, Carl, 103–104*
Smith, George August, 211*
Smith, Jennie Hughes. See Hughes, Jennie Eva
Sophomore Frolic, 91, 94
Sororities, 99–100, 102. See also names of specific sororities
Soulen, Beth, 203*
Spanish–American War, 162, 163, 165, 168–172*, 206

Spanish–American War Memorial, (5), 9, (9), 166, (166), 176*, 188
Spanish Influenza Epidemic (1918–1919), 168
Spaulding, Velma, 167
Spotswood, Mrs. A. T., 43*
Spurs, 105*
Stag Social, 91
Steel House, 100*
Steunenberg, Frank, 42
Stevenson, Edward A., 19, 20
Stivers, Vernon, 117
Student Special (train), 40, (63), (78), (79)
Student Training and Reclassification (World War II), 176
Student Union Building, 14, 54, (59), 95–97*, (96)
Students' Army Training Corps (World War I), 167–169, 167–171*
Students' Athletic Association, 107
Summer School, 42, (232)
Sutherland, Frank B., (160), 160–165*, 210
Sweet Hall, (21), 54, 104*, 174, 186
Sweet, Willis, 16, (16), 19, 19*, 20, 21, 24, 29
Swimming, 134, (140)

Taft, William Howard, 9, 53*
Tanner, George, 98–99*
Tau Kappa Epsilon Fraternity, 6, 176–178*
Telford, Harold, 121
Tennis, (123), 129, 130, (131), 134
Theophilus, Donald R., (72), 73, 103*, 152, 204
Thomas, Esther, (167), 167–172*
Tonnemaker, Kyle, 124
Tourtellotte, J. E., 37, 51
Track and Field, 114, 115–117*, (124), (127), 130, (131), 134
Tsan, Chen–Kueh, (208)

U–Hut, 53
Ullevaalseter, Reidar, 126
University Art Gallery, 7
University Band, 88
University Classroom Center, (59)
University Club, 99*

University Farm, (33), 34, (34), (215), (216), 217, (223). *See also* Agricultural Experiment Stations
University of Idaho South. *See* Idaho State University
University Orchestra, 88, (88)
Upham, Alfred A., 61, 62, 68, (69), 97
Upham Hall, 103*
Upward Bound, 228

Vandaleers, (213), (229)
Vandals (naming of), 115–116
Veterans Villages (post–World War II), (182), 183,(183), 184
Vietnam War, 156, 186–188
Volleyball, 134, (134)

Walker, Wayne, 128, 151*
Washington Agricultural College. *See* Washington State University
Washington State College. *See* Washington State University
Washington State University, 4, 6, 54*, 106–107, 112, 114, 129, 133, 141*, 142, 149–152, 149–152*, 169*, 176*, 188, 226, 229, 231–232
Water Resources Research Institute, 229
Watkins Medal for Oratory, 82, 201*, 211*
Watkins, William W., 200–201*, 203–204*
Websterian Debating Society, 82
Westerwelle, Mary, 134

Wichman, Phillip, (95)
Wiens, A. Gerhard, (177)
Wilderness Research Center, 229
William E. Borah Outlawry of War Foundation. *See* Borah Foundation
Williams, Colleen, 134
Wilson, Nellie. *See* Brigham, Nellie Wilson
Wolfe, Guy, 104, 108
Women's Athletic Association, 133, 203
Women's Caucus, 198*, 202–203, 212
Women's Center, 203
Women's Council, 196
Women's Gymnasium. *See* Gymnasium
Woods, Robert, 95*

World War I, 3, 68, 161–165*, 162, 166–170, 167–172*, 206
World War II, 65, 70, 84, 86, 94, 160, 170–172, 174, 176–179, 181–182, 206, 209–211
Wunderlich, Herbert, 21*

Yarno, John, 129
Y–Hut. *See* U–Hut
Young, Frank, 125
Young, Mary E., 192
Young Men's Christian Association, 53, 86, 94, 103
Young, Virgil, 103*
Young Women's Christian Association, 86, 94, 103, 211*

Zeta Epsilon Fraternity. *See* Beta Theta Pi Fraternity

Designer: Emily Silver
Art and Production Director: Debra L. Moloshok

Typeset in Novarese by Creative Graphics, Inc., Allentown, Pennsylvania.

Printed on 80# Lustro Offset Enamel Dull. Printed and bound by Horowitz/
Rae Book Manufacturers, Inc., New York, New York.

This book was produced by the University of Idaho Centennial Commission,
under the direction of Roy Fluhrer, the university's centennial coordinator.
All of those associated with the project wish to express their gratitude to
Dr. Fluhrer for his enthusiasm and encouragement.